AF564921

Liberation of Women in India and The Work of the NGOs

The present book is about the struggle of women in India to achieve a status of equality which existed in the Vedic Age and in the present Constitution of India. The struggle has been a tough one as it requires the victory of old traditions like caste system and male domination. The book describes the efforts made by the Indian government in the form of Five Year Plans which allots a considerable amount to projects dealing with women and the work of the NGOs (Non Government Organizations) which are heavily involved with defining and raising the status of women particularly in rural areas.

Dr. Tripta Desai was raised in India and she has been here in the USA for the last 45 years. She attended University of Delhi before coming to the USA to do her Ph. D. work at Washington State University, Washington. Her dissertation topic after completing her Qualifying examination in 1964 was INDO AMERICAN WHEAT NEGOTIATIONS OF 1950-1951. She travels often to India which keeps her updated with the events in India. Her specialty in teaching at Northern Kentucky University, USA, is Modernization in India though she handles courses in Europe, Russia and British History too. Her last book, INDIA-USA Diplomatic Relation from 1440-2002 is highly acclaimed by my students.

Liberation of Women in India
and
The Work of the NGOs

Tripta Desai

DEV PUBLISHERS & DISTRIBUTORS
New Delhi

Published by:
DEV PUBLISHERS & DISTRIBUTORS
2nd Floor, Prakash Deep,
4735/22, Ansari Road,
Darya Ganj,
New Delhi-110002
Phone : 011-43572647, 9810236140
e-mail: devbooks@hotmail.com
website: www.devbooks.co.in

ISBN 978–93–81406–00–7
First published 2012

Printed in India

Contents

Preface

It has been realized increasingly that women had been left behind for a long time. Governments and NGOs in different countries are making a great effort to address the issues of women. United Nations drew attention to the women's problems by declaring 1975–85 as Women's Decade. Present work is designed to stress the issues women have faced historically. The Indian government like so many other governments is making an immense effort in the form of Five Year Plans to raise the under-privileged position of women The book goes into all those efforts of the Indian government and also discusses the important role being played by the NGOs in the work of helping women. Since women are half of the world population and bear the responsibility to raise children who would be the future citizens of the country, it makes sense to bring the status of women at par with those of men.

Tripta Desai

New Delhi
12th May 2011

Introduction

The present work covers a long period from the Ancient time around the time of the Rig Veda-1500 BC or 1000 BC to present day. The reason for including a chapter on the status of Women in the Early Vedic Age is to demonstrate that the status of the early Vedic women was high and women were respected as daughters and when married, were respected as co-partners in the family household. Daughters went through the Upanayana ceremony to initiate them into a student's life. Daughters were encouraged to engage in all kinds of activities like music and public oratory. When married, a wife's presence was mandatory with the husband to perform household religious rituals. The status of women began to decline from the later Vedic Age or at the time of the Brahamanas till we come to Manusmriti around 300 BC or so. Child marriage, denial of education to girls, prohibition of widow marriages came to be well accepted. Manu spoke highly in favour of those restraints on women. Subsequent invasions of India by different tribes most of whom were Muslim, further solidified the low status of women as the invaders would rape and tend to carry away young girls.

The low status of women continued during the British rule too because the colonial rulers did not want to disturb the social order and cause any kind of rebellion against their rule. Manusmriti continued to dominate the public thought whenever women were concerned. The British did establish colleges, universities and public elementary and post secondary schools. A few women in the cities did avail of that opportunity. But the bulk of the Indian women remained suppressed as eighty to eighty-five of the population lived in villages. Preceding discussion is in part one which describes the status of women from Ancient time to the End of the British rule.

Part two of the book is a discussion of India after Independence in 1947. It consists of various chapters like the Five Year Plans in the 1950's, 1960's and 1970's and 1980's. Main focus is on the villages and the share allotted to rural women in the Five Year Plans. After independence in 1947, the Indian Constitution gave a fresh start to the Indian women. The enlightened leaders of India were able to point out to the Rig Veda to stress the respect given to daughters and married women. Thus, the Indian constitution declared Indian women equal citizens - equal before law and equal in seeking access to education and to any kind of an opportunity.

However, it is a different thing to enact laws and a different scenario of life wherein women continue to suffer from ancient inhibitions and taboos more particularly in the villages. As we know that even today the vast majority of the Indian population still lives in villages. We have to raise the status of these rural women so that India could earn the title of a modernized country. Women are also almost fifty percent of the entire population. What happens to them is a matter of great concern to any country if a country is to move forward in modernization. Women also deserve a better deal because of their role as mothers which makes it necessary that they are respected and well treated. Women as mothers rear the future citizens of the country. If the mothers receive a decent treatment in society and from the government, they will pass on the right moral values to their children that each human being is worthy of respect and opportunity because we all belong to the same humanity.

The Five-Year Plans are a good example. They seek to assist and uplift women by special projects and allocation of necessary funds. The role of the NGOs or Non Government

Organizations is equally important as they participate in carrying out the Five-Year Plan projects and they also have their own plans and agenda to help the under-privileged women both in urban slums and in the villages.

The first part of part two is devoted to a detailed discussion of the aims of the Five Year Plans, in particular, the projects to help rural men and women.

The remainder of part two deals with the work of the various NGOs. Practical experience has shown that the NGOs interact more positively with the poor than the official bureaucracy assigned to carry out

The projects of the Five-Year Plans as the official bureaucracy vested with the comfort of a secure job and a guaranteed pension along with the colonial arrogance can be half-hearted and callous in their efforts The NGOs represent selfless workers who really have a desire to help the under-privileged.

I had the opportunity to work with NGOs like SEWA in Ahmedabad. SEWA was started in 1970's by Illa Bhatt who was struck by the poverty of women street vendors. Her objective was to organize such women and teach them the advantages of organized power for any social group. When I was in Ahmedabad in 1987, I found various organizations of street vendors and of other poor women groups. They learnt how to deal with the buyer, police and the courts. One of the street vendors, who had been trained to go to the court, told me that police would just carry away in the truck the vegetables of women who were selling on the side walk which was not allowed. The court magistrate was convinced and a shopping area was set aside for these vendors. So, now, they can sell legally.

Other NGO which caught my attention was SEVA MANDIR in Udaipur district of Rajasthan. I was there almost for a week. It was set up by a retired school teacher in 1970's who first went around on his bike to give literacy to these village people around Udaipur. Adult literacy was his passion. That start developed into the present day organization of

SEVA MANDIR. It deals with the tribal people of Udaipur district which suffer from water shortage- being the desert area. Its success is to be noted by the contributions of foreign donors who must be impressed with the achievements.

Other organization is All India Women Conference set up in 1925 which I frequented very much. AIWC is considered the Umbrella organization of the NGOs. It has also been given the consultative status by the United Nations. AIWC carries on research studies among the village poor women and urban slums and also starts a number of pilot projects like Chullah in villages. The idea is to use the manure in the village to create gas for the chullah. Dowry evil is another concern of AIWC. Dowry not only ruins a poor father financially, it also underscores the low status of women in society. Dowry system has also led to female fetus destruction which is inhuman. Let us also mention the constant struggle of AIWC to create a national law for all women in India in case of divorce, alimony and one marriage. It particularly pertains to Muslim women who suffer heavily because of Sharia law of Muhammed which is very much in favour of men and discriminates against women. AIWC is very highly valued by the Indian government. Findings of AIWC are incorporated in the Five Year Plans which shows the importance of AIWC in the history of women organizations. AIWC also has a huge library which I consulted. It also publishes ROSHINI-a periodical- which I found very useful.

CWDS is a research group in Delhi funded by the Indian Government. I found the books published very relevant to my research. CWDS also carries out projects like it has an ongoing project in West Bengal called Bankura project. In this project, those villages were chosen which have a dominant population of scheduled castes. The lesson of Bankura project like of so many other projects is that Village women have to be given a skill to create income on an ongoing basis to raise their status socially.

I also visited the Department of Women and Child Development in the Ministry of Human Resource. I was fortunate to have meetings with different officials. One programme particularly struck me-ICDS or Integrated Child Development scheme initiated in the late 1970's and also heavily supported by the United Nations in order to control the rising population of India. The lesson of ICDS is that if women receive pre-natal and post-natal care, the survival of kids is very likely which will reduce the temptation among the poor people to have a large number of kids not knowing how many would survive.

From Chapter Ten on is the additional information to the older edition which stopped with 1990. In the new edition SEWA, SEVA MANDIR, CWDS, AIWC and the projects supported by the United Nations' Population section are discussed from 1990 on.

United Nations projects are discussed in a separate chapter. One of the interesting findings of these Projects was that to get the young daughter-in-laws to step out of the house to attend Mahila Mandal meetings and to participate in income generation activities, it is necessary to approach the mother-in-law and to convince her first as she dominates the world of the daughter-in-laws. This is the social structure in the villages which are very much tradition bound.

In conclusion , the driving lesson of the various projects is that rural poor women have to develop the capacity to generate income on an ongoing basis for the family to raise their status socially. However, we cannot ignore that school education in the villages must also teach to the kids that two sexes are equal partners in life. It is a long process in terms of time because India is a democratic country. Unlike China which is a dictatorship, a change or a new law cannot be enforced from the top. People's thinking has to be changed through education and by other means like bollywood movies and that takes time.

Acknowledgements

I would like to express my deep gratitude to Dr. James A. Ramage of the Department of History at Northern Kentucky University who has always edited my manuscripts. Dr. Ramage himself is a writer of so many books which are highly acclaimed.

I can never end a manuscript without thinking of my parents—Shree Ram Nath Bali and Mrs. Vidya Wanti Bali-whose inspiration and constant affection had been a big factor in the academic achievements of all of their children.

TRIPTA DESAI

New Delhi
12th May 2011

Section I

1

Ancient and Medieval History of Women in India to 1800–I

One major obstacle encountered in any study of Ancient India is the uncertainty of dating different historical periods. We must accept tentative dates to make the presentation intelligible and coherent. We can accept 2500 BC to 1500 BC as the Vedic age when were composed the four Vedas of the Aryans, of which the *Rigveda* is the oldest and the most revered The period form 1500 BC to 500 BC can be regarded as one of the Brahmanas and the Upanishads, commentaries on, and addendums to the Vedas. When the Aryans, or the Indo-European tribe, entered India around 2500 BC and began advancing across the Jumna and the Gangetic valley to the East near Bengal, many native cults, with their gods and goddesses came to be incorporated into the religion of the Vedas, called Brahmanism, the new assimilated religion faced a strong reaction against it, particularly its Vedic sacrifices, which led to the rise of Buddhism and Jainism around the sixth century BC. From 500 BC to AD 500 can be approximated as the period of the Sutras, early Smritis, the Epics of *Ramayana* and *Mahabharata* and the early Puranas. They all combated the threat of Buddhism and Jainism either by incorporating a few of their ideas (like emphasis upon asceticism as the ideal life for salvation) or by becoming rigid and unrelenting. Around 300 BC the status of women began to decline. Probably dating to the beginning of the Christian era, the *Manusmriti* affords glimpses into the severe restriction of women's activities and status. Form AD 500 to AD 1800 more Smrities and Puranas were compiled which further degraded the existence of women.

Childhood and Education

Marriage laws and social customs reveal clues useful in deciding if women have been regarded as mere market commodities and war prizes, or if men have considered women their indispensable partners in a happy home life. The degree to which a woman is given a voice in the settlement of her marriage and the management of the household and the extent to which her proprietary rights are recognized illustrate a patriarchal society's capacity to balance the loves of self, of power, and of possession with egalitarian ideals. How much freedom a woman is given in society or how often she is allowed to participate in public affairs shows how greatly she may decide what control her progress and development. A litmus test of women's liberty is the measurement of their access to education. The history of India records more denials of women's rights than anyone would have the right to expect.

Available evidence shows that in India, as in other patriarchal societies, a daughter was not as welcome as a son because he was a greater asset to the family. In the obscure epochs of antiquity, men had already developed the superior physical strength essential to successful combat. As adolescents, sons could fight wars which daughters could not. Then after marriage, in contrast to a daughter, a son did not leave his parents but stayed with them. In the Indo-European age, as well as in the Vedic period the same was true. One of the Vedas, *Atharvaveda,* contains charms and rituals to ensure the birth of a son in preference to a daughter. The latter's birth, nonetheless, was not a source of sadness to the family in the Vedas and in the Upanishads. One of the early Upanishads recommends a certain ritual to a householder for ensuring the birth of a scholarly daughter. (That ritual did not become as popular as the other which ensured the birth of a son remains true.) In cultural families, a talented daughter was regarded as a source of pride. Among lower sections of society where the custom of bride-price is known to have prevailed, the birth of a daughter might also have been welcome, although no contemporary evidence has come to light to support this viewpoint.

Daughters were relatively less unpopular during this period because they could be initiated into the Vedic studies and could offer sacrifices to gods. Sons were not absolutely necessary for this purpose. Also the marriage of a daughter was not a difficult issue. The dread of a possible widowhood did not exist, as society permitted remarriage and levirate.

To approximately the third BC century girls could remain unmarried until the age of sixteen. The period prior to marriage was utilized to impart education to them. The *Atharvaveda* observes that a girl can succeed in her married life only if she has been properly trained during *Brahmacharya* or student life. In the *Rigveda* numerous references to educated girls attest to daughter's access to learning. Women students, comprised two groups, the one studying life-long, the other until marriage. Evidence amply shows that women also offered regular morning and evening Vedic prayers. (This practice continued through the Epic period from 500 BC to 300 BC. In *Ramayana*, Sita is cited as offering her daily Vedic prayers.)

When reaction against the sacrificial nature of the Vedic religion prompted intense philosophical speculations as early as 800 BC female scholars contributed to the erudite arguments. In the Upanishads, learned and wise women carry on analytical discussions with their male counterparts. A few of the female scholars remained unmarried, as they did not want to hamper their spiritual development.

An outgrowth of this reaction against the sacrifices of the Vedic religion, Buddhism began to admit women into religious order. This practice gave an impetus to the cause of female education in commercial and aristocratic families. Several daughters of Buddhist families followed lives of celibacy with the aim of fully concentrating on religion and truth. Another religion contesting Vedic rituals and rites, Jainism also mentions a number of women devoted to religion.

Even though to determine the extent of female education from the Vedic time to around BC 300 is impossible, ample evidence suggests that well-to-do parents were eager to have talented and educated girls. *Upanayana* ritual (initiation into studentship) was obligatory for girls, thereby demonstrating that they must have received Vedic and literary education among the three upper classes the Brahmins, the Kshatriyas, and the Vaishyas. (These classes or *varnas* later came to be called castes.) The Vedic and Epic literature also detail girl's recreational activities, which were music, dancing, and a number of courtyard games like hide and seek. To assume that musicianship and dancing expertise would require education is logical.

The cause of women's education began to suffer around 300 BC on account of the child marriages which came into vogue. By the beginning of the Christian era, pre-puberty marriages became the social rule, which gave a serious blow to female education. Gradually in the first centuries of the Christian era, the *Upanayana* sacrament for girls vanished thereby denying access to education. Even in Buddhism, female acceptance and religious initiation declined. Nunneries went out of existence by the fourth century AD as the two renowned Chinese travelers, Fa-Hien and Yuan Chwang, who have given a detailed account of Buddhism in India at the time, do not mention them.[2]

During the first millennium of the Christian era, only a few female scholars and poetesses were renowned. Nothing is known of their family background. Probably, they belonged to the rich and cultured families who could make special arrangements for girls' education even after their marriages. In ruling families, girls received both military and administrative training. This practice was common among Rajputs (a branch of the warrior group which fought fiercely against the Mughals and the British.)

The advent of Muslim rule vanquished the wealthy, cultured Hindu families. Ruined, these Hindus were in no position to make special arrangements for the education of their girls. Female literacy all but disappeared.

During the Medieval Period, Hindu society developed a prejudice against women's education. Patriarchs fueled the fire of the belief that a girl who could read and write would become a widow.

By mid nineteenth century, literacy among Hindu women reached is nadir. Finally, the assumption of power by the British Crown, the government in India took the first, tentative steps to provide at least a minimal education for girls.

Marriage and Divorce

Although traces of promiscuity appear in the Epics of *Ramayana* and *Mahabharata* they are remnants of pre-Vedic times, because the institution of marriage was well-established in the Rigveda, the oldest of the four Vedas. In Vedic Times, marriage assumed the character of a religious and social duty. The married couple was to take particular care in carrying out the rituals connected with the *Grihapatya* fire kindled at the time of their union. The married couple was to perform prescribed, regular sacrifices to gods and manes.

Despite marriages claim to be the best life, spinster women were not unknown. They were not denounced. What compelled these women to remain unmarried can only be guessed. (One reason could have been physical disability.) Even in the age of the Brahmanas and the Upanishads, many young men began to enter monasteries without marrying. A few girls followed suit to achieve spiritual salvation. With the rise of Buddhism in the sixth century BC the number of women entering hermitage grew significantly.

Around 300 BC the social attitude toward marriage radically solidified. Marriage came to be regarded as obligatory for females. Several factors led to this development. During the peak of Buddhism and Jainism, many girls joined the monastic orders, occasionally without the consent of their elders. A few were not able to live up to exacting ideals of asceticism and fell into lapses which shocked society. Social leaders thus, began to make marriage obligatory for girls. For women, marriage came to be considered a rite of significance equal to the *Upanayana* (education) sacrament for boys. To enforce marriage upon girls, patriarchs reduced marriageable age to twelve.

Even in the Epics, *Ramayana* and *Mahabharata*, many stories underscore the point that marriage was indispensable for girls. A woman could not enter heaven without marriage, no matter how virtuous she might be. Society also drew distinction between a fallible man and a woman astray. The former deserved pardon for his indiscretion, the latter condemnation for her sin. To prevent any sinful commission by a girl, religious writers like the Smriti-writers around the beginning of the Christian era began to advocate pre-puberty marriages. Absolute chastity was demanded of a girl, even to the extent that she should not have contemplated a love affair with any male. Pre-puberty marriages could prevent females' eventual sin. Only at peril of potential disgrace would parents permit daughters to remain unmarried after menstruation had begun.

It should be noticed that pre-puberty marriages remained confined to the Brahmin class long after its acceptance around the beginning of the Christian era. Kshatriyas, or the warrior class, did not accept it for many years because, if they married pre-pubescent brides, they would leave behind many child widows. This fact explains the otherwise curious phenomenon that most heroines in the Sanskrit drams from AD 200 to AD 1200 are adults at the time of their marriage. They belong to the Kshatriya families.

The popularity of early marriages increased during the Medieval Period. Eight or nine was the usual age for girls at marriage when the British rule was established in India. By this age, girls could not have received much education; thus, they were in no position to exercise any decision-making power. Women in India had yielded to suppression since the Vedic and the Upanishadic age when girls participated in their marriage settlements and were allowed to have a significant education.

The dowry system, still very much in vogue today, has promulgated the relatively low status of girls in India. Its origin is significant. In the pre-vedic society, the dowry system was probably unknown. Given that girls were regarded as chattels, the bridegroom's family had to give a bride-price to the bride's parents. The dowry system came into vogue in Vedic society when the marriage of a girl was conceived as *dana*, or a religious gift. In the presence of such a gift, the bride's family contributed cash an in-kind payment. In ordinary families, the dowry given was small and was never an impediment to the settlement of marriages. In the Medieval period, however, the amount of dowry began to increase disproportionately, probably because of the exclusiveness of marriages within one's sub-caste. A father would be very eager to pay a handsome price for a bright young man within the sub-caste so that he could discharge his obligation toward a daughter's marriage. When the British took over around the mid nineteenth century, dowry system had grown into a monstrous curse throughout the country.

The caste system in India also has had a great impact on the marriage structure. The origin of this social division can be traced back to the Vedic time when the word *varna* was used to distinguish groups in society based upon vocations. The divisions had not yet solidified into rigid groups based upon birth as they did later. According to Dr. A.L. Basham (listed in the suggested readings at the end of Part One), castes and sub-castes within a *varna* arose historically when the native tribes were assimilated and foreign invaders were allowed a place within the social structure. These castes and sub-castes became so numerous that to enumerate them defies possibility. The rigidity did not occur until the tenth century AD when intercaste marriages went out of existence. Even in the days of Manu (author of the famous Manusmriti in the first century AD), caste did not present an insurmountable barrier to marriages. Alberuni, a traveler who visited India in the eleventh century AD, observed that the Brahmins no longer availed themselves of the permission to take wives from the lower castes. Many other travelers in the sixteenth and the seventeenth centuries, mainly from Europe, mentioned that, in India intercaste marriages were quite unknown.

Inter-caste marriages could take place before the tenth century AD because cultural differences among the twice-born, or *Dvijati* (the three upper classes or Brahmins, Kshatriyas, and Vaishyas) were not there. They all performed *Upanayana* and studied the ancestral sacrifices. Circumstances began to change, as Alberuni related. The Vaishyas no longer performed *Upanayana*, thus abandoning the Vedic studies altogether. Even Kshatriyas, a few studying the Veda, abandoned *Upanayana*. Brahmins were the only *varna* Performing *Upanayana*. They had also ceased the practice of eating meat, a prohibition which the Kshatriyas and the Vaishyas did not accept. These cultural differences became widespread among the different *varna*, thereby rendering inter-class and inter-caste marriage impossible.

In the Vedic age, divorce was permissible. The *Atharvaveda* mentions a woman marrying after divorcing the first husband. Dharamsutra writers of 400 BC to AD 100 describes various situations in which a woman had to wait five years for her husband who left on a long journey before remarrying. In his *Arthashastra*, written in the fourth century BC during the Maurya rule (probably the first unified Hindu Kingdom), Kautilya makes a number of references to divorce rules. He suggests that, if a husband and wife hate each other, divorce is to be granted. Kautilya further recommends that, if a man apprehends danger from his wife, he may ask for a divorce, but he has to return to the former wife all the gifts brought by her to the marriage. In the *Arthashastra* if the wife is the complainant, she has to forfeit her proprietary rights in her husband's family. So states Kautilya. An important point must be borne in mind, however. Divorce was allowed only if the marriage had been performed by any of the unapproved forms prevalent among the lower classes. No divorce was permitted if the marriage had been performed by any of the four approved forms. Unapproved forms were not unknown among the upper classes; thus, to assume that divorce prevailed in one form or another even among the upper classes is safe.

In the last century BC the *Manusmriti* served as the basic Hindu social code (as it would, for many centuries until the modern legislation under the British and independent India demolished its validity). Manu observes that a wife is not to be blamed if she abandons a husband who is impotent, insane, or suffering from a contagious disease. In the *Manusmriti*, this abandonment of the husband amounts to a divorce. Manu permits such a wife to remarry, so long as her previous marriage was not consummated. According to Manu, the children of the second marriage are legal heirs to the parents. In actual practice, we notice that down to the beginning of the Christian era, divorces and remarriages took place now and then in all sections of society even after the consummation of marriage if the marriage had been preformed by the four unapproved forms.[3]

After the advent of the Christian era, the increasingly patriarchal society denied women the option of divorce no matter how unhappy their married life was. A husband could be moral wreck, but a wife could not even contemplate a divorce. In the writings of the Dharmashastras (religious texts) from AD 200 to about AD 1200 society subjected women to unfair treatment. A man was practically permitted to divorce his first wife by contracting a second marriage. He could even avoid the payment of any maintenance to the first wife if she refused to stay with him. He could a self-respecting wife remain with a husband living with a second wife and serve as no better than an unpaid maid at her husband's house? Deserted wives could not even remarry, as their marital tie with their husbands was irrevocable.

In the Vedic time, brides enjoyed affectionate and

respectable treatment in their in-law's house, and they were expected to take over the reins of the household in the new home because they were mature and educated. These relatively pleasant conditions continued until 300 BC or the beginning of the Christian era. Then, the status of the bride began to decline, as she was illiterate and immature at the time of marriage. The prevailing practice of child-marriages doomed women.

In the Vedic age, particularly in the *Rigveda* (the earliest of the four Vedas), wife and husband were referred to as *dampati* or joint owners of the house. This attitude was very much responsible for the high status of the wife during that time. Discord, however, can arise in the married life on account of so many issues, and superior authority was given to the husband. At its heart, Vedic society was basically a patriarchal society. The husband was the senior partner, and the wife the junior partner.

Although supreme command was vested in the husband in the Vedic age, the marriage vow called upon the man to treat his wife with utmost courtesy and regard. She was the ornament of the house. Early literature does not recognize the power of the husband to correct his wife physically. In the Vedic age, such punishment occurred rarely. Indeed, the Vedic texts' stressing of the symbiotic relationship between husband and wife tacitly de-emphasized such severe authority of the husband. The Vedic texts expressly laid down that a complete identity of interest between a husband and a wife should exist. This interdependence was emphasized in the marriage vow which both had to take. The husband and wife promised to cooperate with each other in the realization of their goals and ambitions in life. According to the Vedic passages, a man is incomplete and cannot ascend to heaven without his wife. The husband must treat his wife as his dearest friend. The two Epics, *Ramayana* and *Mahabharta*, agree with this viewpoint.

The wife must also be true to her marriage obligations and must lead the life of a *Pativrata* (one devoted to her husband).

Early literature is full of praises of such *Pativratas.* Sita is the best case in the Epic of *Ramayana.*

Hindu marriage aimed to ensure the full growth and development of husband and wife and to preserve family and society by the procreation of children and their proper upbringing. Sons were indispensable, as they alone could offer monthly oblations to ancestors residing in heaven. Motherhood, therefore, represented the cherished goal of a Hindu woman. The birth of a son heightened her status in family and society. A son was called upon to respect his mother even if she were a widow and could not inherit the property of her deceased husband which passed on to his sons.

Scriptural precepts for marital duties have no ambiguity, but the unanswerable questions remains—did the husbands in ancient India carry out their conjugal responsibilities with a devotion equal to that of their wives? One suspects that a great number of violations transpired, as the male delinquents were not punished by the patriarchal society.

Around the beginning of the Christian era, when child marriages had become a rule, marriage for a woman came to be regarded as equivalent of *Upanayana* (Initiation into studentship), and the husband was considered her *guru* (teacher). A husband could mete out physical punishment to his wife for a violation as a teacher could punish his student in *Gurukula* (the home of the teacher where a student lived as a part of the family to obtain education).

Vedic literature, furthermore, does refer to polygamy. The *Rigveda,* describes the constant troubles of a husband harassed by the wives. Certain passages in the later Vedic literature show that polygamy was well-established in particular sections of society. In the later age, too, society did not have qualms about a man's having many wives. Manu had ten! If a wife, however, transgressed her husband, transferred her affections to another man, and married him, "she" was a sinful person. Polygamy was confined to rich men; the poor man could not afford this luxury.

Common people could take second wives. If the first wife

was barren, a man could remarry to ensure the birth of a son to offer monthly oblations to ancestors residing in heaven. A few religious scriptures go as far as to stipulate that the first wife must urge the husband to take a second wife if she herself is barren. These scriptures also point out that a man must wait for at least ten years to establish that his first wife is barren before taking a second wife. In the Indian society of the epoch, a man was declared to be guilty of the most grievous sin if he took a second wife without just cause. Around the beginning of the Christian era, however, men began to ignore the rule of the scriptures with regard to the second wife, particularly in the well-to-do families. Later Smriti writers from AD 500 on began to atone such actions of men. They began to advocate the shocking doctrine that a man has the right to discard his wife anytime she makes herself disagreeable to him. This principle, along with the lowering of marriage age for girls, proved disastrous for women's status. First wives began to be superseded even after they had given birth to sons. Even though Smriti writers called upon such husbands to provide for first wives if they wanted to live separately, first wives could scarcely countenance the thought of staying away from their husband's homes, as society tended to create scandalous gossip about their conduct. Judicial separation or informal separation became unthinkable if not impossible for the first wives, caught as they were between the proverbial rock and a hard place.

In the Vedic and Epic time, for a widower to remarry was unnecessary, as he could continue his Vedic sacrifices. Around the beginning of the Christian era, or around the time of Manusmriti, second marriage for a widower became mandatory. He could no longer use the icon of his first wife to conduct offerings. Certain rituals, like the pounding of sacred rice, were obligatory. Only a living wife could enact such a ceremony. Ironically, the Smriti writers, at this same time, proscribed remarriage for widows.

The status of a widow reflects the humanitarian element in a society. Is she allowed to remarry? Is she allowed to inherit her husband's property? The answers to such questions help to measure a society's altruism and egalitarianism. In prehistoric societies, the belief prevailed that, in the next life, a dead man needed all his worldly acquisitions, including his wife and concubines. Apparently, the same privilege did not extend to a dead wife; she faced eternity empty-handed and alone. Husbands would not allow wives equivalent customs militating against patriarchal self-interest. In the primitive war tribes, burning of widows was practiced as men were jealous of their women. They could not tolerate that their women should be abducted or raped by the enemy.

These customs might have existed in the Indo-European period when the tribes were probably located in Central Asia before their eastward and westward migrations in India and the European countries around 3,000 or 2,500 BC. When the Aryans (the Indo-European tribe to enter India) came to India, these beliefs and practices had already vanished as no reference to *Sati* appears in the *Rigveda.* In the Atharvaveda, a funeral ritual is described when a widow ascends the funeral pyre of her husband. She alights, and a prayer is offered that she may lead a life of children and wealth. One may, thus, infer that a widow was expected to remarry rather than to immolate herself.

What led the Aryans to discontinue Sati when they entered India can be only surmised. Probably, they had become more refined when entered India. Because the Aryans were invaders, they may have needed women to produce children so as to increase the armies required to conquer to vast land of India.

In the Brahmana and the Upanishad literature (1500 BC to 500 BC) no reference to *Sati* exists. In the period of 500 BC to 300 BC when Grihyasutras (rituals relating to domestic life) were composed, the custom of *Sati* does not appear. From the details of the funeral rite, one may deduce that the widow's relations brought her back to the house from the cremation site. The hope is expressed that she will lead a prosperous life. In the original part of the Epic *Ramayana,* no case of *Sati* occurs. In the Epic *Mahabharata* most of which was composed around 300 BC, few cases of *Sati* gain mention, but the instances of widows surviving their husbands outweigh *Sati* greatly.

The Buddhist literature of the fifth century BC does not mention *Sati.* If the custom were to have existed, Buddha would have condemned it as he condemned all animal sacrifices in the Vedic rituals. A Greek traveler who visited India in the fourth century BC, Megasthenes,. does not mention *Sati,* and Kautilya, the author of *Arthashastra* in the fourth century BC does not mention the custom either.

The authors of Dharmasutras (religious, social and moral codes) in the period of 400 BC to AD 100 and early Smriti writers like Manu and Yajnyavalkya in the period of AD 100 to AD 300 laid down elaborate rules for the duties of widows. None of them states that a widow must cremate herself along with her husband. In the early Puranas, composed around AD 400 cases of *Sati* are mentioned, however. The vast majority of the widows who figure in the early Puranas, survive their husbands, nonetheless. When women did commit *Sati,* they did so out of a mandatory, religious duty. Once a widow committed *Sati,* she altered her own *Karma,* which people in other relationships to the dead man could not. One must bear in mind that transmigration determine the nature of every succeeding birth. Only by birth and rebirth can the individual reach *Nirvana* or salvation. While Smriti writers referred to *Sati,* they did not hold it as an ideal for the widow. They allowed it only as a second alternative and regarded ascetic life as preferable. Certain Smriti writers condemned *Sati.* They allege that a widow could do more good to her husband by staying alive and by offering oblations at the time of *Shraddha* (the annual death-anniversary of a parent or husband) to ensure his happiness in the other world. The same Smriti writers admonished widows against *Sati* because this sin was the gravest of all and would definitely mean a long sojourn in hell for the guilty.

As time progressed, the antagonists of the *Sati* custom lost ground, and the propounders took the field by around AD

700. The latter began to assert that even though the status of present birth was determined by the nature of actions in the past birth, the woman who committed *Sati* was an exception to such Karmic debt. The merit of her self-sacrifice was such that it annihilates all her sins and those of her dead husband. According to such writers, the two could be united forever in perfect *Nirvana* or salvation in heaven. During AD 700 to AD 1100, *Satis* became more frequent in Northern India and Kashmir. The history of Kashmir is replete with cases of *Sati* in royal families; however, in the southern part of India, *Sati* was a rarity, as an Arab merchant, Suleiman, who had spent time on the western coast of India in the tenth century AD, attested. With little or no philosophical compulsion, queens infrequently mounted the funeral pyres of their husbands.

Initially *Sati* was confined to Kshatriya families, or the warrior class. Writers discouraged the Brahmin women from immolating themselves as to do so constituted a grave sin. Around AD 1,000 Brahmin widows also began to perform *Sati*. The explanation for this change in behavior lies in the high value Brahmins ascribed to the trait of being self-sacrificing. They could not let the Kshatriya women excel them in any respect. The writers of the period began to reinterpret the earlier writings which had prohibited Brahmin women from committing *Sati*. Such writers determined that, not *Sati* itself, but the motivation behind the act could amount to sin. Done from irrational sorrow, *Sati* condemned the practitioner; committed logically, *Sati* benefited the widow.

Arguments for *Sati* became so frequent that the custom also spread to the southern part of India after the tenth century AD. Of all the provinces of India, Rajasthan, in the western part of India, became most infamous for the high incidence of *Sati*. Most of the *Sati* women belonged to the royal or Kshatriya families. After AD 1300, widows belonging to the weaver, barber, and mason classes also began to commit *Sati*, as attested by 51 *Sati* memorial stones in the Saugar district.

In Karnataka (a southern province), many inscriptions dating between AD 1500 to AD 1800 testify to the glory of those who committed *Sati*. Concerning the Brahmin widows in general, even though canonical ban was lifted around AD 1000 the practice did not become popular among them, with the exception being those residing in Bengal where the rate of *Sati* among the Brahmin widows was quite alarming as reported in the British census of 1815-28. In the Calcutta division of Bengal, predominantly Hindu, 5,099 cases of *Sati* were reported. In the Dacca division, predominantly Muslim, only 610 cases of *Sati* are registered. The Murshidabad division, a Muslim area, recorded 260 *Sati* cases, while the Patna division, where the Hindus formed a majority, showed 709 cases. Westward to the U.P. province and the Presidencies of Bombay and Madras, the percentage of *Sati* in the Hindu population became much smaller than in Bengal. It was so high in Bengal owing to the existence of the Dayabhaga law which permitted even the childless widows to become a heir to the husband's property. The in-laws chose to eliminate a widow by persuading the forlorn woman to commit *Sati* so as to confiscate her share of the family property.

When the Muslim rulers established themselves in India from the Twelfth century AD to the beginning nineteenth century, they generally discouraged the custom. Humayun, the Mughal Emperor in the sixteenth century, sought to prohibit it in the case of widows beyond the child-bearing age. Another emperor, Akbar, laid down that the permission of a local official be sought before a widow could commit *Sati*. No evidence proves the extent of the success of these royal measures.

That *Sati* became an object of high veneration in the Hindu society is proven by the fact that while earlier writers merely mention the custom, the religious digests written after AD 1500 give details of procedure for the ritual. For example, a widow on her way to commit *Sati* had to gain full public exposure. Loud music would accompany the procession to the cremation grounds. Before saying good-bye to her relatives, the widow would give away most of her gold ornaments to them. Since the most anxious widow might seek to jump out of the funeral pyre, it was arranged in a pit so that she could not climb out.

Did the widows commit *Sati* voluntarily or was force used to compel them? To attempt to answer this problematical questions, one must rely upon the accounts of European travelers like Manucci and Nicoli Conti who state that force was used. Relatives would threaten the widow. If she were to run away, her family would treat the woman as an untouchable, never to be accepted back again. Other Travelers, like Tavernier in the seventeenth century and Ibn Batuta in the fourteenth century, describes the undaunted courage of widows who willingly embraced flames. That this was a religious duty for a widow to commit *Sati* rooted itself so deeply that even a betrothed but unmarried girl would also mount the pyre when her fiance died. The available evidence shows that, with a few exceptions, most of the widows who chose *Sati* did so voluntarily. The life of a widow was so dreary that most of the widows must have decided in favor of *Sati*. Other widows terminated their lives because they revered their husbands like gods—a veneration which the Hindu religion began to teach to young girls at this time. They learned that *Sati* provided for the spiritual good of both the dead husband and the widow.

The *Sati* custom, which horrified the British as the most gruesome of all the practices in India, was on the rise after AD 1300. The percentage of widows who committed *Sati* cannot be determined because of the lack of sufficient evidence; one may speculate, however, that even though later Smriti writers and Puranas deified *Sati*, it was still limited in society. Individually, widows could be persuaded not to choose *Sati*, but the important point to remember is that the Hindu society had not become so morally and collectively conscious of the evils of the custom as to start a public crusade against it. That the practice of *Sati* was not widely prevalent gains credibility in the fact that when William Bentinck, the British Governor-General in India in the early nineteenth century, issued his famous regulations in 1829 against the custom, no large-scale opposition arose. When the regulation was placed before the

British Privy Council for approval, both pro-*Sati* forces and anti-*Sati* forces (led by Raja Ram Mohan Roy)[4] went to England to solicit their cause. Without much difficulty, the resolution was approved.

Though the custom of Sati was abolished in British India, it continued to linger in Rajasthan for about thirty years more. Rajasthan was not within British India but was a subsidiary Princely State in which the British government only controlled the foreign policy and left the internal affairs to the management of the ruler. The princely State of Jaipur prohibited the custom in 1846, and other Rajput states gradually followed suit. The last public case of *Sati* took place in 1861 in the Princely State of Udaipur at the death of Maharaja Sarup Singh.

In October, 1987, one public case of *Sati* took place in Deorala village in Rajasthan. The author was in India at that time on her sabbatical leave. The incident was reported extensively in all the media, and they joined hands to condemn the affair unanimously. The women's organizations in Rajasthan, and the All India Women's Conference, in Delhi, held special sessions declaring the act reprehensible and demanding that the Central Government enact appropriate legislation. The Indian Parliament responded with great promptness signing a strict law which made it a high crime to abet and encourage *Sati* or to participate in the committing of *Sati*. The nearest relatives of the Sati woman were arrested and charges with manslaughter. Major newspapers such as The Hindustan Times and The Times of India gave extensive coverage of the public fury over the incident and of the law passed to control it. In the author's opinion, public sentiment ran so high, enflamed by daily broadcasts on television, that another incident of *Sati* would probably not take place. That the adverse sentiment expressed itself not only in cities but in villages as well was encouraging to witness.

Because widows before 300 BC were not permitted, or required, to die with their husbands, widows either had to remarry or had to live in widowhood and bear children by

Niyoga (levirate) if they had none. The custom of *Niyoga* was fairly common down to 300 BC. Women and children were regarded as property, and women belonged to their husband's families. In the absence of children, women had to be kept within the family by *Niyoga*. Besides, to have a son if the widow did not already have one was essential, as the son alone could perform Shraddha to the dead father.

Around 300 BC, child marriages proliferated, and the religious writers also began to speak against *Niyoga*. Although the custom did not disappear immediately, the number of children by *Niyoga* began to decrease. The period of 300 BC to AD 100 saw an increase in general prejudice against widow remarriage. Opponents of widow remarriage, however, did not condemn child widow remarriages. The Mahabharata states that sons of such remarriages would be fully entitled to offer oblations both to gods and men. The more conservative writers of the period allowed child remarriage only if the first marriage had not been consummated. In the absence of sufficient data, to say how many child widows availed themselves of this opportunity to remarry.

The practice of *Niyoga* continued to decline, going out of vogue by AD 600 the same period when *Sati* became generally accepted and prejudice against widow remarriage in the absolute became deep-rooted. Writers of the period from about AD 600 on began to justify the ban on child remarriages too as the Satyuga or moral age had gone by and the world has entered a new phase called the Kaliyuga or the immoral age.

Since *Niyoga* went out of vogue and widow remarriages wee also banned after AD 600 the implication should have been that widows be given a part of the family's property for sustenance. The in-laws could not have welcomed this implication; thus, the custom of *Sati* came to be strongly proclaimed as the best ideal for a widow. If the widow chose not to commit *Sati*, religious writers encouraged her to adopt the ascetic life of the large number of Buddhist and Jain monks. Society came so much under the spell of these writers that no one dared raise a voice of protest until the nineteenth century with the advent of Western ideas under British rule. One other factor which worked against widow remarriages came in the form of the Medieval Period's growing population of those engaged in lives of religious austerity. Although Buddhism declined with the intense Moslem onslaught against it, the ascetic ideal propagated by it did not. Hinduism would embrace severe self-denial as the ideal life.

Only in the early, and mid-nineteenth century did men like Raja Ram Mohan Roy and Ishwar Chand Vidyasagar speak against the prohibition of widow remarriage. The British government in India responded with the passage of the Widow Remarriage Act in 1856. The general society was slow to change. Even after independence in 1947, social disapproval of widow remarriages acted as powerful deterrent. Finally in the 1960s, the idea of widow remarriage was accepted among the educated classes. Nevertheless, still today the age-old habits and mores persist.

Although we do not gave an exact date for the origin of tonsure, it could not gave existed before AD 600 as widow remarriages were allowed until approximately 300 BC and as child widow—remarriages continued to be allowed in the early centuries of the Christian era. Since monks and nuns used to tonsure their heads as a part of asceticism, widows who did not commit *Sati* and decided to lead an ascetic life were made to tonsure their heads. It was believed if a widow had her hair on her head, she could not be associated with religious rites. Orthodox people would not even drink water she might offer them. This tradition remained quite strong until the end of the nineteenth century when a crusade arose against it.

Bibliography

Ambedkar, B.R., *The Rise and Fall of Hindu Women*, Jullundhar: Beheem Patrika Publications, 1970.

Ashraf, Mohammed, *Life and Conditions of the People of Hindustan*, New Delhi: Munshiram Manoharlal Publishers, 1970.

Auboyer, Jeannine, *Daily Life in Ancient India*, New York MacMillan Company, 1968, 3-28, 143-233.

Baig, Tara Ali, *India's Woman Power*, New Delhi: S. Chand and Company, 1976, 301.

Banerjee, Sures Chandra, *Aspects of Ancient Indian Life*, Calcutta: Punthi Pustak, 1972, 121-39.

Basham, A.L., *The Wonder That Was India*, New York: Grove Press, 1959, 44-79, 137-88, 232-345.

Bhardwaj, S.K. *Women in Veda and Aryan Scriptures*, New Delhi: Malik Ram, 1972, 135-54.

Brijbhusan, Jamila, *Muslim Women*, Delhi: Vikas, 1980; Bhattacharya, S.C., Some *Aspects of Indian Society from Second Century B.C. to Fourth Century* AD.

Chunder, Pratapchandra, "The Position of Women in Kautilya's Arthashastra," Indian History Congress, 3, 1939, Calcutta: B.L. Bannerjee, 1940, 573-63.

Datta, Kalikinkar, "The Great Women in India –1200 to 1800 A.D.," in *Great Women of India*, eds. Swami Madhavananda and Ramesh Chandra Majumdar, Almora: Advaita Ashram, 1953, 320-31.

Gulati, Saroj, *Women and Society: Northern India in the 11th and 12th Centuries*, Delhi: Chanakya, 1985.

Gupta, Sankar Sen, *A Study of Women in Bengal*, Calcutta: Indian Publication, 1970, 69-103, 193-246.

Hussain, Shahnara, "The Position of Women in Pre-Muslim Society, 700-1200 AD," *Journal of the Institute of Bangla Desh Studies*, I, I, 1976, 155-68.

Jayal, Shakamburi, *The Status of Women in the Epics*, Delhi: Motilal Banarsidass, 1966.

Johnson, Donald J. and Jean E. Johnson, *Through Indian Eyes: The Wheel of Life*, vol. I, New York: Cite, 1981, 19-75.

Kamath, S.U., *Studies in India Culture*, Delhi: Asia Publishing House, 1937, 3-117.

Kaur, Inderjeet, *Status of Hindu Women in India*, Delhi: Chugh, 1983.

Kidwai, M.H., *Women Under Different Social and Religious Laws*, Buddhism, Judaism, Christianity, Islam, Delhi: Seema, 1976.

The Laws of Manu, tr. By G. Buhler, Delhi: Motilal Banarsidass, 1964.

Swami Madhavananda and Ramesh Chandra Majumdar, *Great Women of India*, Almora: Advaita Ashram, 1953, 169-81.

Marglin, F.A., Wives of the God King: the Rituals of the Devdasis in Puri, Delhi: Oxford University Press, 1985.

Mathur, Ramesh, "Women in Hindu Society: Status and Image," *Journal of International Studies*, 1-4 (1974-77), 21-42, 42-50, 55-64.

Mazumdar, Vina, "Comment on Sati," *Journal of Women in Culture and Society*, 4, 2 (1978), 269-73.

Mirza, Mohammad Wahid, "Great Muslim Women of India," in *Great Women of India*, Swami Madhavananda and R.C. Majumdar, eds., Almora: Advaita Ashram, 1953, 378-94.

Mishra, Dhira, *Political Role of Women in the Ramcharitmanas*, Delhi: Neha, 1986.

Misra, Rekha, *Women in Mughal India*, Delhi: Munshiram Manoharlal, 1967.

Mitra, Veda, *Happy Married Life in Ancient India*, New Delhi: Arya Book Depot, 1965.

Patil, B.R., "Devadasis," Indian Journal of Social Work, 35, 4 (1975), 377-89.

Radhakrishnan, S., *Women in Hindu Society*, London: George Allen and Unwin, 1947, 39-98.

Sastri, Sri Rao, *Women in the Vedic Age*, Bombay: Bharatiyta Vidya Bhawan, 1969.

Talboys, J., *Indian Under the Muslim Rule*, Delhi: Cosmo, 1975.

Thakur, Upendra, *Some Aspects of the Ancient Indian History and Culture*, New Delhi: Abhinav, 1974, 219-40.

Thapar, Romila, *Ancient Indian Social History*, Hyderabad: Orient Langmans, 1978, 26-105.

Verma, Hari Narian and Amrit Verma, *Indian Women Through the Ages*, Delhi: Great Indian, 1976.

Vreede-De Stuers, Cora, *Parda, A Study of Muslim Women's Life in Northern India*, Assen: Royal Van Gorcum, 1968, 3-112.

References

1 Description of the historical status of women to AD 1800 will be direct avoiding introduction of any of the long-standing controversies among the Indian historians about the dates and interpretations of the classical literature. This monograph seeks not to pose resolutions to such dilemmas but does intend to focus its attention on the present-day problems of the Indian women. The definitive history of the status of Indian women back to ancient times must await further study.

2. In the next section it will be shown why marriage age of girls was lowered during the seventeenth and the eighteenth centuries AD.

3. The reader may read A.L. Basham's *The Wonder that Was India* to obtain more information on the approved and unapproved forms of marriages.

4. Raja Ram Mohan Roy was one of the earliest social reformers of the nineteenth century. His books on social evils are still widely read and are a monument to the human conscience.

2

Ancient and Medieval History of Women in India to 1800–II

ANY DISCUSSION OF THE freedom of women in public evokes the *purda* system, or the veil covering the face and a part of the female body. No reference to *purda* occurs in the *Rigveda*. In the Vedic age, as has been shown, girls were educated along with boys. Love marriages did take place. A young man could approach a young girl to win her love, and the two could go out together to view entertainment and sporting events. Had society practiced *purda*, such public appearances of girls would have faced considerably more censure. Nor, in Vedic times, did the status of girls after marriage demand *purda*. The Vedic marriage hymn requires that the bride be shown to all the assembled guests at the end of the marriage ritual. The hope was expressed that the bride be able to speak with composure in public and public assemblies down to her old age. The presence of women in social and public gatherings was a normal feature of life in the Vedic time.

In the early versions of the Epics around 300 BC or so, one does not come across the veil practice. The three wives of King Dasaratha go out to Chitrakuta to persuade Ram not to go in exile for fourteen years at the command of his father, King Dasaratha. They do so without the veil, or *purda*. When Sita, Ram's wife decides to accompany her husband on the fourteen years' exile in the thick forests infested with demons and enemies, the Epics remain silent about any *purda* difficulties. In the same way ladies like Draupadi, Kunti and Gandhari in the Epic of Mahabharata go out without any veil.

In the later versions of the Epics (written toward the end of the first century BC or early centuries of the Christian era), one finds frequent references to the veil. For example, the later versions describe the embarrassment of Sita embarking upon a long exile with her husband, Ram, when she had been living under the *purda* strictures.

From the existing, and at times conflicting, evidence, the conclusion tentatively emerges the *purda* came into vogue only in the early centuries of the Christian era. In the Arthashastra (written in the fourth century BC), the author does not mention *purda* as a mandatory custom for women, although he describes certain rules for public officials when they had to confront women who despite their having come from decent families, now lived in destitution and were forced to work in royal weaving factories for wages. The officials were to avoid gazing directly on their faces while inspecting goods or paying wages to these women. On the other hand, early Smriti writers like Manu, who laid down elaborate rules for the life of women, no where mentioned that women should not go out in public unless veiled.

Around AD 300 *purda* had come into existence as royal families were thinking it desirable that their ladies must conceal their faces with veils in public and only a select few males should view their countenances. The commentary on *Dhammapada* (written around AD 300) testifies to this preference to *purda*. While traveling, royal women hide their faces behind veils, and girls of marriageable age are segregated—not allowed to be approached by male servants. Royal example must have been cause for imitation by a few families in fashionable society. The custom appears to have been confined to Northern India, as the paintings and sculptures at Ajanta and Sanchi (in the South) represent mixed crowds of men and women moving together in the streets.

From these examples, one discerns that the veil or *purda* extended beyond the mere fabric draped across a woman's face; symbolically, the cloth acted as a force field dividing women from men who had no claim to them. While, outwardly, the veil be tokened the woman's modesty or served to protect her, it invidiously symbolized that she, like the jewel of a wealthy man's fancy, must be hoarded inside a dark, locked box. With the face as the feature of readiest public identity, the woman in a veil became faceless, lacking recognition, and ultimately selfless. Hidden, she was owned.

That the *purda* system must have been confined to royal and prominent families find further verification in the accounts of India recorded by foreign travelers like Yuan Chwang in the seventh century AD. He does not mention the existence of *purda*, which he probably would have noticed, had it existed widely. Another source of information is Rajtarangini, full of details of court life in Kashmir between AD 700 and 1100. An Arab traveler by the name of Abu Zaid visited India in the tenth century AD. He described how most of the women at courts appeared without any veils. One may infer safety that *purda* was confined to a small section of the ruling classes down to the tenth century AD.

Even though no formal *purda* system existed, Hindu women did feel restrained in their free movement. They could go out to visit their friends and relatives, but they had to return at night. Likewise, widows and maidens often avoided going out in public without proper guardians. If a woman's husband was out of town, she would stay home.

In pre-Muslim times, thus, the *purda* custom attract adherents from a small section of the ruling classes and from a few of the upper classes, although the movements of any Hindu woman obeyed strict limitations. The general custom of *purda* came into vogue with the establishment of the Muslim rule in the later Medieval Period around AD 1200. Ruling Hindu families and aristocratic families accepted *purda* either to emulate the conquerors or to provide added protection to their womenfolk. The Muslim *zenana* (quarter of women) was always so well-guarded that a veiled woman came to be accepted as the decent woman in the Northern Provinces of Punjab, U.P., Bengal, Bihar and Rajasthan where the Muslims were entrenched. In the Deccan, or South, Muslim control was far less firm, and *purda* did not obtain a foothold. One exception would be the Marathas who introduced *purda* in their families with a desire to render themselves as respectable as the Muslim rulers, whom they supplanted in the South in the course of time.

Other factors led to the inculcation of the *purda* system in the later Medieval Period. Child marriages at a tender age had cohered into a well-established practice, and husbands easily forced *purda* on them. Besides, the times were unsettled, as the Muslim invaders and marauders constantly molested the Hindu women. Hindu leaders must have felt that *purda* afforded an added security to young brides. In the fifteenth and sixteenth centuries, *purda* had become quite common among the rich and middle class Hindu families of Punjab, U.P., Bihar, Bengal and Rajasthan. Women of lesser classes, such as farmers and manual workers, could not afford to accept *purda*, as they had to move around daily in public in the fields and workshops. They however, would cover their heads constantly and, upon approach of a stranger, would at once throw a lapel of a sari (a long, traditional Indian female dress) across their faces. The boundary between self-protection and numbing shame wore gradually away.

Careers for Women: The high veneration afforded to women in the Vedic era owed partly to the Aryans' need for their cooperation in conquering and subjugating the indigenous people. Women's contributions to the making of bows and arrows and to carrying on civil activities, such as agriculture, weaving, and dyeing, were tantamount to being indispensable. When the task of conquest was completed and the Aryans embarked upon a relatively peaceful life, women in society's higher sections assumed other vocations. A teaching career proved enticing to the intellect of many a woman, well educated as she was. A separate word for a female teacher, acharya, distinguishes her from the wife of a male teacher (called acharayani), and the frequent use of acharya in the early texts demonstrates that several women taught. These teachers specialized in abstract subjects, such as theology and philosophy. In the Buddhist period, women continued to enjoy freedom of vocation; many chose to join the nunneries. Among these women were ranked great theologians and preachers. Other women elected a medical career, while several decided upon thc time-honored role of mid-wife. In the realm of business, no disabilities hampered women; they could freely sign contracts. No evidence shows the extent to which upper-class women participated in family business. Probably, they did not. So far as the women of the lower classes are concerned, they must have taken an active part in carrying on manufacture and related business activities.

Music is yet another vocation which a woman could have adopted. Fine arts, such as singing and dancing, ornamented the cultural life of the Vedic times. Evidence demonstrates, nevertheless, that ladies of upper classes could learn music but did not become music teachers. Male musicians and dancing girls were employed to teach.

When child marriages came into vogue in the first centuries of the Christian era, little time permitted girls to learn music. They could not learn after marriage because of the family responsibilities and the rules of decorum imposed upon them. Music gradually became the exclusive province of courtesan girls who came to have a peculiar position in society. Held in low esteem because of the prevailing social moral, they were paradoxically valued as the custodians of the art of music. Men began to wish for their company as their own wives knew no music. The number of dancing and singing girls swelled as more and more of them entertained in practically all the kingdoms, large or small.

When temples of Hindu gods and goddesses came to be built and endowed on a magnificent scale, dancing and singing acquired significant status as institutions for the expression of joy at religious celebrations. The *devadasis,* or temple girls, became as acceptable as religious iconography. Several Puranas of AD 600 and later adopt the practice of dancing girls to the extent that they recommend that dancing girls be enlisted by temples at the time of divine services. Often, temples would purchase girls to be permanent fixtures of devotion. To be favored with the birth of a child, barren couples would pledge to dedicate their first daughter to a temple, this increasing the number of temple girls.

The South abounded in the number of Hindu temples, as it remained distant from periodic invasions from the North-Western part of India (today's Afghanistan and Pakistan), and the institution of temple girls became widespread and well-established there. In the course of time, men who donated handsome sums to a temple earned the "liberty" of sexually abusing the temple girls. Again the population of the temple girls increased vastly.

Women and Public Administration: The role women played in public administration still remains a matter of controversy among historians. The cases of queens ruling independently by their own right number so few as to be inconsequential. Usually, when a princess had a right to the throne her husband would become the *de jure* ruler. Inscriptions, however, do testify to queens taking an active role in administration. This trend occurred in the Deccan or Southern India.

In the Vedic age, democratic assemblies must have existed as the marriage hymn explicitly states the desire that the bride to be able to speak with composure in public assemblies into her old age. Women must have participated in public gatherings. In the later Vedic age (1500 BC to 500 BC), the state of affairs changed. Women were not mentioned as participating in local assemblies. Gathering at certain levels of organization likely disappeared with the rise of large kingdoms. Village, town and guild assemblies remained the only popular bodies by approximately 300 BC. When women's education disappeared following generations of child-marriages (beginning around 300 BC), women's participation in local bodies became extinct.

Women and Religion: The social status of people often correlates to their place in religion's rites and rituals. In the Vedic age, women received *Upanayana* and the Vedic education. They could also recite Vedic hymns. When the husbands were gone on long trips, wives could start sacrifices on their own. (In the Vedic age, sacrifices paid one's all-important tribute to God; no temples had yet arisen for worship. Nor had the *Bhakti* movement emerged to emphasize devotional religion or intense love of God as a way to salvation.)

In the Vedic epoch, marriage, not renunciation underscored the ideal practical life. A wife's cooperation fulfilled the performance of sacrifices and other religious rites. A husband could not become a spiritual whole or ascend to heaven unless his wife accompanied him in the performance of sacrifices; no god would accept oblations offered singly by a man. As a son was indispensable to the spiritual well-being of a man in life after death—the performance of the *Shraddha* ceremony or offering of oblations to ancestors required male heirs—marriage became obligatory to have a son. The wife was the co-creator in this life. The importance of the wife gained further stature in the fact that she pounded the sacrificial rice, bathed the animal to be immolated, and laid bricks to build the altar. She also chanted the sacrificial hymns which, in a later age, came to be entrusted exclusively to a special class of male priests.

Such participation in sacrifices necessitated the wife's education in the Vedic studies, and indeed women undertook the *Upanayana* ceremony, or initiation into studentship. A girl sank to the rank of Sudra (the fourth class in the social structure) without *Upanayana*. Brahmins, Kshatriyas, or Vaishyas could not be born to her. Society relegated her children to the status of Sudra regardless of the social class of the father.

Anuloma Marriages: These were inter-caste marriages in which a wife belonged to a caste lower than that of the husband. In the Vedic age, such a wife, called a *Dvija* wife, had full religious privileges if she were the only wife of the husband. A Sudra wife, however, had no title to any religious and ceremonial rights.

In the period of the Brahmanas and Upanishads from about 1500 BC to 500 BC the volume of Vedic studies became extensive with the addition of lengthy commentaries written on the Vedas. The spoken dialect of the age had also departed from the language of the Vedic hymns, and the theory became popular that if one committed any error in the recitation of the Vedic hymns, one would produce disastrous consequences for oneself. Society began to insist that only those who could devote twelve to sixteen years to Vedic studies could undertake the project. Girls could afford, at most, eight years until they were married at the age of sixteen, and, hence, lost the opportunity to chant the hymns.

At this time, Vedic sacrifices also increased in complexity. Only those who had carefully studied all the details could perform them. As a result, participation of women in the sacrifices became a mere formality.

In the same period of the Brahmanas and the Upanishads, a wife, who could earlier offer oblations to the *griha-agani*, or house fire, in the absence of the husband, could not do so because a son or a brother-in-law would now do it. The wife, however, continued to perform one sacrifice, the evening one, but she was forbidden to chant the Vedic hymns.

Buddhism and Jainism became strong religions in the sixth and fifth centuries BC. Ascetic by nature, both did not devote much space to the duties and ideals of lay women. The founders and leaders of both shared the contemporary low regard for women. Though Buddha accepted women in the Buddhist philosophy and made them eligible for salvation, Jainism held that women could never have salvation unless first being born as a man. Both Buddha and Mahavira, the founder of Jainism, placed women nuns under strict control. They could not go out unless in groups of twos or threes. A joint meeting of the monks and nuns sanctioned the admission of a novice nun. New monks, however, could be admitted without consulting nuns at all. A nun could never preach before a congregation of monks, though a few selected among the monks could preach to the nuns. The rule most revealing of double standards included the injunction that a nun, even a hundred years old, must stand in reverence to a monk initiated only yesterday.

In spite of discriminatory rules, Buddhism and Jainism admitted women thereby raising their status in comparison to the Brahmanic religion (a later name for the Vedic religion).[1] Sects of Jainism even went to the extent of saying that women need not wed as marriage fetters salvation. As a result, a large number of talented women entered the folds of Jainism and Buddhism and posed a challenge to the Brahamanic religion.

In the period from 500 BC to AD 500 when the two Epics, Grihyasutras, Dharamsutras, early Smritis like *Manusmriti*, and *Yajnyavalkyasmriti* were written, certain basic changes took place in the Brahmanic religion and, consequently, in the status of women. By 500 BC the Vedic sacrifices has become so complex and the Vedic studies had become so time-consuming that women were barred from the performance the Vedic beliefs and rituals, which barred women from becoming recluses of sacrifices, except for a few minor ones. Women could no longer chant the Vedic hymns because any mispronunciation or omission would be disastrous for the entire family. Also, because a few women who joined the Buddhist and the Jainist nunneries began to fall into lapses because of the stern moral code, the Brahmanic religion, under the Smriti writers, eventually denied women a life of *Sannyas* (reclusive existence). Marriage became mandatory for all girls so that they could procreate and discharge their responsibilities to the family. To force marriage upon girls, Smriti writers (by the final century BC and the first century of the Christian era) drastically lowered the marriage age of girls. Manu recommended that *Upanayana* be performed just before marriage and that no Vedic hymns be sung during the ritual. These practices contravened the basic idea behind *Upanayana*. In the early centuries of the Christian era, Smriti writers like Yajnavalkya, thus, began to advocate that *Upanayana* was discontinued, other *Samskaras* (rituals, or sacraments) one-by-one fell into disuse.

Among all the vanished rituals, the lost *Upanayana* harmed women's status most gravely. Without this rite, women plunged to the status of Sudras (the fourth class in the Hindu social structure). Sudra having always been denied participation in the performance of Vedic sacrifices, wives also no longer could partake in the enactment of a sacrifice. The Smriti writers of the early Christian centuries conveniently reinterpreted the right granted to wives in the Vedic time as having been a joint partnership in the performance of a sacrifice. The reinterpretation, furthermore, cleverly and facilely stated that the joint partners had always referred to the husband and the priest taking part in a sacrifice. The mere inability to perform sacrifices did not inflict the greatest damage to the status of women; rather, *Upanayana's* obsolescence, effectively reducing women to Sudras, acted most nefariously. (The Brahmanic religion had also adopted *Ahimsa*, or non-violence, to counter the challenge of Buddhism and Jainism, which were partly based upon a rejection of animal sacrifices as a brutal practice. The Brahmanic religion also popularly came to be called Hinduism as more and more native gods, goddesses, and rituals were endlessly incorporated.)

In the period of AD 500 to 1800 later Puranas, and additional Smritis were written, and the *Bhakti* movement, or devotional religion, also became widespread. Long deprived of education (owing to the growth of child marriages), women heartily embraced unsubstantial superstitions as truth. The Puranas pander stories inimical to a rational mind but believable to credulous, uneducated women married at the age of eight or nine. By ascribing immoral acts to the gods, religious writers disguised vice as virtue, thereby condoning the reprehensible conduct of men. To describe the superstitions and the vices which came to grip Indian society is not this author's purpose. One has only to read the account of travelers and official gazettes to develop an indelible impression of the situation prevailing, around 1800. Patriarchal society has twisted the Vedic religion beyond recognition. By the beginning of the nineteenth century, the status of women has plummeted so low as to bring to the word "degradation" a new and ignominious definition.

Reference

1. Many native ideas and cults would be assimilated within the Vedic religion during the period of conquest and expansion. The assimilated religion came to be called the Brahmanic religion. But the core remained.

Section II

3

Women's Projects in the Five Year Plans in the 1950's

THE MAIN FOCUS in this chapter will be the first two Five-Year Plans from 1951 through 1961 with a preview of the British period. Because the Indian economy is predominantly socialist, as around eight per cent is centrally controlled, the importance of the Five-Year Plans becomes self-evident. The individual states and voluntary organizations all receive the bulk of their funding from these centrally formulated plans.

The British came as traders; they were interested in profits, not the welfare of the native people. The East India Company began as a trading operation and had no intention of permanently settling down in the country. The Company officials insulated themselves from the Indians. They allowed Hindus and Muslims to govern themselves by their own personal laws, while the British and the Europeans followed their own national laws. During the eighteenth century, certain British agencies undertook a few social reforms. For example, the Christian missionaries made a frontal attack on the caste-system and stressed the innate equality of all as embodied in the Christian religion. They also attacked idol-worship. The missionaries also brought in Western education by opening a few public schools. The deplorable condition in Bengal festered away; the caste-system exercised a powerful influence, and the practice of Kulinism licensed a husband of a high caste to marry a number of wives, thereby raising the caste of these women. He could not live with them. Many of these wives had to live the austere life of widows.[1]

Hindus responded to the denunciation of the Western missionaries. Raja Ram Mohan Roy (and others) founded the Brahmo Samaj in 1828.[2] These men advocated a return to the times of purity, as reflected in the Veda and the Upanishads, when the Hindu woman earned high esteem. The Brahmo Samaj admitted members of the untouchables to all privileges. Raja Ram Mohan Roy strongly urged the cause of Western Education and established many educational institutions.[3] In Bengal, men like Dwarkanath Tagore, Devendra Nath Tagore and Keshab Chandra Sen followed him. They participated greatly in social activities, such as improving the conditions of widows and providing of education for girls. The first school for Hindu girls opened it door in 1849. Because of the efforts of such men as Ishwar Chandra Vidyasagar, principal of the Sanskrit College, Calcutta, the British government passed the Hindu Remarriage Act in 1856.[4]

When the Indian National Congress was founded in 1885, its mission concentrated on social reform. Under Hume, the Congress later became a political body. A separate Social Conference convened in 1887 to address the pressing needs of the citizens of India. The Conference openly confronted the most glaring social issues of the day: infanticide, child marriage, widowhood, education for girls, improvement of the condition of depressed classes, and Hindu-Muslim harmony.[5]

As the Christian missionaries struggled to ameliorate the wretchedness of the oppressed classes and set in motion various social welfare agencies in the last two decades of the nineteenth century to help to achieve their ultimate goal of converting the masses to Christianity, the Indian social reformers did not lag behind in their similar efforts. Significantly, these nineteenth-century Indian social reformers did not base their case on the ancient Hindu scriptures but on the intellectual, liberal tradition of the

West. They met annually at the Indian Social Conference to address the lamentable social crises of the day.

The British government responded to these proposals of reform by enacting the following social laws:

1. The Widow Remarriage Act, passed in 1856
2. Civil Marriage Act, passed in 1872.
3. Married Women's Property Act, passed in 1874.

The year 1919 witnessed Mahatma Gandhi's ascension as leader of the Indian National Congress. The halls of the Congress had already admitted women, but now, with Gandhi in control, the participation of women would flourish, as he believed in the enormous moral power of women to influence events. In 1917, Annie Besant and Margaret Cousins had founded the Women's Indian Association; aware of the fomenting activity of such organizations by and for women. Gandhi sought to elevate women from their position beneath the troubled surface of Indian society.

The Congress could not vitally agitate to redress social issues other than untouchability, as its leaders became enmeshed in the political struggle and were held for many years in detention. Other social welfare organizations had to step in and take over the task of social reform. Most prominent were the National Council for Women founded in 1925 and the All India Conference (AIWC) set up in 1927.[7] The AIWC registered a striking growth and, in 1937, arrayed it central office with full-time office-bearers. It bought to the forefront of debate many issues of signal consequence to Indian women—essential questions arising from inheritance and marriage laws.

Pressured to act, the British government passed the following measures:

1. The Child Marriage Restraint of 1924.
2. The Prevention of Prostitution Act of 1923.

3. The Hindu Inheritance Act of 1929.[8]]

During the Second World War, the participation in politics and greater employment opportunities drew a large number of women from the seclusion of their homes. The government of India appointed a commission to consider such issues as Hindu inheritance and the position of women in matter of property right, divorce and monogamy. Sadly, not much came from the recommendation of this Committee because of the gravity of World War II.

After the Independence in 1947, the Congress Government declared India a welfare state—a proclamation that envisaged active participation by the government at both the national and state levels in all areas of national like. To an extent, the government did earnestly attempt to fulfill this sweeping promise. Articles 14, 15, and 16 of the Constitution enumerated the fundamental Right of people and guaranteed to all citizens equal protection of law and equality of opportunity in employment. In the light of these Articles, the government enacted laws to improve the social status of women.[9]

1. Improvement of women's rights and their status in the legislation.
2. Development of Women's education.
3. Health.
4. Economic independence.
5. Legitimate rights in the family and the community.
6. Care for victimized women.
7. Women's welfare organizations.

The Special Marriage Act of 1954 included a provision for obtaining a decree of divorce by mutual consent, provided that the parties have lived separately for a year and that three years have elapsed since the date of the marriage. Apart from the common grounds on the basis of which a divorce may be sought, a wife can seek a divorce if the husband has committed rape or bestiality. Also under this Act, persons who have married under other forms may obtain registration of their marriages and, consequently, be governed by its provisions. Those who marry under this Act (or whose marriages are registered under this Act) come under the purview of the Indian Succession Act of 1925 in matters of inheritance. When a man to whom the Indian Succession Act applies dies, leaving a widow and lineal descendants, the widow is entitled to one-third of the property of the deceased, the lineal descendants get two-thirds. Numerous women prefer to be married under the Special Marriage Act of 1954 because of its benefits. The wife has the right to maintenance the whole of her life, even if she starts living separately from her husband; the specific grounds entitling her to maintenance include the husband's cruelty, desertion, keeping a concubine, having another wife, suffering from leprosy, conversion to another religion, or any other cause justifying her living separately.

Under the customary law, the right of a Hindu wife to obtain a divorce confronted many more obstructions than that of a husband. Among Muslims, a husband can divorce without giving any reasons but simply saying, "I divorce you," three times. The Muslim wife, however, must run the gauntlet of securing a judicial pronouncement of divorce—and that, too, on specific grounds.

The divorce provisions of the Hindu Marriage Act of 1955 give equality to both sexes. The Act applies to Hindus, Buddhists, Jains, and Sikhs. The Act also provides for regular monthly maintenance favor of either of the two spouses. Further, if the recipient of the alimony is the wife, she must remain chaste. If maintenance is granted to the husband, he is enjoined from having sexual relations with any other women. Like the Special Marriage Act of 1954, the Hindu Marriage Act of 1955 helps to engender the spirit of egalitarianism.

Before the adoption of the Indian Succession Act of 1956, when a woman succeeded to the divided property of a deceased Hindu male, she took only a limited interest, as the law prohibited her from being a coparcener in a Hindu joint family. The Hindu Succession Act of 1956 (which applies to Hindus, Buddhists, Jains and Sikhs) determines the heir of a deceased person on the basis of affinity without any regard to sex. It gives a woman full ownership in the property inherited or acquired by her. This Act further prepares present-day India to accept equality of the sexes.

The Hindu Minority and Guardianship Act of 1956 provides that, even if a father appoints a guardian for minor children, any such appointment will not be effective during the lifetime of the mother if she survives the father of the children. It will take effect only after her death, provided she has not appointed a guardian by her own will. A Hindu mother also acts as the natural guardian of her minor children if the father ceases to be a Hindu or renounces the world by becoming a hermit.

In 1956, the Adoption Law applicable to the Hindus changed substantially. Now a Hindu woman can adopt a child—a right she had not enjoyed before. Previously, only a male could adopt, but, under the present Act of 1956, the law recognizes the competency of a woman to adopt a son or daughter. The Act further specifies that, except in certain circumstances, a man cannot adopt without the consent of his wife. Under the earlier law, her agreement was immaterial. Now, a court waives her consent only when she has renounced the world, has ceased to be a Hindu, or has been judicially declared to be of unsound mind.[10] A Hindu woman not of unsound mind and not a minor may adopt a son or daughter, provided she is a spinster, divorcee, widow, or one whose husband has renounced the world, has ceased to be a Hindu, or has judicially been declared to be of unsound mind. During the course, this succession Act aimed toward egalitarianism, the Suppression of Immoral Traffic in Women and Girls Act came into law in 1956; as its title stipulates, the prostitution of women finally faced proscription.

The Planning Commission chartered by the Indian Government and entrusted with the formulation of the Five-Year plans described the main objectives of the planning in India initiating a new process of development to raise living standards and to open new opportunities for a richer and varied life. Programs were to ensure a more equitable distribution of wealth; thus, the whole process of development traces a broad perspective—to guarantee to everybody the right to work, a decent living, and insurance against old age, sickness and disability. The Indian Constitution has provided a veritable cornicopia of special actions and plans for women and children. Likewise, it has set a priority to identify, and to protect, the interests of the weaker sections of the people, such as Scheduled Castes and Tribes far behind the national mainstream. The Planning Commission also realized that mere passage of laws does not necessarily lead to desired results—that many a proverbial slip occurs between the legal cup and the lip. A conducive public opinion had to form to enforce the essential social change.[11]

Because eighty percent of the Indian population lived in villages in the 1950s, the government embarked upon an ambitious rural development program. As laid down in the First Five-Year Plan (1951-56) the basic aims of the Community Development Program became these:

1. To provide for a substantial increase in the country's agricultural production and to improve the system of communication, rural health and hygiene, and village education.
2. To initiate and direct a process of integrated cultural change designed to transform the social and economic life of the villages.

The Community Development Program did not proffer outside aid or charity; rather, it encouraged village self-help.

It sought to arouse in the rural population a burning desire for a higher standard of living and the will to live better. Prime Minister Nehru wanted the rural people to be invested with a sense of intimate partnership in this national effort, and, with this aim in view, they were to be associated not only with the execution of the Five-Year Plans but also with their formulations. As its share in the effort, the government would provide technical aid and modest financial assistance; notwithstanding, the Community Development Program urged villages to realize their own needs and to evolve their own leadership for their progress and welfare. The government hoped that, after an initial period of subsidizing and directing, the Community Development Program would regulate and support itself. The assumption that the village people were eager to improve their way of life prompted such optimism. The government believed that the villagers wanted only the opportunity to see what they could accomplish with their own efforts. Officials did not naively overlook the fact that the villagers would be reluctant to accept the news in the beginning, but the government did assume that, once convinced, the rural people would plunge headlong into a program of reform and growth. The reluctance of the villagers to accept reform grew from their long suppression under foreign domination, which had mercilessly exploited the village masses. These people, thus, tended to look with great suspicion upon everything coming from the government.

Because the Community Development Program also proposed to further democracy, its framers stressed popular participation in planning and implementation. Program directors, thus, solicited the cooperation of all existing village organizations, such as the *Panchayat* (village council), Cooperative Societies, and other voluntary associations.

Projects of the Community Development Program addressed:

1. Agriculture and related matters.

2. Communications.
3. Education (including adult education).
4. Health (including pre-natal and post-natal care, midwife services, and public health services and education).
5. Social Welfare (including community entertainment and sport facilities, organizations of cooperatives and self-help movements, and provision of audio-visual aid for instruction and recreation.
6. Supplementary Employment (including encouragement of cottage industries and crafts as main or subsidiary occupations, providing incentives for medium and small-scale industries to employ surplus labor and to provide products for outside project areas, and improved housing on a self-help basis).

To implement a program of this magnitude, adequate administrative machinery equipped with technical knowledge and effective methods of mass contract proved essential. Personal contacts and discussions with individuals and groups and other effective means of communication, such as books, posters, plays, radio, exhibition, motion pictures, sought to reach out to the rural masses. Of all the workers, the V.L.W. (Village Level Worker) could most readily establish a daily contact with the people. His main responsibilities were:

1. To guide the villagers to identify their own needs while inspiring them with the desire to change.
2. To help villagers to plan their own programs so that they could bolster their own self-worth.
3. To discover and train local leaders so that the village development project could become a true program of self-help.
4. To complement the work of various government agencies, so those villages could develop organizations, such as women's associations (called

> Mahila Mandals) and youth and children's clubs which would actively participate in the Community Development Program.

The government anticipated that, by the end of the Second Five-Years Plan in 1961, the Community Development Programs or the National Extension Service would reach to the furthest extents of the rural landscape. Officials posited the even higher ideal of seeing the whole of rural India under intensive devélopment by 1966, the end of the Third Five-Year Plan.

Under the auspices of the Community Development Program, adult classes were started for women. Besides reading and writing, the curricula featured sewing and knitting, as homemade clothing was, and is, popular in India. Beyond this limited program, however, women were left to fend for themselves.[13]

Because the Community Development Program stemmed from the democratic concept of self-help, the foremost task challenged officials to educate the rural people about the need to change and the possibility of change. Given the rural elite's urban contact either with various political parties or with their relatives and provided with their solid knowledge of the development projects initiated by the government, the program directors could persuade the elite to inspire the masses that worked in their homes or in their fields. Controlled and run by the Central Government, the All-India Radio aired a number of programs to explain the new projects to the rural folk. In 1954, Panchayat Raj Department opened to distribute information about the development programs to the village elite, who, in turn, would inform their workers.[14] Speeches by political leaders echoed the same these that the vast developmental work undertaken by the government could succeed only if the people accepted the challenge and assumed the responsibility for their own destiny. Still a major source of entertainment in India, movies conveyed the goal of the projects. Exhibitions and conferences, tournaments and competitions among the villagers, and propaganda meetings by voluntary organizations stocked the arsenal of promotional devices. Officers received orders that they must fraternize with the people on religious festival days to break down the centuries old alienation between the bureaucracy and the people.

Coercion was, thus, not to be the basis of the developmental progress. For the rural people to act on their own initiative, adult literacy had to become a reality. Only by learning to read could the masses become competent enough to participate wisely in the village institutions, whose help the government officials had to seek at every stage of the development.

The years 1951 to 1961 of the first two Five-Year Plans enclose a period of experimentation during which the Indian Government learned crucial lessons from the reports of the official committee and from the experiences of V.L.W.s, both male and female.[15] Often, mistakes spawned insights:

Adult classes: Social education did not play as important a role as had been anticipated in conveying the aims of the Community Development Program. Education restricted itself to improving adult literacy and lost sight of the goal of convincing villagers to lead a better life. For that matter, adults failed to take much advantage of literacy courses, because they thought it ridiculous for adults to attend classes—the pastime of school children.

Women's education made little headway, as teachers employed were the same who taught in local girls' schools. These teachers could instruct women only after their regular school hours had ended. At that time of day, women forfeited attending class in favor of preparing supper. Besides, village constraints prevented a young daughter-in-law from wandering around to attend classes, while a woman with two or three children might do so. This woman, however, could not attend classes, for she could not bring the children to school or leave them at home. Women of upper castes refused to attend literacy class with women of lower castes and untouchables. Adult classes for men were discontinued after one year; with the pedagogical method the same as in elementary school, the lessons failed to hold the men's interest.[16]

Community Centers: Because religious and devotional singing served as virtually the sole activity of the Centers, they attracted mainly children. With more important chores to attend to at home, adults stayed away.

Group Discussions and Individual Contacts: Limited to village leaders supposed to instigate change, these gatherings and conversations involved only those individuals wishing to enhance their own self-interest.

Leadership: The Community Development Program aimed to identify natural leaders within a village, to educate them about the objectives and process of the development, and thereby to prepare them to serve as a catalyst generating a strong and compulsive desire in the whole of the village community to change on the basis of self-help. The Program Officials, however, found themselves associating with the traditional families of landowners. The common villagers had never liked these families because of their exploitative habits. When these families urged the people to support development projects, the latter did so from fear, not from conviction. This motivation tended to defeat the central goal of then Development Program—to create a burning desire for change among the people. This caste affiliations of these landowning families caused commoners to feel less conviction and more contempt. The Program Officials had to negotiate cautiously so as not to appear to favor one caste more than another. The alienation of certain castes menaced the best efforts.[17]

Association with traditional families posed another disadvantage in that many natural leaders were ignored who might have been considerably more amenable to change than the conservative traditional families. Logically enough, officials sought the help of the traditional leaders who had sway over the common villagers and thus helped the officials achieve targeted results by their deadlines. This official approach, however, tended to undermine the basic purpose of the Community Development Program—to instill in the people the voluntary desire to seek change.

Public Participation: A part of public participation was *Shramdan*, or the contribution of voluntary labor to carry out projects like road and canal construction or building a schoolhouse. Acting out of political self-interest, the village leaders assumed the primary responsibility for organizing the drives for *Shramdan*. The poor people who contributed did so reluctantly because they lost their daily wages. Also, the Project Officials did not concern themselves with *how* the labor contribution proceeded—only *that* the deadlines were met. This attitude did not foster that spirit of voluntary participation among the people, which the Community Development Program sought.

Village Panchayat, or Councils: The government hoped to resurrect a historic institution democratic in function and concept. In real life, however, village *Panchayats* became arenas for different castes and factions to battle for village domination. The hitherto dispossessed castes also entered the fray to gain a footing in the power structure of the village community. Competition supplanted cooperation.

Cultural Habits: So many times, officials had to modify projects to suit the cultural milieu of a village. For example, the construction of a drinking-water well in a village might gain the support of the leading caste, as such a public work could propagandistically enhance caste's community image. The Harijans, or untouchables, might support the well project because it would elevate their social status by their participating equally in the construction of the well.

The tenacity of old habits and the continued existence of age-old superstitions further complicated the carrying out of projects. For example, people attributed cold to the use of new seeds. Another illustration was the failure of an attempt by the officials to introduce the growing of vegetables as in the kitchen gardens of the United States. As vegetables were considered a part of a rich man's diet, poor people resisted eating them. Construction of public latrines (dry) proved a wasted effort; not accustomed to them, the villagers used them once then eschewed them thereafter. The project officials argued for applying cow dung as fertilizer to the fields, but the people customarily regarded manure as fuel and could not adjust their perceptions. Sanitary wells thwarted the women, as the wall stood high and the rope fixed over a pulley hung still higher, which made it necessary for women to adopt an uncomfortable posture while drawing water. Women justifiably refused to strain their muscles excessively. On the outskirts of the villages, workers dug compost pits to contain the village refuse. Even though the village *Panchayat* decreed that anyone not depositing leavings in the pit would be fined, the new system failed because women, who cleaned the house and the cowshed, would have to carry the refuse all the way from the house to the compost pits. Women of higher castes particularly rejected this effort, and the system fell into disuse. Again and again, villagers balked at new health and hygiene methods.[18]

Economic Factors: The lower classes refused tractors, as such machinery reduced employment opportunities for them. The attempt by the Project Officials to recruit and train leaders from the youth drew the censure of the elders, as leadership was associated with age in the traditional set-up. The lower classes often showed opposition to new methods because the elite groups in the villages would identify themselves with the officials and the city way of life. When the Project Officials chose leaders from poorer sections, the upper classes resented the selections and refused to acknowledge such leader. Thus the V.L.W. found himself needlessly embroiled in the factional and caste politics of a village. Naturally, his zeal rapidly waned.[19]

Past Bureaucratic Experience: The average person in a village tended to regard the developmental plans as political stunts on the part of the Congress Party to win the next general parliamentary elections or as attempts on the part of the government to increase agricultural production so as to satisfy the ulterior motive of increasing taxation or revenue. A few even viewed the whole development process as a passing fancy; after all, had not the British Government initiated a number of welfare projects which soon became moribund because of lack of support? The villagers also viewed the V.L.W. as working for salaries and not from any humane motivation. The V.L.Ws. also drew criticism as the representatives of a distant government who had come to fleece the poor villagers, even as the agents of the British Government had exploited them in the past.[20]

Non-involvement of people: In planning, villagers were not consulted. The officials condescendingly presumed that the common people in the villages possessed no experience in such work. As one would expect, however, planning done from outside and forced upon people meets resistance. Project officials had target and cut-off dates; they could not afford to spend too much time in discussion. The luxury of efficiency doomed many a project.

Wasteful Expenditure: One of the ideas behind the development plans had been to create enough funds within a village so that the whole process of construction could be self-funded in the long run. This objective faltered, largely because the people habitually spent wastefully on marriages, funerals, and other family functions for social display.

Positive Responsiveness

Although several factors hamstrung development efforts, the general responsiveness of the villagers led to certain positive results:

The national agitation of the early twentieth century had prepared the people for changes, and Gandhi deserves the primary credit. When radical changes began to transform India after Independence, people were not totally unprepared for them. A village might accept a new idea because the "good name" of the town was at stake rather than the "felt need" for the innovation. Also, upper-caste villagers might support the introduction of new educational institutions because they wanted their children to learn modern urban skills to compete for jobs in the cities. The same upper classes, however, looked with disapprobation upon education for lower classes because education would make them untraditional, thereby disrupting the social order dominated by the upper castes. The patriarchal tradition condemned education for women because they would acquire immoral urban traits, such as competing with men for jobs.

Received enthusiastically in the initial stages, the powers of *Panchayats* shortly proved disastrous because, instead of initiating grass-root democracy, these village councils shored up the authority of those upper families who had historically enjoyed social leadership. In a few instances, new families gained power by corruptly manipulating the voting of the villagers. Intense factional fighting came to mar these councils, the basic purpose of which was to extend to the common man the opportunity to participate in village planning. Though the *Panchayats* failed to produce the anticipated results, their presence did introduce the people to a democratic concept. They restrained the hegemony of the traditional families upon whom the British had conferred sovereign power by electoral competition from other families.

A number of other insights sprang into being by the end of the First Phase from 1951 to 1961:

1. Planners had to understand the close relationships between agriculture and industry and between the urban and the rural populations.
2. New techniques resulted in the poorer sections' loss of jobs, such as chaff cutters. New jobs had to be created for them.
3. The number of youth going to institutions of higher

learning had been increasing. They expected to find jobs; otherwise, they became frustrated and could pose political dangers.

4. Personnel of the development projects had to be adequately trained so that they could demonstrate with conviction the superiority of new skills and techniques.
5. Close cooperation between the social scientist and the Project Planners had to ensue. The former could conduct vital pre-project surveys of the area in terms of values, habits, needs, and population where projects were to be undertaken.
6. The V.L.Ws. complained that, after training when they went to work in various villages, no one came to provide them with on-the-spot guidance to deal with problems. For example, a female V.L.W. called *Gram-Sevika* was to open a *Balwadi*, or a pre-school center, for children from three to six years of age. She was supposed to start the day washing the children's hands and faces. The water scarcity, however, was so serious that it had to be fetched from far away. Another problem she describes in her diary grew from the constant presence of older girls in the *Balwadi.* The working mothers had left these girls behind to look after their younger brothers and sisters. The girls would bring three-to-six-year olds, but they would also sit around the center. The *Balwadi* soon became a recreational center for all. The same *Gram–Sevika* also describes how, at first, the mothers were reluctant to send their youngsters to her. She then conceived an ingenious way of overcoming this difficulty. In the evening, she would call upon the mothers socially and chat with them about their problems. After thus winning their confidence, the *Gram-Sevika* could persuade the mothers to bring their children to the center.
7. *Problems of Training*—Owing to the fact that the

> Community Development Program was dynamic, the training program for the workers had to change continually so as to keep up with the new, unforeseen objectives. Also, the same courses could not be offered to all the workers, as their assignments varied according to the needs of the villages.[21]

In concluding the 1950s or the first phase of the Community Development, it may be pointed out that the Rural Development Program on such a massive scale was the first of its kind on a massive scale. It not only won world acclaim but also led to increased participation by the United Nation's agencies in the rural regeneration program. For all it faults and blunder, the program encouraged Indian Villages to take that all-important first steps into the modern world. In turn, women in India began slowly to regain their lost equality.

References

1. One may consult the following books on British India in the Nineteenth Century. Mill, James, *The History of British India,* Chicago: University of Chicago Press, 1975, 72-190.
   Ray, N.R., *Western Colonial Policy: A Study on its Impact on Indian Society,* Calcutta: Institute of Historical Studies, 1981, 173-82.
   Robb, Peter G., *The Government of India and Reform,* 1916-1921, New York: Oxford University Press, 1976.
2. Raja Ram Mohan Roy (1772-1833) was one of the first Indian who rallied a group of people against the attacks of the Christian missionaries on Hinduism. He founded the Brahmo Smaj in 1828 which opposed idolatry which had crept into the practical Hindu religion. He also attached the existing social customs like *Sati* (widow burning) and casteism and admitted the untouchable castes to all the privileges of the Brahmo Samaj. He strongly urged the cause of western education and established many educational institutions. The efforts of the Brahmo Samaj led to the legal abolition of *Sati* in 1829 by the British Government.
   Other British legislation of the century included the Caste Disabilities Act of 1850 under which no person could be deprived of any right or

property by reason of his renouncing or being excluded from the communion of religion or deprivation of caste; and the Special Marriage Act of 1872 which applied to intercaste marriages. Under this act parties were given protection from forfeiture of the rights of succession by extending to them the Caste Disabilities Act. Kincaid, Dennis, *British Social Life in India, 1608-1937,* Port Washington, New York: Kennikat Press, 1971.

Basu, A.N., "Women's Education in India in the Nineteenth and Twentieth Centuries," in Calcutta Review, 3rd series, 60, 1 (1936), 67-80. The author denotes four periods. (1) 1820-50, government inaction and lack of policy for women's education, only minor private efforts; (2) 1850-80, beginning of government initiative and policy; (3) 1880-1900, great influence of religious, social and political movements; (4) 1900-on, various groups continue to support demand for women's education which led to some very concrete results.

Madan, G.R., *Indian Social Problems,* Bombay: Allied Publishers, 1966, 407-9.

Nehru, Rameshwari, "Early Marriage," in Shyam Kumari Nehru, ed., *Our Cause: A Symposium by Indian Women,* Allahabad: Kitabistan, 1938, 250-67.

Panigrahi, Lalita, *British Social Policy and Female Infanticide in India,* Delhi: Munshiram Mahoharlal, 1972, 204. The Act of 1872 prohibited infanticide in British India.

3. Chowdhury, D. Paul, *Voluntary Social Welfare in India,* New Delhi: Sterling Publication, 1971.

   Clifford, M. "Social Work During the British Period," in *History and Philosophy of Social Work,* 1961, 29.

   Gore, M.S. and I.E. Soares, "Historical Background of Social Work in India," in *Social Welfare in India,* 1960, 2.

   Madan, G.R. *Indian Social Problems, Bombay:* Allied Publishers, 1966.

   Majumdar, R.C. "Social Work in Ancient and Medieval India," in *History and Philosophy of Social Work,* 1961, 17, 22.

   Natarajan, S., "A Century of Social Reform in India," in *Social Welfare in India,* 1959, 23-24, 51.

4. Ishwar Chandra Vidyasagar was a great advocate of social reform in the nineteenth century. He was greatly instrumental in the enactment of the Hindu Widow Remarriage Act of 1856.

   Ali Baig, Tara, India's Woman Power, Delhi: S. Chand and Co., 1976, 272, 281.

   Naidu, Muthyalayya, "Beginning of Widow Remarriage Movement in India," in *Modern Review,* 118, 6 (1965), 490-92.

5. All India Congress Committee, *Congress Varnika: One Hundred Years of the Indian National Congress,* New Delhi: AICC, December, 1985.

   Andrews, C.F., *The Rise and Growth of the Congress Party in India,* London: George Allen and Unwin, 1934, 91-141, 201-90.

Gautam, Ram Sakha, *Indian National Congress and Constitutional Changes, 1885-1975*, New Delhi: Chetna Publications, 1981, 1 15.

Ghose, Sankar, *Indian National Congress, Its History and Heritage*, New Delhi: All India Congress Committee, 1975.

The Indian Nationalist Movement, 1885-1947: Selected Documents, B.N. Pandey, ed., New York: St. Martin's Press, 1979

6. Bose, Pramatha Nath, *Education Under British Rule: A History of Hindu Civilization*, vol. l. II, New Delhi: Asian Publication Services, 1978, 205-16.

   This book discusses the missionary efforts in the nineteenth century in the realm of educational institutions for women like the establishment of the Bethune School in 1849 and progress of education in Bengal from 1849-93; advance of education in Bombay to 1892; education in Madras from 1841-92, education in Punjab from 1855-92.

   India: Bureau of Education, *The Beginning of Female Education. Selections from Educational Records*, part 2 (1840-59), Delhi: Manager of Publications, Government of India, 1965, 32-63.

   Sen, Hannah, "Education of Women and Girls," in *Our Cause*, Shyam Kumari Nehru, ed., Allahabad: Kitabistan, 1938, 93-110.

   Wasi, Muriel, "Education," in *Women of India*, Tara Ali Baig, ed., New Delhi: Publications Division, Ministry of Information and Broadcasting, Government of India, 1958, 53-60.

7. Asthana, P., "A History of Women's Movement in India from 1857 to 1957," Thesis, Agra University, New Delhi: Indian Council for Social Science Research or ICSSR.

   Bagal, Jogesh C., "Women in Indian's Freedom Movement," in *Modern Review*, 93, 6 and 94, 1 (1953), 53-61, 467-73.

   Bala, Usha, *Indian Women Freedom Fighters 1857-1947*, New Delhi: Manohar Publications, 1986.

   Basu, Aparna, "The Role of Women in the Indian Struggle for Freedom," in *Indian Women: From Purdah to Modernity*, B.R. Nanda, ed., New Delhi: Vikas, 1976, 16-40.

   Chakravarthy, Renu, *Communists in Indian Women Movement 1940-1950*, New Delhi: People's Publishing House, 1980.

   Chattopadhyaya, Kamla Devi, *Indian Women's Battle for Freedom*, New Delhi: Abhinav Publications, 1983.

   Chopra, P.N., *India's Struggle for Freedom: Role of Associated Movements*, Delhi: Agni, 1985.

   Swami Madhavananda and Ramesh Chander Majumdar, eds., *Great Women of India*, Mayavati, Almora: Advaita Ashram, 1953. This is a voluminous work as it has contributions by experts on different historical periods.

   Jain Devika, ed., *Indian Women*, New Delhi: Publications Division, Ministry of Information and Broadcasting, Government of India, 1975.

Kaur, Manmohan, *Women in India's Freedom Struggle*, New Delhi: Sterling Publications, 1985.

Mathew, P.M., *Women's Organizations*, New Delhi: Ashish, 1986.

Nethercot, Asther, *Last Four Lives of Annie Besant*, Chicago: university of Chicago Press, 1963.

Shah, K., "Voluntary Organization and Women's Liberation," Thesis, South Gujarat University, Anand, 1980, New Delhi: Indian Council for Social Sciences Research.

Shah, Kalpana, *Women's Liberation and Voluntary Action*, Delhi: Ajanta Publication, 1984, 43-96.

8. *Index to Proceedings of the Ministry of Home Affairs* housed in the National Archives, New Delhi is a listing of issues regarding Indian women which engaged the attention of the British Government. Some of these listings are given below as an illustration:
   (i) Women—Convicted of infanticide in the Punjab in 1884, Police, November 16, 1885, 101-3.
   (ii) Women—Remarrying whose husbands have not been heard of for more than seven years, Ecclesiastical, June 1876, 203.
   (iii) Women—Sentenced to imprisonment for helping girls for immoral purposes, Police, February 15, 1902, 187-90.
   (iv) Women Police Officers—Proposed adoption of measures for the prevention of inhuman practices obtaining in betrothals. Proposal for the appointments of women police officers to aid in the suppressions of betrothals, Police, April, 1919, 173-89.
   (v) Women's Medical Service—Recommendations of the Medical Services Committee regarding Women's employment in Medical Services, Medl., August 1, 1919, Deposit.
   (vi) Women—Resolution by the Women's India Association asking for removal of the disqualifying bar against women legal practitioners, F. 816, Judl., 1922.
   (vii) Women—Resolution in the Legislative Assembly to amend the criminal law with regard to offences against the person in case of women, such as kidnapping, abduction and rape, so as to enable more deterrent punishment being inflicted on culprits, F. 6801: Judl., 1926.
   (viii) Women, Right of—Resolution in the Council of State regarding the appointment of a Committee to consider the question of giving women the same rights as men in matters of succession to deceased Hindu's estate, F. 631, Judl., 1928.
   (ix) Women—a bill to amend the Hindu Law of Inheritance so as to make better provision for certain heirs especially women, F. 858, Judl., 1928.
   (x) Women's Conference—All India Resolution passed by the Women's Conference regarding the right of women to inheritance, polygamy, and the right of Muslim women to divorce,

F.No. 1069/29, Judl. 1992.

(xi) Women—Resolutions passed at the Eleventh Session of the All India Muslim Ladies Conference regarding the appointment of a department of Quzzat and regarding the rights of Muslim women in respect of Inheritance and Divorce, F.no. 359/29, Judl., 1929.

(xii) Women—Resolution passed by the Indian National Social Conference regarding marriage of children, status of women and other aspects of social reform, F. no. 99/29, Judl., 1929.

(xiii) Women—Resolution to be moved in the Legislative Assembly regarding the appointment of a Committee to examine the law relating to the status of rights of women, F. 58., Judl., 1930.

(xiv) Widow Remarriages—Resolution in the Legislative Assembly that exorbitant demands in connection with marriage dowries be penalized, and that all *Panchs* (village elders) who punish those, who marry widows, should be punished, F. 58, Judl., 1930.

(xv) Women—Questions in the Legislative Assembly regarding Franchise Qualifications for Women, F. 1/16/33, Pub., 1933.

(xvi) Women—Crimes Against—Proposed Question in the Council of State regarding crimes against women and the steps proposed by the government to eradicate evil, F. 853/33, Judl., 1933.

(xvii) Women's Legal Disabilities, F. 19.IV/35, Judl., 1935.

(xviii) Women—Steps Government proposes to take against outrages on women, F. 20/3/35, Judl., 1935.

9. Banerjee, Anil Chandra, *A Survey of the Indian Constitution*, Calcutta: A. Mukherjee, 1957.

Gledhill, Alan, *The Republic of India: The Development of its Laws and Constitution*, Westport, Greenwood Press, 1970.

Gupta, S.N., *Personal Laws*, Delhi: Commercial Law Publications, 1983.

Minattur, Joseph, "Women and Law," in Alfred de Souza, ed., *Women in Contemporary India*, Delhi: Manohar, 1975, 96-109.

Mitter, Dwarka Nath, *The Position of Women in Hindu Law*, New Delhi: Inter-India Publication, 1984.

Appendix 1 of the Indian Constitution established justice, liberty, and fraternity for all. Article 14 of the Constitution prohibits discrimination on grounds of religion, race, sex or place of birth. Article 16 guarantees equality of opportunity in matters of public employment. Article 23 prohibits traffic in human beings and forced labor. Article 39 includes Directive Principles to the Indian States to ensure that men and women have equal right to an adequate means of livelihood and equal pay for equal work for both men and women. Article 42 provides for just and human conditions of work and maternity relief.

10. Ali, Firasat, *Divorce in Mohammed Law*, New Delhi: Deep and Deep Publications, 1983.

India: Hindu Law Committee, *Report*, New Delhi: Manager of Publications, Government of India, 1947, 188. (This Committee was appointed in 1947 to propose a code on Hindu Law. The Report of the Committee lists public objections to some of the provisions of the Hindu Code Bill introduced in the Indian Parliament.)

Kaur, Inder Jeet, *Status of Hindu Women in India,* Delhi: Chugh Publications, 1983.

Minnatur, Joseph, "Women and the Law," in Alfred de Souza, ed., *Women in Contemporary India,* Delhi: Manohar Book Service, 1976.

Mitter, Dwarka Nath, *The Position of Women in Hindu Law,* New Delhi: Inter-India Publication, 1984.

Vreede-De Stuers, Cora, *Parda, A Study of Muslim Women's Life in Northern India,* Assen: Van Gorcum, 1968, 41-98.

11. Planning Commission was set up by the Indian Government in 1950 to undertake the drafting of the Five-Year Plans to develop the country economically and generally. The drafts of the Five-Year Plans are available in the Central Secretariat Library, New Delhi, which houses the official documents.

Hanson, A.H., *The Process of Planning: A Study of India's Five-Year Plans, 1950-1964,* London: Oxford University Press, 1966.

Nehru, Jawaharlal, *The Discovery of India,* New York: The John Day Company, 1960, 317-30; Nehru, Jawaharlal, *Independence and After: A Collection of Speeches 1949-1953,* Freeport: Books for Libraries Press, 1971, 50-56; *India's Independence and Social Revolution,* New Delhi: Vikas, 1984, 103-59; *Jawaharlal Nehru's Speeches,* 1953-57, New Delhi: Publications Division, Ministry of Information and Broadcasting, Government of India, 76-82, 90-105, 472-76.

Shenoy, Sudha R., *India: Progress or Poverty: A Review of the Outcome of Central Planning in India, 1951-1969,* London: Institute of Economic Affairs, 1971.

Singh, Tarlok, *Towards an Integrated Society: Reflections on Planning, Social Policy and Rural Institutions,* Westport: Greenwood Publishing Corp., 1969.

12. *Action for Rural Change, Readings in Indian Community Development,* New Delhi: Munshiram Manoharlal, 1970, 99-161.

Bhattacharya, S.N., *Community Development,* Calcutta: Academic Publishers, 1970, 1-64.

Community Projects—First Reactions, 1954, New Delhi: Publications Division, Ministry of Information and Broadcasting, Government of India.

Dube, S.C., *India's Changing Villages,* London: Routledge and Kegan Paul, 1961, 1-56.

Evaluation Report on first Year's Working of Community Projects 1954: Community Projects—First Reactions, 1954; Evaluation Report on Second Year's Working of Community Projects, 1955; Evaluation Report, 1957, New Delhi: Planning Commission Government of India.

Five-Year Plan, A Draft Outline, New Delhi: Planning Commission,

Government of India, 1951, 82.
A Guide to Community Development, New Delhi: Ministry of Community Development, Government of India, 1957.
Jawaharlal Nehru's Speeches 1953-1959, New Delhi: Publications Division, Ministry of Information and Broadcasting: Government of India, 90-105.
Karve, D.G., *Community Development and Cooperation,* New Delhi: Ministry of Community Development: Government of India, 1957.
Krishnamachari, T.V., *Community Development in India,* New Delhi: Publications Division, Ministry of Information and Broadcasting, 1958.
Marriott, McKim, *Village India: Studies in the Little Community,* Papers by Alan R. Beals and others, Chicago: University of Chicago Press, 1955.
Nehru, Inaugural Speech at the Development Commissioner's Conference, New Delhi, May 1952, 2; New Delhi: Publications Division, Ministry of Information and Broadcasting, Government of India.
Pattern of Rural Development: Report of a Seminar, February 1958, New Delhi: Indian Institute of Pubic Administration, 1958.
Taylor, C., Ford Foundation Consultant on Community Development, *A Critical Analysis of India's Community Development Program,* issued by the Community Project Administration, Government of India, September 1956, 13.
Wilson, M.L., *Community Development in India: Report of Survey,* New Delhi: Ministry of Community Development, Government of India, 1956.

13. Coldwell, M.J., R. Dumont and M. Read, *Women and Village Programs: Report of a Community Development Evaluation Mission in India,* New Delhi: Ministry of Community Development, Government of India, 1956.
Jawaharlal Nehru's Speeches, 1953-1957, New Delhi Publications Division, Ministry of Information and Broadcasting, Government of India, 472-76; *Jawaharlal Nehru, An Anthology,* Sarveppalli Gopal, ed., Delhi: Oxford University Press, 1980, 242-88.
National Committee on Women's Education Report, New Delhi: Ministry of Education, Government of India, 1959.
Subbalakshmi, G., "Role of Mahila Samaj, Some Suggestions," in *Kurukshetra,* vol., XIII, July, 1965, 16-17. *Kurukshetra* is a publication of the Ministry of Agriculture, Government of India.
"Women in Community Development," in *Kurukshetra,* June, 1964.

14. Article 40 in the Directive Principles of the Indian Constitution makes a provision for the formation of village *Panchayats* or elected village councils as units of self-government.
Action for Rural Change: Readings in India Community Development, New Delhi: Munshiram Manoharlal, 1970, 189-223.
Bhattacharya, S.N., *Community Development,* Calcutta: Academic

Publishers, 1970, 65-81.
Dube, S.C., India's *Changing Villages,* London: Routledge and Kegan Paul, 1967, 85-102.
Mehta, Ashok, "Development: Address to the Community Development and Panchayat Raj." In *Kurukshetra,* August 1964, 6-7.
Nehru, Jawaharlal, "Men the Ultimate Objective," in *Community Development, Panchayat Raj and Cooperation,* Delhi: Publications Divisions, Government of India, 1965, 1, 7, 90, 92; *On Community Development and Panchayat Raj,* Delhi: Government Press, 1963; *Nehru's Speeches,* 1957-1963; New Delhi: Publications Division, Ministry of Information and Broadcasting, Government of India, 92-93.
"Population Participation," from *Evaluation Report on Second Year's Working of Community Projects,* vol. I, New Delhi: Planning Commission Evaluation Organization, Government of India, 1951, 37-42.
"Reasons for Disorganization of the Gram Sabha," from the *Report of the Study Team on the Position of Gram Sabha in Panchayat Raj Movement,* New Delhi: Ministry of Community Development Government of India, April 1963, 13.
Report on the Panchayat Election in Rahasthan, 1960, Jaipur: Evaluation Organization, Rajasthan Cabinet Secretariat, 1961; "Panchayat Raj," in *Kurukshetra,* April 1959, 13.

15. *Action for Rural Change, Readings in India Community Development,* New Delhi: Munshiram Manoharlal, 1970, 352-84.
Bhattacharya, S.N., *Community Development,* Calcutta: Academic Publishers, 1970, 110-36.
Dube, S.C., *India's Changing Villages,* London: Routledge and Kegan Paul, 1969, 102-36.
16. "Govind Sahay Committee," as reported in *Kurukshetra,* March 1961, 17-18.
Report of the Team for the Study of Community Projects and National Extension Service, (Balvantray G. Mehta, leader), 1957, vol. I (November 1957), 44, 125-61, vol. III, parts I, II (December 1957), 2, 3, 7, 11, New Delhi: Committee on Plan Project, Government of India.
Reserve Bank of India Bulletin, New Delhi: Government of India, January 1961.
17. Dube, S.C., *India' Changing Villages,* London: Routledge and Kegan Paul, 1958, 177, 22-30.
Krishnamachari, V.T., "The National Extension Movement and Community Projects," in *Sainik Samachar,* January 1957.
Kurukshetra, April 1959, 13; January 1961, 4.
Mehta Report, vol. I, 115, 117, 125-61, New Delhi: Committee on Plan Project, Government of India.
Nanavati, M.B., *Group Prejudices in India: A Symposium,* Westport: Greenwood Press, 1970.
Nation-Buildings in India: Socio-Economic Factors, R.C. Dutt, ed., New

Delhi: Lancer International in Association with India International Center, 1987.

Sharma, Miri*am, The Politics of Inequality: Competition and Control in an Indian Village,* Honolulu: University Press of Hawaii, 1978.

18. Kapp, William K., "The Retardation of Economic Development," in *Hindu Culture, Economic Development and Economic Planning in India, A Collection of Essays,* Bombay: Asia Publishing House, 1963, 41-66.

Srinivas, M.N., *Caste in Modern India and Other Essays,* Bombay: Asia Publishing House, 1962.

Tilman, Rovert L., "The Influence of Caste on Economic Development," in *Administration and Economic Development in India,* Ralph Braibanti and Joseph L. Spengler, eds., Durham: Duke University Press, 1963, 213-23.

Wiser, Charlotte M., *Behind Mud Walls 1930-1960,* Berkeley: University of California Press, 1971.

19. Carstairs, Morris, "Hindu Personality Formation Conscious Processes," in *The Twice-Born,* London: Hogarth Press, 1961, 137-51.

Bhattacharya, S.N., *Community Development,* Calcutta: Academic Publishers, 1970, 97-109.

Dube, S.C., *Indian's Changing Villages,* London: Routledge and Kegan Paul, 1958, 157-220.

"Gram-Sevika and Mukhya-Sevika," in *A Guide to Gram-Sevika and Mukhya-Sevikas,* New Delhi: Ministry of Community Development, Government of India, 1961, 47-51.

"Popular Participation," from *Evaluation Report on Second Year's Working of Community Projects,* vol. I, New Delhi: Planning Commission Evaluation Organization, Government of India, 1955, 37-42.

20. *Action for Rural Change, Readings in Indian Community Development,* New Delhi: Munshiram Manoharlal, 1970, 406-11.

Bahattacharya, S.N., *Community Development,* Calcutta: Academic Publishers, 1970, 97-109, 137-58.

Chakravarti, S., "Block as a Unit Planning," in *Kurukshetra,* April, 1964, 9-10.

Coldwell, M.J. and M. Reed, "Problems of Staff and Supervision," from *Report of a Community Development Evaluation Mission in India,* New Delhi: Ministry of Community Development, Government of India, 1959, 41-46.

"Community Development," from *Report 1963-1964,* New Delhi: Ministry of Community Development, Government of India, 1963, 34.

Dube, S.C., *India's Changing Villages,* London: Routledge and Kegan Paul, 1969, 157-222.

"Gram-Sevika—The Useful Link" from *A Guide to Gram-Sevikas and Mukhya-Sevikas,* New Delhi: Ministry of Community Development, Government of India, 1961, 11.

"Importance of Atmosphere in Training," from *Report on Training*

Center Visited by the High Level Team on Training, New Delhi: Ministry of Community Development, Government of India, 1961, 8.

"Importance of Block Staff Team Work," in *A Guide to Community Development,* New Delhi: Ministry of Community Development, Government of India, 1962, 113.

Mukherji, B., "Problems of Training," in *Kurukshetra,* June 1961, 5.

"Problems of Trainees During and After Training," from *Report on Training Centers Visited by High Level Team on Training,* New Delhi: Ministry of Community Development, Government of India, 1961, 19-20.

Shiwalkar, R.S., "Problems of Community Development Workers," in *Kurukshetra,* 1964, 17-18.

"Some Considerations in Training for Community Development," from *Study Kit on Training for Community Development,* New Delhi: Ministry of Community Development, Government of India, 1962, 157.

Taylor, Carl C., "Training Personnel for Community Development," from *India's Roots of Democracy,* New Delhi: Orient Langmans, 1965, 222-26.

Vithal, B.P.R., "The Gap Between Training and Field Conditions," in *Kurukshetra,* June, 1961, 10.

"Weeding out of Unsuitable Staff" from *Main Recommendations, Proceedings and Agenda Notes on Annual Conference on Community Development and Panchayat Raj,* New Delhi: Ministry of Community Development, Government of India, 1964, 219.

4

Women's Situation in the Five Year Plans of the 1960's

THE SECOND PHASE from 1961-66 saw further intensification of village institutions such as *Panchayats*, cooperatives, and village schools. To help foster a further growth of understanding between the official hierarchy and the elected officials in the villages, block and district levels were emphasized. Planning and action focused on the interest, initiative and leadership of the people themselves. It was also realized that the economic base of a village should be strengthened through increases in agricultural production; in turn, development in other areas of rural life would occur with more speed and quantum. Agriculture, thus, came to occupy the highest priority. However, despite the lessons learned from past mistakes, serious problems persisted in the second phase.

The V.L.W., or Gram-Sevak, found himself impeded. In the beginning, village people had admired him, as he brought government money and other materials for projects. Later village people became suspicious of the V.L.W.; they questioned if he were on their side or government's. The V.L.Ws. contributed to the climate of distrust, for, early on, they assumed the bureaucratic posture of expecting the villagers to come to their offices for their needs. The V.L.W. also found himself short of time to attend to village problems, as he had to make frequent visits to block headquarters for odds and ends requested by the village people.

The role and status of the V.L.W. also suffered because the bureaucratic hierarchy took over the ladder of development, on the lowest rung of which stood the V.L.W. The village *Panchayats* failed to become effective instruments of planning and action. With the V.L.W. initially assigned to work in a team spirit with the *Panchayats,* to him the villagers imputed the *Panchayat's* corruption.

Inequities inland ownership hindered the creation of a community spirit among the poor. The Land Reform Act had placed a ceiling on the amount of agricultural land to be owned by previous Zamindars, many of whom were absentee landlords under British rule. Several connived with government officials to conceal the real extent of their land ownership. The ignorance of the poor people had also played into their hands to help them maintain large tracts of land. Whatever land the government ceded to the poor landless farmer was bought right back by the landlords at a pittance. The poor rural father counted so many social responsibilities, such as giving dowries, sponsoring expensive funerals, or hosting other social festivals enjoined by the unwritten caste and village codes, that he all too quickly grasped any ready cash from his new lord.

Because only a few farmers at the top benefited economically by securing easy credit for purchasing tractors and seed, the marginal farmers also tended to lose their lands to the few rich. As a result, they had no choice but to migrate into cities where urban slums sprawl sullenly across whole landscapes.

Rural development ran afoul of Hinduism. Given the belief that each present birth results from the cumulative effects of all past births, the votary accepts the current status with a resignation detrimental to the concept of democratic development. The respect for individual in communities carries with it the concomitant belief in the individual's desire to improve and that person's ability to do so. Honored by the religious sanctions of the past's sages, the caste system stands as a formidable obstruction to the emergence of that wider, national solidarity necessary for economic development and political democracy. In a society divided by caste and birth, and with many so accustomed to oppression as to be submissive, each group fears that an anticipated change will place a rival group in an advantageous position. A caste-controlled society also fails to develop that identification with national objectives which should override family, caste and kin considerations. A people dominated by caste could hardly initiate those self-help institutions for their betterment that the Community Development Program envisaged.

The Joint-family system also weighed as a massive encumbrance. Despite its benefit as a social insurance agency, its wrong have been many. It promotes a high rate of fertility while the rate of mortality has gone down with the control of epidemics and with other health improvements. It instills in the individual a sense of subservience to the group—an obsequiousness that produces a regimented being, not an individual willing to take the initiative. This dependency explains why the village people came to expect so much from outside sources like the government instead of creating their own self-help institutions for their advancement. The joint family also induces wasteful expenditures like costly funerals, weddings, and other social occasions hurting the member's ability to save for economic investment.

Rural Industries Program: After the high priority given to agriculture in the second phase rural industries came next. The State Khadi (handloom) and Village Industries Board took responsibility for encouraging the production and sale of rural goods through the Community Development Blocks. The task of the B.D.O., or Block Development Officers, entailed the registering of village artisans as the main participants in the program. He was to help them from cooperatives, to supply them with tools and raw materials, and to teach them new skills whenever necessary.

The State Khadi and Village Industries Board opened

short-term training facilities in village centers. The State Industries Departments had also been imparting training through their Industrial Training Institutes. While the concepts undergirding these programs had merit, their reality suffered from the shortage of trained hands to serve as instructors. No one had predicted the numbers of extension officers of the State Industries Department needed at the block level to provide technical assistance to build up rural industries.[1]

The second phase laid added stress on the importance of social education in the Community Development Program. Besides promoting literacy, social education aimed to prepare people to be good citizens and to take a meaningful part in the democratic institutions. Because one of the missions of education concentrates on the provision of vocational opportunities for people to learn skills to raise their economic status, social education encompassed this goal, too. Three village institutions—the *Panchayat*, the Cooperative, and the school—promoted such education.

But the village school floundered in a quagmire of difficulties:

1. Children could not attend school because they had to work to contribute to the basic needs of the family.
2. The youth who did attend school grew dissatisfied with village life and moved to cities.
3. Both the curriculum and the pedagogy bore little relevance to the village life. Being educated did not automatically imply that a youth would be more effective cultivator, a better artisan, or a wiser leader in the community.
4. The scarcity of good reading material for village schools created a serious problem.
5. Village people could not understand why they should be literate or how literacy was inter-linked to their economic advancement, the only goal of the villagers.
6. The village teachers complained of their overload.

They had to run adult literacy classes in addition to their regular school duties. They resented doing so for no additional financial compensation.

7. The bureaucracy choked the improvement of village schools. After each General Election, even as the nation split asunder politically, the Panchayat Samitis shattered into factional fragments. Even the Extension Officers of the State Education Department had to play roles subordinate to the contending political divisions within a state.

As with the village schools, reforms generally sunk under tradition or stirred up controversies. In this turbulent sea of change, women had to steer a careful course. The Community Development Program sought to involve women in the challenge of nation building. To achieve this objective, women were to gain such knowledge (through practical demonstration wherever necessary) as would make them better housewives and mothers. The organizational structure set up in the first phase (1951-61) consisted of a *Mukhya-Sevika* (chief female official) at the block level who supervised Gram-Sevikas (female officials) in the work of the villages. With the help of rural women's organizations (called Mahila Mandals) and the village *Panchayats*, the *Mukhya-Sevika* and the *Gram-Sevika* concentrated their efforts on the following:

1. Literacy centering on crafts, such as spinning, weaving, embroidery, and the cutting and sewing of garments.
2. Improvement of homes through provision of clean drinking water and protection of food-stuffs.
3. Introduction of cottage industries.

Programs for women looked to the Mahila Mandals for implementation. To enable women to join Mahila Mandals, *Gram-Sevikas* identified the best time when the most women would conveniently attend. The most progressive women received appointments as *Gram-Lakshmis*, or village leaders, who would conduct the regular activities of the Mahila Mandals. To help women attend, *Balwadis* (pre-school centers) had to free mothers from a few of their most time-consuming familial obligations.

Officials recommended that the village *Panchayats* duly acknowledge the existence and importance of the Mahila Mandals by forming sub-committees to assist the women. Following steps were suggested for the *Panchayats* to help Mahila Mandals:

1. By providing a building and equipment, such as sewing machines, to the Mahila Mandals.
2. By dedicating financial assistance to the Mahila Mandals' programs.
3. By helping to select the *Gram-Lakshmi* (village leader) and particularly by facilitating training camps.
4. By finding suitable accommodations for *Gram-Sevikas* and midwives.
5. By assisting the Mahila Mandals in teaching women knitting, sewing, and other home-based activities to contribute to family income. To organize activities like these, block level officials needed to offer their guidance and help. Regrettably, the *Mukhya-Sevika* (chief female official at the block level) could not visit villages as often as she should have because she did not have access to a speedy conveyance to take her around frequently. *Gram-Sevikas* (village level female workers) could not devote sufficient attention to the Mahila Mandals, for they numbered too many villages within their jurisdictions.

The lessons of the first phase (1951-61) suggested certain changes in the second phase (1961-66). Officials realized that women should form their own farmers' clubs for receiving instruction in their roles in agriculture, as they were tired of the knitting and the sewing that constituted women's activities in the first phase. Program directors encourage women to join local cooperative marketing consumer goods. Here *Gram-Sevikas* and *Mukhya-Sevikas* could be the contact between various state agencies and the Mahila Mandals to ascertain current demands for designs and handicrafts.

The Mahila Mandals deserved greater support. Their presidents hardly participated in meetings and activities. Ordinarily, the president was usually the wife of the president of the *Panchayat*. Illiterate, she did not comprehend the importance of attending the meetings. Besides, coming from an upper-caste family, she thought it below her dignity to attend gatherings of low-caste women. That Mahila Mandals should elect women from their own ranks as their presidents became increasingly obvious. To identify such women, however, prove difficult, as the poor and suppressed women of the villages could not be expected to have qualities of leadership. Besides, not many rural women enjoyed the freedom to undertake such responsibility. Most of them had to work in the fields to contribute to the family income and could not even attend the meetings. To overcome this problem, the suggestion arose that productive activity should transpire while the women were attending the Mandals' meetings; the principle employed could be "learning and earning."

The Mahila Mandals could not use the village school as a meeting place. In the 1950s, schools had no electricity, and the Mahila Mandals met mostly in the evenings after the women had cooked the evening meal. The woman village teacher also did not take much interest in the Mandal's meetings in the evening, as she felt exhausted after a day of school teaching.

That village schools be electrified and that the teachers participate more ensued as the next recommendation. To make a Mandal's meetings more attractive, a movie or a dance show could be added. The rationale worked—no matter how tired people might feel in the evening, they would come to watch a movie, arguably the most popular form of entertainment in India.* Exhibitions of articles made by the Mahila Mandals could create interest and better attendance. To promote Mahila Mandals, officials suggested that educational tours be offered. The Mandals could also celebrate national holidays with cultural programs and communal feasting. Such festivities could engender the sense of social harmony in the village.

Functional literacy had to be a significant goal of the activities of the Mahila Mandals. For growing girls to be able to attend school, the economic status of the average rural family had to rise. Reformers lamented that children labored to contribute to the basic survival of the family. Mahila Mandals could help avert the disastrous flood of destitution by combining a productive activity for women with literacy classes. These women could then supplement the family income enough so that their young daughters could attend school.

To promote social education, the *Gram-Sevak* and the *Gram-Sevika* continue to sponsor folk singing, folk dancing, and rural stage shows that drew people because these events served recreational purposes. Incrementally, social education recognized its comprehensive nature that sought to awaken an awareness among the people about undesirable social customs deserving change or rejection.[2]

Family Planning—The Second Phase gave a great deal more importance to family planning than the first phase.

In 1951, the Planning Commission had appointed a Committee on Population Growth and Family Planning. It conceived of three stages in the development of family planning schemes and, thus, ushered in the all-important concept of curbing the population explosion.

Stage One, 1956 to 1961, during the Second Five-Year Plan involved the establishment of various Family Planning

*Next to the United States and the Soviet Union, India is the third largest movie producing country, with three-hundred movies produced every year.

Bureaus at the central and the state levels. The Minister of Health chaired the Central Family Planning Board, and, in practically all the states, similar Boards sprang into action by 1959. The first priority emphasized the training of family planning officers; the second, the need to carry on research to develop new contraceptives for native conditions.

In the training part of the Program, medical colleges and schools of nursing took the lead, and, under the auspices of the central government in certain instances and at the instigation of the state governments in other circumstances, training centers were set up. In addition, travelling teams of trainers were formed, usually including a physician and a health educator, who worked with camps of local leaders in the Community Development Program and in other backward areas.

Although the first stage emphasized planning, training, and research, several clinics began to operate in cities and rural areas. By 1961, approximately 1,500 such clinics functioned throughout India. Several mobile surgical teams performed operations at sterilization camps. Mass Publicity advertised the financial rewards for the patient choosing sterilization. The minority in the Mudlair Committee Report proposed that those who refused to practice family planning should suffer penalties, such as forfeiture of maternity benefits and of tax incentives.

During Stage Two (1962 to 1966), to reach out to the masses, the Director of Family Planning recognized the program from the "clinical" to the "extension" approach. Under the former system, women came to clinics for medical examination and prescription of contraceptives. With the latter method, trained officers fanned out to educate the masses about the methods of family planning. The magnitude of the projected task equaled the size of the Indian population. India has twenty-five states, four Union Territories, and 324 districts. In all, there are five thousand Rural Development Blocks with the number of villages exceeding 500,000. Each Rural Development Block contains approximately eighty thousand people. Given such staggering statistics, officials proposed that, at the village and the block levels, female workers, auxiliary nurses, and midwives should assist and that a male worker should provide education in family planning, organize sterilization and I.U.C.D. camps, and maintain an adequate supply of contraceptives.

The report of the Evaluation Committee in 1964 hailed the success of the extension approach. Drawbacks, nonetheless, marred the system. For example, the presence of far too few supervisors at the block and the district level hamstrung efforts. In the service units, workers did not know what they were supposed to do to induce the people to accept the idea of small families. Local leaders in the villages had not been mobilized to promote family planning. Finally, the states worried about how long the central government would continue to fund the family planning program.

The Third State began in 1966 with the Fourth Five-Year Plan. The Planning Commission wrote its blueprint, given below:

1. The decentralization of power which would allocate more authority to the states in managing their family planning programs. Each state would compose a master-plan for the entire family planning program. For a unit started under the Program, the central government would guarantee the states a budget, at least for ten years irrespective of the Five-Year Plan. The states could disburse funds to voluntary organizations and other bodies that had undertaken the task of family planning for poor people.
2. The share of central government should be at least seventy-five percent in state-level programs related to family planning. This share could be raised to one hundred percent whenever possible.
3. At the central level, the administrative and financial strength of the main agency should increase. A five-

member Family Planning Executive Board would include such high officials as the Secretary of the Ministry of Health, the Director General of Health Services, the Joint Secretary of the Ministry of Finance, the Joint Secretary of the Ministry of Home Affairs, and the Director-General of Family Planning.

Once again, the problem of rural illiteracy endangered the family planning initiatives, as it had so many other reforms. Even those rural people who moved to the cities did not surrender their village psychology to have large families. According to Hindu tradition, only a son may perform the last rites of a deceased family member. Scriptures bar daughters from this privilege. Even today illiterate, poor people did not feel satisfied with one son, as the mortality rate runs high. They must have three or four sons to ensure the survival of at least one. Large families also tend to be favored because farming is still done by hand, although tractors and other farm equipment have appeared on the large estates of the wealthy landowners. As India lacks a comprehensive system of social-security payments for all those who are engaged in active, productive work, the village farmers and others have to resort to old-age protection by fathering sons. The more sons a family has, the more certain is security in later life. The pressures of religion, tradition, and poverty, thus, threatened—and continue to menace reform.[3]

The success of all the plans depended on the performance of the V.L.Ws. and *Gram-Sevikas*; therefore, the Indian Government launched a program of rewarding the best among them. Their success was to serve as an inspiration to others to achieve the same high goals.[4] In the 1960s, numerous award-winning exemplified the following characteristics, worthy of emulation by future V.L.Ws.:

1. A V.L.W. should have a cheerful face, patience, and a tendency to listen to others.

2. A V.L.W. must anticipate what the villagers need. For instance, if farmers were not to receive supplies in time, they would be disappointed and would lose interest in the development.
3. Village leaders' camps should be encouraged as they enable a V.L.W. to establish a personal and continuous discussion with the other village leaders about the development projects. Such a periodical dialogue would generate popular participation, the keystone of the Community Development Program. One V.L.W. explained how he enlisted the youth to be the leaders in his village for various social projects. To one youth, he entrusted a poultry development project, to another, improved seed utilization, and to yet another, kitchen gardens. While a particular youth would serve as the leader, he would form a club by enlisting the support of his friends. These projects earned the enthusiastic support of the people and attained great success.
4. A V.L.W. should carry on constant advertisement of the projects to inform village people about the projects' accomplishments and, thus, to receive continued support.
5. A V.L.W. should take the initiative in devising persuasive arguments. One V.L.W. reported how his village people opposed the introduction of a new farming technique called dibbling. He, then, decided to convince one young farmer to lay aside a certain part of his land to test the new method. When the experiment succeeded, many other villagers followed the lead.
6. A V.L.W.'s success should depend not only upon the support of village people but also upon the continued guidance of the Block Development Officer and extension officials of the State Development Departments.

One female V.L.W., or *Gram-Sevika*, reported how the illiteracy of women posed a major obstacle. The *Gram-Sevika's* voice, not unlike one crying in the wilderness, warned that, homebound girls and brides could not attend classes; women of lower classes were too tired to come to literacy classes at night after a full day of work in the fields and of toil at home. How to break they syndrome was a gigantic task.

References

1. Dandekar, Hemlata C., *Men to Bombay, Women at Home; Urban Influence on Sugao Village, Maharashtra, India, 1942-1982,* Ann Arbor, Michigan: Center for South and South-East Asian Studies, University of Michigan, 1986.

   Hayes, Samuel P., "Extract from Measuring the Results of Development Projects," from *A Manual for Field Workers,* New York: UNESCO, September 1961.

   Jawaharlal Nehru's Speeches, 1963-1964, New Delhi: Publications Division, Ministry of Information and Broadcasting, Government of India, 134-52.

   Johnson, B.L.C., *India, Resources and Development,* New York: Barnes and Noble, 1997.

   Mishra, J.N., *Small Scale Cottage Industries,* Saugar: University of Saugar (India), 1963.

   Ramanathan, S., "Village Agricultural Plan," in *Kurukshetra,* vol. XII, December, 1963, 10-13.

   Vasudeva Raju, V.S., "Rural Industries Program," in *Kurukshetra,* vol. XIII, June, 1965.

2. *Aid of Social Education in Community Development,* New Delhi: Ministry of Community Development, Government of India, 1961, 71-77.

   Chaube, M., Developing Rural Youth Leadership, in *Kurukshetra,* vol. X, August, 1962.

   Coldwell, M.J., R. Dumont and M. Reed, "Women and Village Programs," in *Report of a Community Development Evaluation Mission,* New Delhi: Ministry of Community Development, Government of India, 1959, 61-62.

   "Development of Village School as a Community Center," from *a Guide to Community Development,* New Delhi: Ministry of Community Development, Government of India, 1962, 134.

   Jawaharlal Nehru's Speeches, 1963-1964, New Delhi: Publications Division,

Ministry of Information and Broadcasting, Government of India, 157-59.

Madhu, Kishwar, *Gandhi and Women*, Delhi: Manushi Prakashan, 1986.

"Program for Women and Children," from *Report on National Conference on Community Development at Mysore City*, New Delhi: Ministry of Community Development, Government of India, 1959, 31-33.

"Summary, Recommendations," from *Report of the Working Group on Evaluation in the States*, New Delhi: Planning Commission, Government of India, 1964, 38.

"Village Schools," from *A Guide to Community Development*, New Delhi: Ministry of Community Development, Government of India, 1962, 74.

"Women in Community Development," in *Kurukshetra*, June, 1964.

3. *Action for Rural Changes, Studies in Indian Community Development*, New Delhi: Munshiram Manoharlal, 1970, 412-26.

Ali, Tariq, *An Indian Dynasty: The Story of the Nehru-Gandhi Family*, New York: G.P. Putnam, 1985, 111-209, 275-87.

Cassen, Robert, *Indian, Population, Economy and Society*, New York: Holmes and Meier, 1978.

Chandrasekaram, C. and Moye W. Freyman, "Extract from Evaluating Committee, Family Planning Program," presented at symposium on *Research Issues in Populations Change*, at University of Pittsburgh, School of Public Health, June, 1974.

Chandrasekhar, S., *Infant Mortality, Population Growth, and Family Planning in India*, Chapel Hill: University of North Carolina Press, 1972.

Desai, A.R., *Urban and Family Planning in India*, Bombay: Popular Prakashan, 1980.

Ensminger, Douglas, "Assessing Progress in Community Development," in *Kurukshetra*, January, 1965, 6-7.

Evaluation of the Family Planning Program in India, New Delhi: Program Evaluation Organization, Planning Commission, Government of India, 1965, 27.

"Family Planning Plan and Action," in *India Journal of Public Administration*, vol. XI, no. 4, New Delhi: Planning Commission, Government of India, 683-97.

Gangrade, K.D., *Development by Persuasion: An Integrated Approach to Family Planning in Rural India*, Delhi: Marwah Publishing, 1980.

India, Family Planning News, New Delhi: Ministry of Health, Government of India, August, 1965, 3.

Jawaharlal Nehru's Speeches, 1963-1964, New Delhi: Publications, Division, Ministry of Information and Broadcasting, Government of India, 126-28.

Manohar, Kamla, *Abortion: A Social Dilemma*, Delhi: Vikas, 1973.

Nayar, Sushila, *Family Planning*, Delhi: Government Press, 1963.

Patil, R.K., "Community Development Achievement and Failures," in

Kurukshetra, January, 1965, 5-6.

Raina, B.L., *Family Planning Program, Report for 1962-63,* New Delhi: Ministry of Health, Government of India, 1964, 86-131.

Response to Population Growth in India, Marcus F. Franda, ed. New York: Preager, 1975.

"Some Aspects of Social Change," from *Evaluation Report on Working of Community Projects,* vol. I, New Delhi: Program Evaluation Organization Planning Commission, Government of India, April, 1957, 53-69.

5

A New Approach to Women's Projects in the 1960's and 1980's—Emphasis on Income-Generation

A NUMBER OF FACTORS prompted the Indian Government to alter its rural strategy in the 1970s, even though the 1960s had seen the "Green Revolution" in agriculture, which made India self-sufficient in grains. The Congress Party had split in 1969, and Indira Gandhi, India's Prime Minister, wanted to strengthen her electoral prospects by doing something for the poor. Also the Indian Government attempted to benefit from past experiences. In the General Election of December, 1971, Indira Gandhi adopted the slogan "Garibi Hatao" (remove poverty). Her faction won, and, in July 1972, the chief ministers of the states were called to work out a new program and guidelines for land reform to meet the electoral promise of "Garibi Hatao."[1]

Between 1971 and 1978, the government set up new agencies and institutions, either group-oriented or area-oriented, to meet the needs of the landless and marginal farmers who had failed to benefit from the Five-Year Plans and the Green Revolution of the 1960s. In selected areas, the government introduced the Benor System as a new approach to extension work in agriculture. Mr. Daniel Benor of the World Bank was the creator of this idea targeted toward small farmers who usually use "low level" technology and traditional methods. A new administrative structure took effect. A district agricultural officer supervised a number of agrarian specialists expert in fertilizers, pest-control, and minor irrigation. Agricultural extention officers functioned under these authorities. Each V.L.W., or Gram-Sevak, took charge of eight hundred families divided into eight groups. The V.L.W. had to visit each of his groups once every fortnight for a full day's counseling.

About six to ten V.L.Ws. reported to one Agricultural Extension Officer. He had to spend three days in his office doing routine administrative work. One day he spent on his own training with his subject-matter specialist at the district level. He spent one day training the V.L.Ws.

The World Bank urged the government of India to expand the Benor System. In 1970-80, the government responded by introducing the system in ten states. The remaining states were to adopt it during the Sixth Plan period (1980-1985). In 1981, the World Bank supplied a credit of over 100,000,000 dollars for this purpose.

The 1970s also witnessed the growing involvement of commercial banks in the field of rural credit (In India, banks are nationalized). By applying this credit to the purchase of fertilizers and improved seeds, a farmer could considerably increase his yield even on 0.5 hectares of land. A small farmer not only could create jobs for landless laborers, as he would need field hands to work with the larger crops.[2]

Because middle-and upper-class farmers could afford the expensive, sophisticated technologies, the government proposed to aid marginal and poor farmers by making available simple, inexpensive devices. Laboratories and industries began to devote more and more research to the manufacture of low-cost technologies.[3]

Small Industries: In the 1970s, the government gave a great impetus to small industries that could supplement the incomes of marginal farmer and give employment to landless laborers. The state governments played a principle role in the marketing of these products.

The India Government also resurrected the 1950s concept of Integrated Rural Development, ignored in the 1960s, to achieve the "Green Revolution" in agriculture.[4] The programs included:

1. "Food for Work Program"—Started in 1977 to provide employment to rural poor in lean months of the year so as to create durable assets in the community, this program adopted the title of National Rural Employment Program or NREP in October 1980. A centrally sponsored plan on a fifty-fifty sharing basis between the central and state governments, the NREP set three objectives: to generate additional gainful assets, and to raise the nutritional standards of the people.
   The village Panchayat listed projects addressing the felt needs of the community. DRDAs, or District Rural Development Agencies, implemented these programs. This project expanded during the Sixth and Seventh Five-Year plans, 1980-90.
   This program has helped in ensuring payment of minimum wages to the rural laborers and in improving their nutritional standards. It has also helped in slowing the exodus of the rural population to cities. Under this program, the building of roads has facilitated trade.
2. "Minimum Needs Program"—Introduced in the late 1970s, this project set reasonable deadlines for improving the villages' educational facilities, drinking water, electrification, public roads and health. The central government issued high yield bonds to encourage public investment in long-term rural development.
3. TRYSEM—This national program for the Training of Rural Youth for Self-Employment had already begun in 1979 with the principal objective of eliminating unemployment among rural youth. The Sixth and Seventh Plans (1980-90) target funds specifically for women. During the Sixth Plan 10.11

lakh youth received training under this project. Of them, 3.32 were scheduled castes, and 3.3. lakh were women.

4. CARI—The Council for Advancement of Rural Technology was created in 1986 to act as a nodal point for the transfer of appropriate technology to the villages. Voluntary organizations constituted the driving force behind this project. Not the least among CARI's lessons was the teaching of new methods of easing housework chores so that women could have more time to devote to constructive and productive activities not only empowering them economically but also leading to that comprehensive development of human personality, the raison d'etre of the national development plans.
5. RLEGP—The Rural Landless Employment Guarantee Program, launched in August, 1983, provided more employment opportunities for the rural landless. Typically these agricultural laborers remain out of work during lean agricultural months. The central government fully financed the project, although the state governments had to prepare specific projects for specified allocation. Today, the wage component in the project must not fall below fifty percent of the total cost. Farmers received food grains at a subsidized rate, as in the case of the NREP. The Central Committee of the NREP/RLEGP organized within the Department of Rural Development, approves projects. The agency for the implementation of the program is to be decided by the state governments. During the Seventh Plan (1985-90), the central government has granted an allocation of Rs. 1,743.78* crore. The Seventh Plan provided for Rs. 100[t] core for construction of housing units for scheduled castes, scheduled tribes and freed

[t]A rupee is the basic unit of currency in India like a dollar in the U.S.A.

bonded laborers in 1985-86 under RLEGP. During 1986-87, Rs. 125 crore have inaugurated projects under RLEGP; of the amount, the government has earmarked twenty percent annum for social forestry and has set aside Rs. 6 core for Rural Sanitary Latrines.

6. IRDP—The Intergrated Rural Development Program was expanded in the Sixth Five-Year Plan, 1980-1985. It assisted families below the poverty line to attain an income level above that line. To achieve this goal, IRDP extended to such families productive assets and inputs. Subsidies from the central government and loans from the banking institutions financed this program. Today, IRDP sets aside thirty percent of its grants for families belonging to scheduled castes and scheduled tribes and another thirty percent for women beneficiaries.

   The DRDA (District Rural Development Agency) oversees the IRDP. At the state level, a coordinating committee, headed by the chief secretary, monitors the overall program. At the central level, a governing body includes members of Parliament, representatives of the state legislative assemblies, the Chairman of the Central Cooperative Bank, the Chairman of the Land Development Bank, and two delegates from the disadvantaged sections of society, and a representative of scheduled castes and tribes, the other a woman.

   The Zila Parishads (elected assemblies at the district level) and the Panchayat Samits (elected councils representing a certain number of villages) closely cooperate in the planning and implementation of this program.

   The final selection of the beneficiaries of this program takes place in the meetings of the village Panchayats.

   The strategy of the Seventh Plan (1985-1990) is twofold: first, it seeks to consolidate the gains of the beneficiaries under the Sixth Plan and to help those families of the Sixth Plan who could not rise above the poverty line, and, for this purpose, a house to house survey was to be carried out. Secondly, new beneficiaries are to be sought. They are to be assisted in such a way with one time help they could cross the poverty line.

The Seventh Plan has laid aside a sum of Rs. 2,358.81 crores, with the central government contributing Rs. 1,186.79 crores and the states contributing Rs. 1,172.02 crores. The Plan has set a target of 2 crore families to cross the poverty line by 1990.

The Seventh Plan also recommended a revamping of IRDP as follows:

To coordinate various training programs, composite rural Training and Technology Centers were to be set up at block, district, and state levels.

Voluntary agencies were to step up their involvement in the IRDP as well as in TRYSEM in order to create family-oriented projects to increase incomes.

A new system of monthly evaluation of the IRDP was to assess any thirty-six districts, any seventy-two blocks, and a group of ten current beneficiaries and ten former beneficiaries. In October of 1985, this monitoring system began to take effect.

7. DPAP—The Drought Prone Areas Program covers 615 blocks in ninety districts of thirteen states. In the Sixth Plan (1980-85), there was a provision of Rs. 350 crore to be shared equally by the central and state governments.
8. DDP—In the Sixth Plan (1980-85), the Desert Development Project selected eighteen districts to benefit from a budget of Rs. 100 crore to be shared equally by the central and state government.

   The Program included the following objectives:

   Forestation with emphasis on shelter belt plantation, ground water development and utilization, rural electrification for tube wells and development of agriculture and husbandry.

9. Rural Water Supply—The provision of safe drinking water has been included in the Minimum Needs Program or MNP. This project occupies a top position in the priorities of central government. The Seventh Plan (1985-90) aimed at providing an adequate water supply to the entire rural population on the basis of the existing standard of forty liters per person per day within a distance of 1.6 kilometer.
10. Rural Roads—As a part of the Minimum Needs Program, the Sixth Plan (1980-85) envisioned road connections to all villages having a population over 1,500 and to fifty percent of villages with a population between one-thousand and fifteen hundred by the end of the Seventh Plan, or by 1990. During the Seventh Plan (1985-90), 24,000 villages will have become interlinked with new roads.

The central government has also sponsored a plan, during the Sixth and Seventh Plans (1980-90), to provide one hundred percent financial assistance to states for the development of roads in tribal areas. The Sixth Plan provided Rs. 6.50 crore for this purpose. The Seventh Plan has earmarked Rs. 14 crore for the same.[5]

The mid-1970s marked a watershed era for women, as the United Nations declared 1975 to 1985 as the Women's Decade. The United Nations' designation alerted India's official planners and social researchers to the fact that women had been ignored in the planning of development work. Special emphasis was now needed at all levels of planning on specific women's programs. In 1975, the central government consequently appointed a Committee on the Status of Women that presented its report in 1976.[6]

The Report on the Status of Women candidly acknowledged that, as Indian society has been male-dominated, main beneficiaries have been men. If women were to benefit, specific programs with definite appropriations for women would have to occupy prominent places in each Five-Year Plan. The Report also stressed that development could no longer afford to have a narrow definition as in "economic" growth. Development should encompass the full growth of all human faculties so that a just and equal society could blossom.

The far-reaching, forthright recommendations of this Committee created separate projects for women:

DWCRA, or *Development of Women and Children in Rural Areas:* DWCRA improves the socio-economic status of women in families below the poverty line through income-generating activities. DWRCA envisages the formation of groups with fifteen to twenty women in each village for carrying on income generating activities. Since the scheme is a sub-scheme of IRDP or Integrated Rural Development Program, the DWCRA draws funds from the IRDP budget. In addition, each women's group is sanctioned Rs. 15,000 which acts as a revolving fund. The central and the state governments and the UNICEF (United Nations International Children's Emergency Fund) share the sum equally.

DWRCA achieved considerable progress during 1984-85 with the formation of 4,754 groups. The amount of Rs. 630.70 lakhs brought immediate benefits to women. During 1985-86, DWCRA reached twenty-five more districts in the states. The set target of forming 7,500 groups necessitated the budgeting of Rs. 1,005 lakhs. In the Seventh Plan, the total outlay is Rs. 48.05 crore.

For wider coverage of women under DWRCA, the services of forty-two voluntary organizations was enlisted. During 1986-87, Rs. 100 lakh was granted to these organizations as grants-in-aid.

At the direction of DWCRA, construction of Community Centers was extensively taken up. With these centers as meeting places, women could convene for their group activities, training and demonstration of new technology.

The emphasis on the formation of elected rural bodies at the village, block, and district levels has continued. These bodies are responsible for the promotion of medical relief, maternity help, women and child welfare, the maintenance of common grazing grounds, the improving of village roads, the digging of wells, and the provision of sanitation. They occasionally provide primary education and collect land revenue. It was mandated that rural elected bodies include women members who would look after the women's projects.

In 1977-78, Training Centers for the Rehabilitation of Women in Distress has been started to rehabilitate such women. In non-traditional areas training would be for a year and residential facilities were provided. The central government shared expenses with the state governments and voluntary agencies in the ratio of 45:45:10.[7]

Family planning has been the next important concern with the central government. Family planning, as mentioned earlier, was adopted in 1952. During the First and Second Five-Year Plans (1951-61), family centers took the clinical approach in their services and the advice to visitors. During the Third Plan, (1961-66), the extension strategy supplanted the clinical method in reorganization of family planning. Under this novel approach, family centers widely distributed information about family planning and supplies of contraceptives. A full-fledged Department of Family Planning began operating at the central level in 1966, and the program again recognized and became more target-oriented. In the Fourth and Fifth Plans (1967-79), the program assumed a higher profile. During these years, the program was expanded and integrated with maternal and child care. Maternal care included supervision and treatment of pregnant women, safe delivery, post-natal care, proper breast-feeding, and an immunization and nutrition program for children. A large amount of money is spent on the control of such diseases like diarrhea, a notorious slayer of Indian children.

With greater visibility, the family planning effort incorporated the maternal welfare and childcare projects because rural people and urban people would not consent to having small families unless they could be certain about the survival of their first two or three children. The central government wisely foresaw the need to introduce a plan called ICDS, or the Inegrated Child Development Scheme, in 1975.

Implementation Machinery: The family planning program has been implemented through state governments for which a hundred percent of the central government's financial assistance is available. It has been extended to rural areas through primary health centers and sub-centers operating at block and village levels. The Sixth Plan (1980-85) envisioned the establishment of an additional 35,747 sub-centers, and the proposal to establish another 54,883 sub-centers during the Seventh Plan (1985-90) has warranted favorable consideration.

Assessment: Since the inception of the program, 5.38 lakh sterilizations and 186 lakh I.U.D. insertions have been done, giving a rate of 71.2 per thousand for sterilization and 24.6 per thousand for I.U.Ds. up to March 31, 1986. The oral pill program was extended to all the urban centers. Voluntary organizations and other local bodies participated fully in the program. In the rural areas, it was extended to those primary centers where patient follow-up could be done. The pills are now distributed to 22,015 centers functioning in urban and rural areas.

To ensure that the family planning program reaches far and wide in rural areas through the network of primary centers and sub-centers, the training of multi-purpose workers was launched during the Sixth Plan to educate the people since the program depends upon the voluntary acceptance of the people. In 1972, the Parliament endorsed the Medical Termination of Pregnancy Act, which allows a woman to seek an abortion if two doctors testify that continuation of the pregnancy is hazardous to her present and future physical and mental well-being.[8]

In 1984-85, the Ministry of Social and Family Welfare presented its report, the Third Chapter of which dealt with specific issues concerning women. On the basis of its report, the Ministry of Social and Family Welfare next prepared a National Plan of Action for Women to serve as a guideline at the national and the state levels. The ministry also kept in close touch with other ministries involved in the women's program. Periodic meetings among the representatives of state governments and voluntary agencies considered and reviewed important issues affecting women's development.[9]

The following programs received considerable attention:

1. *Functional Literacy for Adult Women (FLAW)*: From January 1, 1985, the Ministry of Education accepted the primary responsibility for funding the project under the auspices of the National Adult Education Program. The Ministry of Education has enlisted a great deal of help from voluntary organizations and colleges.
2. *Hostels for Working Women*: In cities, working women, if from out of town, have difficulty in finding secure places to live. In 1984-85, a budget of Rs. 270 lakhs went to voluntary organizations to build forty new hostels for two thousand working women.
3. *Employment and Income-Generation Units:* In 1982-83, this program started to train women belonging to weaker sections of society and to secure their permanent employment in public sector undertakings or in private industries. This program was implemented with the assistance of NORAID, or the Norwegain Agency for International Development. Under this program if a new production unit is opening, its training component can apply for assistance under this plan. An existing production unit, planning to expand, can have financial assistance for the additional training program of the unit.
4. *Women's Training Centers for the Rehabilitation of Women in Distress:* Begun in 1977-78 with the objective to

rehabilitate such women, these centers offer a year's training in non-traditional areas and supply residential facilities. The central government shares expenses with the state governments and voluntary agencies in the ratio of 45:45:10. These centers expanded in the 1980s, and voluntary organizations are playing a vital role in their success.

5. *Women's Development Centers:* Women's Development Centers were set up in six colleges of Delhi University with the objective of using students and teachers as targets to bring about change in social attitudes. The colleges provide the infrastructure facilities, whereas the Ministry of Social and Family Welfare gave financial assistance for counseling and guidance.
6. To underscore the growing awareness of women's issues, the Indian Government again decided to send a delegation to the international meeting held in February, 1984, to prepare for the world conference to review the achievements of the U.N. Decade for Women from 1975 to 1985. In 1985, the Indian Government also contributed $20,000 to U.N. Fund for Women.

The need for more national programs for children gained increasing recognition along with the concentration on the status and well-being of women. Such synchronism stems from the synergism of mother and child—of matriarchal welfare and well-adjusted children.

The National Policy for Children: Proclaimed in 1974, this national doctrine described children as the "supremely important asset." A National Children's Board was set up under the aegis of the Prime Minister to provide a forum for planning, review and proper coordination of services striving to meet the needs of children.

Integrated Child Development, or ICDS: This program began in 1975-1976 on an experimental basis when thirty-three ICDS projects were started in different areas. Today, its aims are:[10]

1. To provide supplementary nutrition, immunization, and periodic health check-ups to children below six yeas of age and to expectant and nursing mothers.
2. To make available non-formal, pre-school education to such children.
3. To teach health education and nutrition to women.

This program earned wide support, and the Sixth Plan (1980-85) increased the number of ICDS centers to 1,019 by 1985. Besides, some state governments had taken the initiative and started 117 centers of their own.

The focal point for delivery of the ICDS package of services is an *Anganwadi* in every village or in a ward of an urban slum. Generally, one *Anganwadi* serves a village of one thousand population or an urban ward. For the tribal population, as *Anganwadi* reaches a population of seven hundred. An *Anganwadi* worker, a female volunteer worker from the community, runs each *Anganwadi.* A helper assists her. A *Mukhya-Sevika,* or chief female worker, supervises every worker. A Child Development Project Officer (CDPO) directly inspects the proceedings of every ICDS project. In an *Anganwadi,* health care obeys rules and norms laid down by the Ministry of Health and Family Welfare.

UNICEF (United Nations International Children's Emergency Fund) continues to assist ICDS projects in the areas of consultation services, training, communications, supplies, equipment, research and evaluation.

NORAD (Norwegian Agency for Aid) is assisting twenty-two ICDS projects in the state of Uttar Pradesh. USAID (United States International Development) is helping eleven ICDS projects in Gujarat and eight in Maharashtra. CARE and WFP contribute supplementary nutritional support for selected ICDS projects.

To study the impact of ICDS more closely, a monitoring and evaluation division has been set up in the National Institute of Public Cooperation and Child Development (NIPCCD).

Training of ICDS Functionaries: To carry our projects successfully, officials must take part in expert training. The Child Development Project Officers study at the National Institute of Public Cooperation and Child Development and at its regional units in the cities of Lucknow and Bangalore. The training of supervisors is provided through Middle Level Training Centers, or MLTC, located in several states. *Anganwadi* workers are trained at centers run by the Indian Council for Child Welfare in New Delhi and at training institutions selected by state governments. Centers for the training of *Balsevikas,* or pre-school workers are also run by the Indian Council for Child Welfare, funded entirely by the central government.

Special Nutrition Program, or SNP: Launched in 1970-71 to provide supplementary nutrition to children under six years of age, expectant women, nursing mothers, the SNP has energetically pursued its goals. By the end of the Fifth Plan (1974-79), 28,000 feeding centers operated from a budget base of Rs. 38 lakhs.

The SNP originally served as a central government program. Then it was transferred to the states through the Fifth Plan (1974-79). In 1975-76, when the ICDS program was launched, its nutritional component was funded from the SNP budget.

Balwadi Program or Pre-School Centers in Urban Slums and Rural Areas: Since 1970-71, this program has functioned under the auspices of five national organizations: the Central Social Welfare Board, the Indian Council for Child Welfare, the *Harijan* (scheduled caste) Sewak Samaj, the Bharatiya Adimjati Sevak Sangh (Indian Scheduled Tribes Association), ad the Kasturba Gandhi (Mahatma Gandhi's wife) national Memorial Trust. These organizations extend assistance to voluntary organizations as the Indian government has realized the effectiveness of these bodies in identifying with the common people more readily than government officials can. The grants pay Balsevikas (children's care-takers) in charge of Balwadis and supply nutritional programs for children.

About seven thousand Balwadis grew from the efforts of voluntary organizations in 1984-85. UNICEF has greatly helped the ICDS program. For 1985-89, the UNICEF assistance from the general resources was estimated t 175 million U.S. dollars and totalled 52.3 million dollars from supplementary resources.

The Ministry of Social and Women's Welfare underwent reorganization in November, 1985. With its new name of the Ministry of Human Resource Development, it boasted the following Departments:

1. Department of Women and Child Development
2. Education
3. Youth Affairs and Sports
4. Arts
5. Culture

The Department of Women and Child Development reviews, coordinates and guides official and non-official programs for women and children's development, as children and women comprise the more disadvantaged sections of society. The Department has two bureaus: Nutrition and Child Development and Women's Development.

An increased investment from Rs. 117.90 crore in the Sixth Plan (1980-85) to Rs. 738.12 crore in the Seventh Plan (1985-90) shows the central government's deep concern with women and children's integrated development—particularly rural women and women in urban slums who do not benefit much from national development.

Until the end of the sixth Plan, i.e., 1985, 1019 centrally sponsored ICDS projects had been sanctioned . In addition, 131 projects had been taken up by the state governments. These projects were taken up in selected blocks in the most backward rural and urban areas and in tribal villages.

The créches are a part of the ICDS program and the children of the age of 0-5 years of working and ailing mothers are provided with sleeping facilities, day care, nutrition, and recreation. Voluntary organizations, through which the program is implemented had made a modest beginning in 1974-75 with 247 créches to cover approximately five thousand children. The program gained momentum, and, in 1985, over eight thousand créches benefited 200,000 children.

The SNP or the Special Nutrition Program, has been a very important aspect of ICDS. By 1985, 110 lakh beneficiaries had received aid. The SNP supplements its food supplies under CARE (Cooperative for American Relief to Everywhere) and the WFP (World Food Program). All these projects received added funding in the Seventh Plan (1985-90).

The National Children's Fund: This began in 1979, the International Year of the Children, and grew in the Seventh Plan. The fund purposed to create a source of assistance to the voluntary organizations for innovative programs in child development. Children today constitute about forty percent of the Indian population, and the central government realizes that is must develop diverse projects rapidly.

Training Centers for Women in Distress: This started in 1977 for the age-groups of eighteen to fifty years and implemented through voluntary organizations which are given ninety percent assistance in equal portions from the central and state governments were greatly increased in the Sixth and Seventh Five-Year-Plans.

Employment and Income Generation Production Units: This program which was started in the 1982-83 fiscal year to generate income and employment for needy women was expanded in the Seventh Plan. (This program draws assistance from the Norwegian Agency for international Development, or NORAD). Grants go to both public-sector undertakings (or the governmental sector of the economy) and to autonomous or private business for the training part of their projects. Beneficiaries include rural poor women,

women belonging to scheduled castes and tribes and war-widows.

Condensed Courses of Education for Adult Women: This program was started to provide courses in the shortest time possible for the needy women who could be trained for employment, particularly for projects in rural areas.

Designated courses last for two years so as to help women to pass the primary level, secondary level, or high-school examinations conducted by the state governments. The maximum number of students to be admitted is twenty-five. Only socially handicapped and other deserving needy women candidates in the age group of eighteen to thirty qualify for admission.

Registered voluntary institutions for women who have had three year's experience in conducting welfare activities and recognized educational institutions such as middle and high schools are eligible to receive funds under this program from the CSWB which has State Advisory Boards in the states where applications are submitted and screened with their recommendations.

Vocational Training Program for Adult Women: Designed for needy and deserving women, these training programs rely heavily upon voluntary agencies. The State Social Welfare Board in consultation with state governments, selects the vocational training courses in each state. The choice of vocations should be made after full consideration of the scope of immediate employment opportunities following the completion of the training course. Women between the age groups of eighteen and thirty qualify, if they have undergone a basic, general education necessary for vocational training.

Socio-Economic Program for Needy Women and Physically Handicapped Persons: Under this plan, women can gain training to upgrade their skills and to set up production centers. Their activities can vary from traditional jobs to modern vocations, such as electronics and assembly line work.

Training of Leadership for Mahila Mandals: Voluntary

organizations first undertake surveys in rural, urban and tribal areas to identify and assess the welfare of women. Next, they identify women leaders from among the neighborhood. Third, they set up training camps to educate them in social welfare activities. This program recognizes that grassroot leadership afford the most effective means to bring about the needed change in thinking and action.

Family Counseling Centers: They provide preventive and rehabilitative services to women and children (primarily in the cities) who are victims of atrocities and exploitation. Such centers give counseling in marital and family disputes, create awareness about the laws relating to women and children, and provide facilities, such as free legal aid, short stays, medical treatment and vocational training.

The Seventh Plan has also greatly stressed Awareness Generation Projects for Rural and Poor Women. Awareness Generation Camps represent the forum for rural women to get together, exchange their experience and ideas and develop an understanding of reality. The final step remains to devise ways to deal with the issues affecting women. These camps differ from formal training programs in that the organizer of a camp, a representative of a voluntary organization, plays a vital role as a facilitator. The local situation determines the theme for discussion. Free and open dialogue is the main method of communication to deal with the issues. The general status and role of women in family and society spark these discussions.

Awareness Camps induce rural women to think about their social problems, analyze them, and initiate actions to tackle them.[11] The current problems of domestic violence against women, infanticide, dowry murders, molestations, rape, and discrimination against women with regard to property and employment are very much rampant in spite of rigorous debate. Women become aware of their rights, laws pertaining to marriage and divorce, child labor, and the Suppression of Immoral Traffic in Women Act. They pay attention to daily life—community health, hygiene, improvement of housing, and sanitary conditions. They discuss the latest rural technology, such as water fetching devices, smokeless ovens, and non-conventional energy sources. Village institutions like *Panchayats,* and block-level organizations are explained to encourage women to participate in the political process. Because the economic well-being of women determines their success in other areas of life, discussions of women's cooperatives, local resources like poultry, improvement of storage facilities, local crops, and marketing facilities takes up much time at these camps.*

The organizers of the camps, create a cadre of socially conscious leaders from among the rural women themselves. At the recommendations of these organizers, the CSWB also has written to the officials of the local governments where the Awareness Camps were held to invite those leaders to attend these camps to give a profile of development activities relating to women in that region.

Camp organizers design follow-up activities; for example, to cope with the issue of nutritional deficiency, the villagers learned to grow food like drumsticks, *mitha neem,* colocasia leaves, papaya, lemon, and mango which are less labor-intensive. The women visited a nearby nursery to obtain seeds, and they experimented with recipes incorporating local produce.

In one of the Awareness Generation Camps tribal women realized that they could not apply for the official loans because of illiteracy. They had to be helped by the village teacher in any paperwork. By practical demonstration, the village

*The author of the book was in India in the Fall of 1987 to conduct on-the-spot studies of the Indian women. She talked to Miss Shashi Bhatnagar, the Assistant Director of the CSWB. Miss Bhatnagar revealed that she had participated in the work of the "Committee on the Status of Women" appointed by the central government. She had also organized a number of the Awareness Generation Camps. Her experiences are recorded on a tape in the holdings of the History Department of Northern Kentucky University. She also talked about a publication of the CSWB called *Chetna*, which deals extensively with the Rural Awareness Projects.

teacher convinced the women of the need for functional literacy, and such classes were started.

The follow-up activities also cast the spotlight on women's low-income levels. Generally speaking, tribal families of the region own two to three acres of land. As this land cannot produce enough food for the family, men tend to migrate to nearby industries or to enter construction work. Women till the land, but they still cannot harvest enough to feed their families. In the follow-up program, women were helped to set up a center for preparing spices which were marketed to the employees of Surat cotton mills and other major industrial cities. Kitchen gardening was another activity tapped for additional income. Since the women were already familiar with it, the activity picked up in short time. Additional money led women and men both to accept other developmental programs such as literacy classes. All of these endeavors garnered women's rich comprehension.

The Awareness Camps also took up the issue of the fuel shortage, as so many trees had been felled from unscrupulous development. Through Mahila Mandals, solar cookers, smokeless *chullahs*, and *gobar* (cow-dung), gas cookers drew the attention of women in the follow-up activities. Villagers could buy a solar cooker with only Rs. 60, for they were government subsidized.

One can study the literature of women's organizations like the AIWC, or All-India Women Conference, to get a good perspective of the range of the follow-up activities among the rural and the tribal women after the completion of the Awareness Generation Camps.

The author also conducted a formal interview with Mrs. Susmita Srivastava, the Chairperson of the CSWB, which is providing large funds for these camps. In her hour-long interview, she stressed the following points. First, rural women are more capable and responsive than generally believed. Once approached persuasively, they reveal their intelligence. Second, rural women, or any other woman, have to organize to regain, and to protect their rights. That reason explains the vast emphasis on creating Mahila Mandals in rural areas and in urban slums. Mrs. Srivastava also pointed out that Mahila Mandals are most effective when the leadership emerges from the rank and file of local women. That is the reason why rural women's projects appropriate a part of their funds and activities to evolve such grassroot leadership. Lastly, Mrs. Srivastava explained, Mahila Madals can remain viable and on-going organizations only if socio-economic programs are attached to them to improve the economic strength of the rural poor and tribal women. (The tape is available with the Department of History and Geography of Northern Kentucky University.)

Parliamentary Legislation in the 1970s and 1980s: In Pursuing the recommendations of the Committee on the Status of Women (1975), the Hindu Marriage Act of 1955 and the Special Marriage Act of 1954 were amended by the Indian Parliament in 1976 to accept mutual consent as a basis of divorce. The amended law also gave the right to a girl to repudiate her marriage as a child whether or not the marriage has been consummated. The Child Marriage Restraint Act was amended in 1983, the Criminal Law made the offence of rape more severely punishable than earlier.

The Dowry Prohibition Act of 1961 was amended in 1986 to make the provisions of the Act more stringent. The punishment for taking or abetting dowry now carries five years in jail. The government encourages the states to set up special Dowry Prohibition Officers for effective implementation of the Act. The Dowry system, nevertheless, persists with full force. Evidently the girls' parents are unwilling to report demands of high dowry by the bridegroom's family, and government officials neglect to enforce the law.[12]

To siphon off money wasted in expensive marriage celebrations, the Indian government has established high-yield bonds for parents to purchase in the girls' name for their dowry. Such bonds have produced only a marginal effect, as parents still compete, either voluntarily or by pressure, in the amount of money spent in a marriage ceremony; the dowry, the expensive feasts, and the large scale illumination and decoration of the house and the street devour vast sums. (Reference here is not to the poorer sections but to the educated middle-class, both rich and medium.)

SITA, or the Suppression of Immoral Traffic in Women and Girls Act, became law in 1956. It did not attempt to abolish prostitution but only to control it. Section 7 (1) states that a woman, twenty-one years of age or older who carries on prostitution on the premises within two hundred miles of a public place is liable for punishment with imprisonment up to three months. Only the prostitute finds herself subject to punishment; her client, who happens to be on the premises, escapes punishment under the Act. Prostitutes have been forced to work in places like the "ghettos" away from pubic places. Daughters raised in the ghettos often adopt the night's profession of the woman when they grow up.

SITA is basically a penal statute. The punishments directed at persons other than the prostitute appear in sections three to six, nine, ten, and eighteen. Section three provides punishment for brothel keeping. Owners of premises being used for prostitution are liable only "if they knowingly" allowed the use of premises for such purpose. If keepers of brothels plead ignorance, they are not convicted.

The other drawback of SITA is that it mainly penalizes and barely mentions welfare for a prostitute. Section nineteen offers the only legal assistance to a woman who might choose to free herself from this demeaning profession. She can apply to the court to be placed in a protective home or in the custody of a court. This helping provision amounts to little, as she is so tightly bound by her keepers or may be entirely ignorant of her rights under SITA. All too often, the police apprehend a prostitute, the courts send her to a protective home, she leaves, and soon she returns to the ruthless hands of the brothel keepers posing as her guardians.

The SITA Amendment Act of 1986 fails in that it merely punishes traffickers. The other drawback is the retention of Section eight which is detrimental to a prostitute. The acceptance of prostitution as a profession because prostitution is nowhere declared illegal and, at the same time, the treatment of the prostitute as a criminal reveal SITA's serious flaws. The Act does have positive sections; for example, Section two widens the definition of a brothel to include any place used for the purpose of sexual exploitation or abuse. This broad definition would make it easier to prosecute brothel keepers under Sections three of the act for all kinds of sexual exploitation or abuse falling outside of prostitution.[13]

SITA more effectively protects children; the younger the age of the exploited child, the greater the punishment. Section three of SITA of 1956 has also been amended. This section had earlier given immunity to landlords or managers of premises where prostitution took place, on the grounds of ignorance or lack of knowledge. Now, with the amendment, a landlord cannot shield himself behind ignorance, if a local newspaper has reported that the premises in questions have been used for prostitution. In India, change for the better may resist reformers' sense of urgency, but transformation comes albeit in its fits and starts.[14]

References

1. Shah, C.H. and C.N. Vakil, eds. Agricultural Development in India, New Delhi: Oprient Longmans, 1979.
Bhalla, G.S., "Transfer of Technology and Agricultural Development in India," in *Economic and Political Weekly*, December, 1979.
Dantwala, M.L., "*Agricultural Policy in India*," in Indian Journal of Agricultural Economics, no. 4, 1976.
Etienne, Gilbert, *India's Changing Rural Scene, 1963-1979*, Delhi: Oxford

University Press, 1984, 152-215.
Krishna, Raj, "Small Farmer's Development," in *Economic and Political Weekly*, May, 1979
Nair, Kusum, in *Defense of the Irrational Peasant: Indian Agriculture and the Green Revolution*, Chicago: University of Chicago Press, 1979.
Report of all India Rural Credit Review Committee, Bombay: Reserve Bank, Government of India, 1969.
Sen, B., *The Green Revolution in India*, New York: Wiley, 1974.
Small Farmer's Development Agencies, A Field Study 1972-1973, Bombay: Reserve Bank of India, Government of India, 1975.

2. Bhattacharya, M., "Administrative and Organizational Issues in Rural Development," in *Journal of the Indian Institute of Public Administration* no. 4, 1978.
Kurien, C.T., "Paradoxes of planned Development: The Indian Experience," in *India 2000: The Next Fifteen Years*, James R. Roach, ed., Maryland: Riverdale Company, 1986, 179-82.
Census of India, Government of India, part I, 1971; part II, 1981.
Miltra, A., *India's Population*, New Delhi: Abhinav Publications, 1978;
National Commission on Agriculture, New Delhi: Ministry of Agriculture, Government of India, 1976.
Bose, A., P.B. Desai and J.N. Sharma, eds., *Population in India's Development—1947-2000*, New Delhi: Vikas, 1974.
On Panchayat Raj Institutions, New Delhi: Ministry of Agriculture, Government of India, 1978.

3. Asian Development Bank, *Asian Agriculture Survey*, Manila, 1977; F.A.O., *Report on Agrarian Reforms and Rural Development in Developing Countries*, Rome: World of Conference, 1979.
I.L.O. (International Labor Organization), *Poverty and Landlessners in Rural Asia*, Geneva, 1977.
Scott, W., *Concepts and Measurements of Poverty*, Geneva: U.N. Research Institute for Social Development, 1981.
Srinivas, M.N. "Village Studies, Participant Observation and Social Science Research in India," in *Economic and Political Weekly*, Delhi: August, 1975.
World Bank, *Small Farmers and Landless in South Asia*, Washington, 1979, World Bank, "Towards a Theory of Rural Development," *in Development Dialogue*, no. 2, 1977.

4. Desai, Neera, *India Women: Change and Challenge in International Decade*, New Delhi: Sterling, 1985
McNault, Gail, *The Extended Family: Women and Political Participation in India and Pakistan*, Delhi: Chanakya Publishing, 1981.
Report of the National Seminar on Role of Women in Rural Development, November 5-7, 1981, New Delhi: National Institute of Public Cooperation and Child Development, Government of India, 1981.
Singh, Andrea Menefe, *UNICEF-Assisted Women's Programs in IndiaÖ*,

Paper for Seminar on Role of Women in Rural Development at Hyderbad, March, 1980, New Delhi: Center for Women's Development Studies.

5. India 1986: A Reference Manual, New Delhi: Publications Division, Ministry of Information and Broadcasting, Government of India, 160-79, 361-75.
   State-Cum District Level Workshop on Development of Women in Rural Areas (DWCRA), A Collection of Papers in a seminar held at Rabindra Bhawan, 28th and 29th February, 1984, New Delhi: Center for Women Development Studies or CWDS.
6. Committee on the Status of Women in India, *Roles, Rights and Opportunities for Economic Participation from 1975 on*, New Delhi: Center for Women's Development Studies, 1976.
   Committee on the Status of Women in India, *Toward Equality: Report*, New Delhi: Ministry of Social and Women's Welfare, Government of India, 1976.
   Status of Women in India: A Synopsis of the Report of the National Committee, New Delhi: Allied Publishers for the Indian Council of Social Science Research, 1977.
7. Gangrade, K.D., *Social Work and Development*, New Delhi: Northern Publisher, 1986.
   India, 1986: A Reference Manual, New Delhi: Publications Division, Ministry of Information and Broadcasting, Government of India, 169-205.
8. Medical Termination of Pregnancy Act of 1972 is a great victory for women as it allows the doctors to terminate pregnancy on grounds of any anticipated physical and emotional hazard to the expectant woman.
   Manohar, Kamla, *Abortion: A Social Dilemma*, Delhi: Vikas, 1973.
   Population Education of Parents through Parent-Teacher Associations, New Delhi: Central Institute of Research and Training in Public Cooperation (CIRTC), Government of India, 1980.
9. *Chapter Three, Report 1984-1985*, New Delhi: Ministry of Social and Women's Welfare, Government of India, 26-49.
   India, 1986: A Reference Manual, New Delhi: Publications Division, Ministry of Information and Broadcasting, Government of India, 26-49.
10. Beneria, Lourdes and Gita Sen, "Accumulation, Reproduction and Women's Role in Economic Development" *Signs*, Winter, 1981, 279-98.
    Boserup, Ester, *Women's Role in Economic Development*, New York: St. Martin's Press, 1970.
    "Children Slave over Fireworks," in *India Abroad* (U.S.A.), December 1, 1989, 17.
    Dandekar, V.M., "Integration of Women in Economic Development,"

Economic and Political Weekly, October 30, 1982, 1782-86.
India, 1986: A Reference Manual, New Delhi: Publications Division, Ministry of Information and Broadcasting, Government of India, 206.
India Association of Women's Studies, Report of a *Workshop on women, Work and Employment*, presented at the Second National Conference on Women's Studies, University of Kerala, Trivandrum April, 1987.
"Indira Prize for UNICEF," in *India Abroad* (U.S.A.) December 1, 1989, 2.
"Indira, Rajiv, 'A Great Legacy' Nehru Left for India," in *News India* (U.S.A.), November 24, 1989, 18.
Papanek, Hanna, "Class and Gender in Education-Employment Linkages," Boston University Press, *Center for Asian Development Studies*, Discussion Paper, 22, 2-4.
Prospective Plan on Child Development (1980-2000 A.D.), New Delhi: National Institute of Public Cooperation and Child Development (NIPCCD), Government of India, 1984.
Report of the National Seminar on Social Action with the Poor, New Delhi: National Institute of Public Cooperation and Child Development (NIPCCD), Government of India, 1982.

11. Basu, Amrita, "Two Faces of Protest; Alternative Forms of Women's Mobilization in West Bengal and Maharashtra,: in Gail Minault's *The Extended Family, Women and Political Participation in India and Pakistan*, Delhi: Chanakya, 1981, 217-62.
The Central Social Welfare Board or CSWB has *Chetna* and *Project Profile* as some of its publications at the main office, New Delhi.
Jain, Devaki, "Street Vendors of Ahmedabad," in her *Women's Quest for Power*, New Delhi: Vikas, 1980, 20-76.
Omvedt, Gail, *We Will Smash This Prison! Indian Women in Struggle*, Delhi: Orient Longmans, 1979, 91-97.
Project, Profile, 1986, New Delhi: Central Welfare Board, Government of India, 9-13. It describes the money released as of March, 1986 to set up 7,082 units for providing employment to 88,800 women in urban poorer sections.
Report of the National Committee on Role and Participation of Women in Agriculture and Rural Development, New Delhi: Ministry of Agriculture, Government of India, 1980.

12. Carroll, Lucy, "Muslim Family Law in South Asia," *Islamic and Comparative Law Quarterly*, New Delhi: 1, 2, 1981, 95-113.
Diwan, Paras, *Dowry and Protection to Married Women*, New Delhi: Deep and Deep, 1987.
"The Dowry Prohibition Act, 1961: The Struggle for an Amendments," *Samya Shakti*, 1, 2, 1984, 131-34.
India, 2000 A.D.: A Symposium, conducted by the Center for Asian Studies, University of Texas, 1986, James R. Roach, ed. Maryland: Riverdale Company, 1986, 215-25.

Manohar, Murali, *Women's Studies and Development in India,* Warrangal: Society for Women's Status and Development, 1984.
Mehta, Sumit, "Dowry Law: Debating the Delay," *India Today* (U.S.A.), April 15, 1984, 39.
National Seminar on Status of Women, 1975-1976 held in New Delhi and sponsored by the National Council of Educational Research and Training, New Delhi: Center for Women Development Studies.
Report: United Nations Economic and Social Commission on the Status of Women, held at Vienna, February 24-March 5, 1986, New Delhi: Center for Women Development Studies.
Report of Workshop on Child Marriages, New Delhi: Council for Social Development, 1986.
Srinivas, M.N., *Some Reflections on Dowry,* Delhi: Oxford University Press, 1984.

13. Baxi, Upendrí, *"Patriarchy, Law and State,"* Paper presented at a workshop on Women and Law, Second National conference on Women's Studies, Trivandrum, April 1984.
Baxi, Upendrí, "Talking Suffering Seriously: Social Action Litigation in the Supreme Court of India," *Delhi: Law Review* (New Delhi), 1997-80, 91-116.
Kaur, Inderjeet, *Status of Hindu Women,* Delhi: Chugh, 1983.
Mukherjee, Santosh K., *Prostitution in India,* New Delhi: Inter-media Publishing, 1986.
Report of National Seminar on Atrocities on Women, Role of Community, New Delhi: National Institute of Public Cooperation and Child Development, Government of India, 1982.
Sakhare, Seema, *Platform Against Rape,* Paper Presented at Second National Conference on Women's Studies, University of Kerala, Trivandrum, April, 1984.
Sethi, Sunil, "Rape: Controversial Code," India Today (U.S.A.), December 31, 1983, 34-35.

14. *The Equal Remuneration Act, 1976,* New Delhi: Ministry of Law and Justice, Government of India, 1978.
Festival of India in the United States 1985-1986, James R. Roach, ed., Riverdale, Md.: Riverdale company, 1986, 215-26.
India, 1986: A Reference Manual, New Delhi: Publications Division, Ministry of Information and Broadcasting, Government of India, 212-17.
Bose, S. N emai, ed., *India in the Eighties,* Calcutta: Firma KLM, 1982, 125-48.
Mishra, R.K., ed., *India Towards 1990s,* New Delhi: Patriot Publishers, 1986, 1-15.
Jain, Devika, *India Women,* New Delhi: Publications Division, Ministry of Information and Broadcasting, Government of India, 1975; *India Women: Today and Tomorrow,* New Delhi: Institute of Social Studies

Trust, Nehru Memorial Museum and Library, 1982.

Mahajan, Amarjit, *Indian Police Women*, New Delhi: Deep and Deep, 1982.

Minault, Gail, "Scholars and Activists: The Indian Association of Women's Studies Conference at Trivandrum," *Choice* (India), August, 1984, 37-38.

6

Development of Education for Women After Independence

BECAUSE THE STATUS OF women depends upon economic power, the extent of a women's access to education largely determines her position in the hierarchy of prestige. Education also plays a significant role in changing the general societal attitude toward women. With education, both men and women can develop their personalities, thus enabling them to fulfill their economic, political and cultural functions. Education helps remove inequality of sexes. So crucial is education that it ranks as one of the Human Rights in the constitution of UNESCO.

In the history of women's education in India, those who have stood for women's emancipation since the nineteenth century have emphasized women's desperate need for learning. The Indian reformers of that century, however, wanted to educate women to better them in their roles as wives and mothers but not to make them direct participants in the national development of the country. The British Government also supported this limited viewpoint of women's education, as the Victorian model of the angelic and perfect female held sway. In the twentieth century, the need arose to train women as teachers and nurses with the expansion of schools and medical facilities. These two professions had to be incorporated in a general plan of female education that went well beyond the mere uplift of motherhood.

The Independence of India in 1947 and the preparation of its Constitution in 1949 built a different conceptual framework for women's education, Declared equal with men, women had to play equal and multiple roles in the political, social, and economic life of the nation. This new attitude led the central government to appoint various committees to frame the goals of the national education.

The First Five-Year Plan (1951-56) stated that the general purposes of women's education should not differ from those of men. At the secondary level and at the university level, women's education must have an occupational content. So proclaimed the First Plan, and the National Committee (appointed in 1958) presented its report in 1959 with the following recommendations.

1. Girls' education should assume the prominence of a unique need, and special measures should be undertaken on behalf of girls.
2. At the central level, a National Council for Women's Education should take form to look after the national educational system for women. At the state level, State Councils for Women's Education should be created.
3. To provide teachers for primary schools, particularly in rural areas, intensified courses for adult women (prospective teachers) should fill curricula on as large scale as possible.
4. Women hostels should be attached to secondary schools (grades VI to XI) so that village girls could attend classes distant from their villages.
5. Special inducements should be offered to girls, like free books, clothing, and attendance scholarships, to encourage them to enroll in schools. The National Committee noted, that frequently, girls between the ages of six and fourteen could not attend schools during regular hours. The Committee advised that volunteers and schoolteachers should give them non-

formal education.

6. Female teachers working in rural schools should have access to special facilities.

In 1959, the central government created a National Council for the Education of Women, and a Special unit in the Ministry of Education began to concentrate on the issues of female education in both urban and rural areas. The state governments did the same.

These female institutions soon began to manifest a series of shortcomings, the major flaw being the poor quality of science and mathematics teachers and equipment in the middle and high schools. The girl students in the cities could not earn scores high enough to enter technical colleges. This fact was defeating the Constitution's expressed promise of achieving equality of men and women. Certain academicians, therefore, recommended co-education as the possible remedy. Opponents stated that the lack of discipline and boy's rowdyism would act as deterrents to girls. Besides, the custom of *purda*, or the wearing of the veil, among some sections of communities would stand as a barrier to girls' entry into co-educational institutions. The supporters of co-education, nevertheless, stated the following reasons in support of their case: first, co-education would allow for economy and full utilization of the existing infrastructure in science and math; second, it would foster a spirit of respect for girls among their male peers, thus helping to change societal attitudes toward women.[1]

The National Committee on the Status of Women (appointed in 1975) recommended a series of evolutionary steps to compromise the divergent views on co-education.

1. To adopt co-education as a general policy at the primary level.
2. At the university level, to bar new colleges exclusively for women so as to force female candidates to enter male colleges.

3. To promote the ideal of co-education by including a high percentage of female teachers on the teaching staff in existing co-educational institutions.
4. The National Committee on Women's Education had stated in 1958 that girls' colleges followed different curricula as influenced by traditional thinking. Most of these institutions provided domestic science, household skills, needle work, and fine arts. This slate of courses produced an adverse effect on the concepts of equalization of educational opportunities for girls and deprived them of career-oriented courses in science and mathematics. The National Committee on the Status of Women, therefore, recommended that colleges move toward the co-educational system.

Although urban attitudes toward women's education changed dramatically in the 1960s, a survey conducted by the Committee on the Status of Women revealed that a few of the respondents believed that girls should receive no education at all. The survey found that middle-class respondents accepted girls' education more readily than did either the affluent or the poor. Affluent sections opposed education on grounds of tradition; poorer sections rejected girls' education for economic reasons. Paradoxically, the lower middle-class respondents supported girls' education to increase the family's income. The strongest advocates of girls education came from parents influenced by the demands of the marriage market where good bridegrooms wanted educated brides.

The census of 1971 published frightening figures about female literacy; 29.8 million or 67.5 percent of women between the ages of fifteen and eighteen were illiterate. The number of illiterate women in the age group about twenty-five was 94.5 million, or 88.6 percent. Such statistics led the central and state governments to launch an aggressive program of adult literacy for working mothers.

The Fifth Five-Year Plan (1974-79) included a large appropriation to start adult literacy classes. This program has enjoyed vigorous follow-up in the succeeding Sixth and Seventh Plans, (1980-90). In the census of 1981, the percentage of illiterate women to the total illiterate population remained a disappointing 56.4 percent.

The literacy program among women has crept forward slowly, owing to the unattractive environment of the classes, the lack of adequate publicity, and the lack of motivation.

In 1980-81, only twenty-nine percent of girls in the age group of eleven through fourteen received schooling as against the coverage of 50.5 percent in the case of boys. Worse is the dropout rate among girls. Of every one hundred girls enrolled in the first grade, only thirty, on an average, reach the fifth grade. In grades nine to twelve, the proportion of girls in the age group of fourteen through seventeen is only thirteen percent as against thirty-five percent in the case of boys.[2]

For every one hundred men attending a university, only thirty-eight women share the opportunity for advanced education. Moreover, female education in colleges is confined to upper-and-middle-class women living in towns and cities.

The all-India dropout rate for girls at the elementary level is seventy-four percent, owing to such factors as early marriage in rural areas and in urban slums and parents' unwillingness to educate girls. In the rural areas, girls cannot attend middle and high schools, for such institutions are usually located in areas distant from their villages. Lack of transportation and hostels and parents' relentless refusal to allow girls to travel unescorted every day to school account for the high female drop-out rate after primary education. Girls in poorer sections stay home to look after siblings and housework while mothers go away to work in the fields or in the houses of the upper classes. Parents inculcate the inequality of the sexes during upbringing by exhibiting different patterns of behavior toward male and female children. While boys continue their schooling after the primary level, girls find themselves kept at home to attend to their traditional roles as defined by society.[3]

Given that education alone can change these stereotypes about women, the 1980s found the cabinet of Prime Minister Rajiva Gandhi endorsing the National Policy on Education (1986) subsequently submitted to the Parliament for approval. The highlight of the Action Plan was the launching of an effective program for ensuring that no child between the age group of six and eleven would remain outside the structure of formal and non-formal education throughout the country by 1990, the end of the Seventh Five-Year Plan. The Action Plan envisaged that the enrollment of the school children in the age group of six to eleven would be 99.2 percent, while, for the age group of eleven to fourteen would be 59.76 percent. The percentage of children in schools in the age group of six to fourteen, thus, would be 85.88 percent of the total population of children.

For the year 1987-88 an outlay of Rs. 825.00 crores (as compared to Rs. 352 crores in 1986-87) enhanced education. To offer special relief to scheduled castes and scheduled tribes, 20.9 percent and 13.0 percent of the total outlay for education for 1987-88 targeted these groups. The Ministry of Education has undertaken a number or promotional steps to help educationally backward minorities.

The National Policy on Education declared that the following strategically decisions would achieve the national goals on education:

1. Single schoolteachers be converted to double schoolteachers.
2. Appointment of more women teachers.
3. Special attention to children and girls of weaker sections of society.
4. Provision of incentives like free supply of books, stationery, uniforms, mid-day meals, and scholarships for regular attendance.

Non-formal Education for the Elementary Age Group: Non-formal education complements the formal system of elementary education for children. Nine educationally backward states, Andhra Pradesh, Assam, Bihar, Jammu and Kashmir, Madhya Pradesh, Orissa, Rajasthan, Uttar Pradesh, and West Bengal, benefit most directly from non-formal education. The central and state governments share these expenses. The Parliament sanctioned a budget of Rs. 712 lakhs for 1986-87. To encourage voluntary organizations to participate in this program, the central government extended Rs. 4 lakhs to them for 1986-87 (upon the recommendations of the state governments). Officials projected that approximately 38.87 lakhs would be enrolled through 155,455 non-formal centers including 20,500 non-formal centers exclusively for girls in 1986-87.

To increase girls' enrollment, the government since 1983-84 has liberalized the program of non-formal education. Under it, the central government provides ninety percent assistance, and the states' share is ten percent. A total grant of Rs. 144 lakhs addressed the needs of 1986-87.

Appointment of Women Teachers in Primary Schools in the Educationally Backward States: The central government contributes eighty percent of financial assistance to such states, which carry the remaining twenty percent., during the fiscal year 1986-87, total grant of Rs. 200 lakhs went to the states for appointment of eight thousand women teachers.

Population Education Program: In 1980, the National Population Education Program was launched to create an awareness among the youngsters about their responsibilities toward the nation with regard to population control This program collaborates with the United Nations Fund for Population Activities and with the active involvement of the Ministry of Health and Family Welfare. Until now, the project restricted its focus to the formal education sector. During the Seventh Plan (1985-90), the program is gearing up to cover the adult literacy program and non-formal education section.[4]

Besides taking care of educationally backward social classes and areas, the National Policy on Education has proposed that physical fitness center and center for talented children in every district be set up by the end of the Seventh Plan in 1990.

Recognizing that teachers must update their information, in a 1986 in-service telecast for teachers, translated in thirteen different provincial languages, reached a wide audience with the help of the Ministry of Broadcasting and Information. Certain high schools have ushered in the computer age by introducing sophisticated, new technologies to able students.

Higher Education: Student enrollment in universities and colleges increased from 35.39 lakhs in 1984-85 to 35.71 lakhs in 1985-86. The enrollment of women students was 10.59 lakhs in 1985-86, as compared to 10.21 lakhs in 1984-85. Higher education among scheduled castes and scheduled tribes continues to receive special emphasis with the establishment of special programs for these groups.

Technical Education: All the Five-Year Plans have laid great emphasis on technical education to produce enough trained people for the economic development of the country. By the end of the Sixth Plan in 1985, technical educational facilities accommodated thirty thousand students annually in degree courses, sixty thousand students in diploma courses, and seven thousand students in postgraduate courses.

These figures do not fail to impress even the most pessimistic observer of India. The author witnessed the large increase in the number of female students in these technical institutions. Although these figures may represent unfortunately low proportion of the entire population, they attest to change more rapid than anyone has the right to expect.

Scholarships: The government of India awards scholarships

to enable students to carry on studies both in India and abroad. Scholarships are usually awarded to meritorious students without adequate means. Under the National Merit Scholarship Program, scholarships enabled 27,000 students to undertake studies beyond the high school level. Rural children received 38.000 scholarships for carrying on studies up to the high school level. Out of the 38,000 scholarships, 23,000 went to children of landless laborers, scheduled castes, and scheduled tribes. Five hundred scholarships were awarded to poor but meritorious students so that they could gain a good education in approved residential schools. India recognizing that investment in education and banking on a better future go hand-in-hand; luckily, more and more women will have a hand in that stronger tomorrow.[5]

Summary

India has made significant progress. A vast number of poorer sections' children, however, cannot attend school for long because they must work to contribute to the family income. These children live in a doldrums of continued poverty and persistent ignorance, both greatly contributing to a high rate of fertility. Poor families must have as many earning hands as possible; children go to work at young age. The twin statistics of lack of education and of population growth spiral higher. National development cannot forever keep pace with the rise in population, and a vast bulk of population continues to live in a state of utter poverty. Education dashes ahead, but the population runs faster. The Indian government must decide who will win the race.

References

1. Brijbhushan, Jamila, *Muslim Women*, Delhi: Vikas, 1980.
   Hans Mehta Committee was appointed in 1964 to make recommendations about removing inequalities between the male and

female curricula at college. Some of the recommendations pointed out that in a democratic and socialistic society education should be related to the interest and capacities of individuals and not to sex. Since India was going through a transitional period, traditional subjects should be retained at the university level as options for girls and not as compulsory subjects. Girls should be encouraged to study science and mathematics at the secondary and high school levels so that they could enter technical colleges later on.

Majority of the Hindu and Moslem parents are reluctant to accept co-education because of the traditional emphasis on female virginity before marriage. Parents want to take no risk, which could lead, to any infraction of this moral guide for girls ready for marriage.

Siddiqui, M. Iqbal, *Islam Forbids Free Mixing of Men and Women,* Delhi: Adam, 1986.

2. Bhandari, R.K., *Educational Development of Women in India,* New Delhi: Ministry of Edncation and Culture, Government of India, 1982, table 17, p 44; table 20, p 48

   Commission on Higher Education for Women, Report, Madras: University of Madras, 1977.

   Jesidasom, Victor, *Non-formal Education for Rural Women to Promote Development of Young Children,* New Delhi: Allied, 1981.

   National Council for Women's Education, *Differentiation of Curricula for Boys and Girls,* New Delhi: Ministry of Education, Government of India, 1964.

   People's Participation in Adult Education: Report, New Delhi: Central Institute of Research and Training in Public Cooperation (CIRTPC), Government of India, 1971.

   School in the Community, New Delhi: Central Institute of Research and Training in Public Cooperation (CIRTPC), Government of India, 1970.

   Tellis-Nayak, Jessie B., *Non-formal Education for Women,* New Delhi: Indian Social Institute, 1980.

   Vocational Training in Residential Institutions, New Delhi: National Institute of Public Cooperation and Child Development (NIPCCD), Government of India, 1979.

3. Bhandari, R.K., *Educational Development of Women in India,* New Delhi: Ministry of Education and Culture, Government of India, 1982, 33, table 13, p. 35; table 14, p. 37; table 15 , p 39.

   Dropout rate for girls was reported much higher than that for the boys in the census of 1981.

4. *Challenge of Education,* New Delhi: Ministry of Education, Government of India, 1985.

   Education—National Policy on Education 1986: Annual Report, 1986-76, part I, V to X, New Delhi: Department of Education in the Ministry of

Human Resources Development, Government of India.
Mass Media in India, 1981-83, New Delhi: Publications Division, Ministry of Information and Broadcasting, Government of India, 1984.
New Perspectives of Women's Vocational Training, New Delhi: Ministry of Labor and Rehabilitation, Government of India, 1983.
Selected Speeches and Writing of Indira Gandhi, vol. III, 1972-1977, New Delhi: Publications Division, Ministry of Information and Broadcasting, Government of India, 1984.

5. "Decline in Birth Rate is Stagnant, Population Experts Affirm," in *Time* (New York), November 13, 1989, 53-54.
Desmond, Edward W., "Puppies and Consumer Boomes," in *Time* (New York), November 12, 1989, 53-54.
"India's First All Woman Crew," In *India Tribune* (Chicago), September 23, 1989, 1.
Marthandum, Nambi, "T.N. Plans University for Women," in *India Abroad* (New York), October 6, 1989, 25.
"Poverty Still a Stubborn Fact," in *India Abroad* (New York), November 17, 1989, 18.

SECTION III

7

Special Plans and Issues for Women in Villages

THE DEVELOPMENT concept has evolved through distinct phases. In the first phase in the fifties, there was a heavy emphasis on the economic improvement of the under-developed countries (now called the Third World) by the injection of foreign investment and technology transfer, with voluntary organizations having a negligible role to play. Development in the first phase meant raising per capita income and an increase in agricultural production to meet acute food shortages. Soon it was realized that along with per capita income, vital areas of life, such as health, nutrition, education and sanitation must also improve. A number of new official agencies were also created to provide the social services. Official agencies boasted of the number of social facilities created instead of realizing the importance of reaching out to the poorer people in a meaningful way, though women were offered courses in craft within the household. The social service of teaching women certain household crafts reinforced the old thinking that the main function of women is to become a good wife and a mother. *Gram-Sevikas,* or village level workers, received training in food preparation, nutrition, kitchen gardening, poultry raising, child hygiene, tailoring, and knitting. Soon, classes in these subjects became irrelevant to a large number of rural women who had to work all day to earn a bare living. In the fifties, no real attempt was made to change the village infrastructure, as the focus centered in increased industrialization and agricultural production.

In the sixties, development gained a new dimension. The official planners began to discuss the importance of "integration" in any development process, that term implied that the Third World countries must carry on development from within, instead of acquiescing to development imposed from outside. Still this phase suffered from one serious drawback. The urban elite planners could never understand the problems of rural women who remained "invisible" to them.

This phase had another flaw in presuming that the benefits of development would automatically "trickle" down from the top to the bottom of the social scale without any major changes in the social structure in the villages and urban slums. In other words, the presumption was the "haves" would be willing to make necessary sacrifices and concessions to the "have-nots." This view also pre-supposed that the poor would gladly accept development and change from above, thus giving up their traditional beliefs.

Women's programs greatly suffered in the 1960s and the minimum staff of two lady workers per block remained unchanged. The country faced foreign threats from China and Pakistan and suffered reported food shortages. At the same time, the Indian Government decided to free the country from dependence on foreign food by launching the so-called "Green Revolution" in the sixties.

In the seventies, awareness grew that solid and lasting development could take place only if people at the bottom of the social scale also benefited. Phrases like "grass-root changes" and "grass-root organizations" became very popular. The poor people thus became the point of reference. If they could improve, the country could claim stable development. The people would also have to participate in decision-making, which affects their lives. Popular participation, in turn, would require that masses should be organized to make them aware of their situation and, then, these organizations should act as pressure groups from below to bring about the needed reforms. In this vital task of organizing the people, the role of voluntary bodies would assume major proportions.

In 1971, the central government appointed a Committee on the Status of Women* to review changes in women's status. The Committee included eminent women like Veena Mazumdar, the current Director of the CWDS; the chairperson of the Central Social Welfare Board; Kumud Sharma, Assistant Director of the CWDS; and Lolita Sarkar, an attorney at law. This Committee carried on work for four years. In its research, the Committee toured many states of the country to talk to women of different backgrounds, from those holding high positions in the government, academic institutions, and various skilled professions, to landless agricultural workers in villages, women workers in factories, mines, and plantations, and housewives. The Committee also held discussions with representatives of governments at both central and state levels and met delegations from political parties, women's organizations, and trade unions. In addition, the Committee also sought the support of scholars from universities and research institutes to undertake specific studies.

The report was submitted to the Minister for Family and Social Welfare in 1975 who, then, presented it to the Parliament, which set up a Division for Women's Welfare and Development in the Ministry of Family and Social Welfare to coordinate and initiate policies for women's development. The Parliament also passed the following laws: The Equal Remuneration Act of 1975, which mandated equal salaries to both the sexes; SITA or the Suppression of Immoral Traffic in Women Act, amended in 1978 to make penalties more stringent; the Hindu Marriage Law, amended to introduce new grounds for divorce, like no-faults; the anti-Dowry Act, amended to make sanctions more severe;

*The report is available at the CWDS library in New Delhi.

and the family courts were set up to help arbitrate family disputes.

The impact of the report went beyond the realm of legislation. In the academic world, a number of renowned universities inaugurated separate centers for women's studies. The National Council of Educational Research and Training began to revise books to remove prejudice against women.

The India Press gave great coverage to the main text of the report, thus helping in creating an awareness of women's issues and problems. One member of the Planning Commission, Professor Raj Krishna, was so impressed with the findings contained in the report that he remarked to his colleagues that women who had been left out of the planning, i.e., Five-Year Plans, must now receive their due share. Outside of India too, the report made a great impact, as the agencies of the United Nations concerned with women used it extensively for reference. The U.N.O. also declared 1975 as the Women's Year and 1975 to 1985 as the Women's Decade.

The report of the Committee on the Status of Women emphasized that women's problems would not take care of themselves. The report stated that a concerted effort would be needed to deal with them and that Mahila Mandals would have to play a vital rule. Thus rural women and women in urban areas had to be organized with the help of external agencies like *Gram-Sevikas* and voluntary organizations. The report also emphasized that income-generating projects would be necessary to make rural women aware of their dignity and rights. Since agriculture had long been their main occupation, modern skills in agriculture should be taught to them. The report went on to point out that, so far, the government's laws had mainly affected the organized sector of the economy; the government would have to pay equal attention to the unorganized sector which exists massively in rural India and urban slums.

The report also contended that women should participate

in trade unions and village *Panchayats* so that they could achieve just rights in a democratic society. The Committee report called upon all women's organizations to carry on a relentless war against age-old, anti-female social prejudices sanctioned by the Hindu scriptures like *Manusmriti* and the Holy *Koran.* Laws alone, however, would not change social attitudes towards women. Social education had to accompany the legalities, and this education had to begin at home and in schools where the idea of men and women being equal partners in life should be taught.

Last, the report called upon women organizations to remain in close touch with judicial decisions. Since the judges are in visual contact with the misery of exploited women, their rulings would favor women against male abuse.

The official planners in the 1970s, nevertheless, adhered to a narrow conception of women's role in society, which was considered to be basically homemaking and child rearing. A few of the projects initiated for poor women in rural areas and urban slums were not worked out with much output from the people. They were externally conceived and imposed upon the people.

The Planning Commission appointed a Working Group on Employment of Women, which presented its report in 1978. It stressed the importance of giving employment to women in jobs, which brought decent incomes—jobs in agro-based industries, animal husbandry, and large-scale poultry and livestock operations. The Ministry of Social and Family Welfare had also presented a National Plan of Action for Women in 1976 before the Parliament. It advocated the participation of women in those jobs where they are as productive as men. This would help change women's general status in society to a great extent. The above recommendations were embodied in the Sixth and Seventh Five-Year Plans (1980-90) which provided substantial funds for economic-generation programs for rural women.

In this chapter we shall focus on those issues repeatedly the subject of studies done by the Center for Women's

Development Studies (CWDS), the Indian Council for Social Science Research (ICSSR), the Self-Employed Women's Association, Rural Wing (SEWA), and *Kurukshetra,* a journal published by the Ministry of Agriculture, Government of India.

Uttar Khand, in the hilly area of U.P. at the feet of the Himalaya Mountains, comprises eight districts, two of which are Garhwal and Kumaon.[1] The study gives a background of the region under the British rule. Once replete with forests and forest products, the area supplied timber as a source of livelihood for the natives. With the drive for railroad construction, the British began to fell trees indiscriminately. Later on, sprawling tea plantations further eradicated the trees on a massive scale. The male laborers began to leave the area in the nineteenth century to seek jobs in towns and later on to serve in the British army during the two World Wars.

After Independence, the Indian Government did not make much change in the British forest policy in Uttar Khand, although it professed to be saving forests. In 1960s, the DGSS (Village Association) protested against the tree-felling practices of the government's greedy contractors who cleared forests even in the banned regions by bribing local officials. After the Chinese war of 1962, the Indian Government also undertook a policy of destroying forests to build defense roads to these inaccessible regions near the Chinese border. Women's hardships increased, as they had to go a long way and along steep paths to collect fuel for cooking. These women fought to take care of large households, as the men had migrated to towns for jobs.

In the 1970s, the Chipko Movement, the organized protest of the DGSS, saw the involvement of more women whose help the movement's leader solicited to act non-violently against the government's policy and the greedy contractors. Local youth also joined the movement, as contractors were bringing in cheap labor from the neighboring state of Himachal Pradesh, which caused unemployment among the locals.

In the late 1970s, the Chipko Movement assumed a much wider dimension, emphasizing the planting of trees necessary for soil conservation, prevention of floods, and curbing of the soil-erosion which causes droughts. In other words, it beams an ecological movement. In 1977 and 1978, the DGSS planted ten thousand broad-leaf trees in a number of villages with the active involvement of voluntary organizations representing the women's cause.

Chipko became a women's movement representing environmental protection and addressing economic issues, such as the loss of jobs for men who had relied upon forest produce and the great struggle of women to secure wood for fuel. Since women became so heavily involved, the movement has also come to articulate their other social problems. For example, women of the Chipko Movement participated in the Prohibition Movement.

Women took part in the Prohibition Movement largely for social reasons. Village men were wasting away their meager earnings on alcohol. Then, upon returning home, they were beating their wives at little or no provocation. The organizers of the Prohibition Movement found that, if they kept women in the front line of protest, demonstrations would not become violent. The Prohibition Movement also brought out two other important points. Not only did the police threaten women demonstrators with arrest, but also their family men threatened them. Efficiently organized, women carried on, and, finally the U.P. State Assembly passed a law in 1972 prohibiting alcoholism in the Garhwal region of Uttar Khand.

Carrying on the organized process of effective change, the women's movement today is creating Mahila Mandals or Women's Organizations in villages and urban slums to achieve positive effects. The chairperson of the Central Social Welfare Board, which allocates funds to voluntary organizations for work in women's and children's advancement, also emphasized the importance of organizing women to make their power felt.

The Chipko Movement also discovered how to overcome the difficulties in organizing women. Women were nowhere in the leadership or decision-making positions. Asked why they had joined the Chipko Movement in 1977, when the government had decided to give a huge contract to deforest the area, the women answered that they had to resort to direct action as their men were away in cities. This response showed that women thought they had to play only a supportive role to their men. They assumed that they could not be the initiators or the leaders because they had not had any education, nor had they inter-acted independently with the outside world. The Chipko Movement did reveal a difference in the 1980s about women's power and willingness to act when the state government decided to convert a forest into a potato farm in a remote village of Chamoli district. These women had never heard of the Chipko Movement in the Garhwal and Kumaon districts in 1970s. Women in the village Dungri Paitoli decided to undertake a direct action against the State's Horticulture Department because their own husbands were willing to accept the government's plan. These men calculated that a potato farm would bring a road, a bus connection, a school, a health center, and employment to local men. Women activists confronted harassment from the village *Panchayat,* exclusively male in composition. The state bureaucracy also intimidated the women activists by having arrest warrants issued against them.

When the Chipko Movement's leader, C.P. Bhatt, heard of the protest, he decided to offer his good services to help negotiate a settlement. Whatever the government had cut so far could be used as a potato farm, but the remaining forest would be left untouched. C.P. Bhatt also pointed out how the village *Panchayat* became very hostile to the Mahila Mandal for its activity. Mr. Bhatt concluded that the male-dominated *Panchayatas* could be as bad as the bureaucracy when it came to women's issues and rights.

The Chipko Movement also showed that bureaucracy, in

general, was callous because women were not consulted before any decision to level forests was taken, although they were going to suffer from deforestation, The development officials also has a perception of development different from that of women; for example, in a reforestation plan, local men insisted upon planting fruit trees while women wanted fuel and fodder trees. Fuel, fodder, and firewood were women's urgent needs as construction of roads, buildings, fuel for the army, and an increasing influx of pilgrims to hilly areas had created an acute shortage of fuel. Women were also afraid that, if the fruit trees were planted, their men would get the employment to sell fruits for earnings which they quickly spent on liquor and, then, beat their wives.

Now it was left to the State Forest Department to make a decision between the conflicting pressures of local men and women. The Department favored men by giving only fruit saplings to plant while saying they had no other trees.

The CWDS study included one other event, which occurred in the Gopeshwar town of the Chamoli district in Uttar Khand. Gopeshwar had been declared a "town" because of a change in the zoning. As a result, a great part of the forests were cut down to construct town buildings. Women faced the same problem—less fuel and less fodder for cattle, which meant a great decline in nutrition. The Mahila Mandal got involved and highlighted one other problem facing women as a result of deforestation. Women had no place to go to the latrine. The efforts of Mahila Mandal prevailed; the remaining forest was saved. Women guarded it vigilantly and did not allow even the local people to exploit it. Mahila Mandal became so confident with success that they began to report it to the forest officials of any illegal felling of trees.

The preceding discussion of the Chipko Movement in the Garhwal and Kumaon districts and other incidents in the Chamoli district of Uttar Khand in the state of U.P. would lead the reader to ask the following questions, also raised by the CWDS team in the final part of its report: first, when the Women's Movement became so strong, why did it not try to enter the local power structure and control it fully or partially? Second, when the women's movement became so successful in the Prohibition struggle, why did it not create a network of women's groups for different issues facing women?

An answer to the above two questions requires a more detailed investigative study, although the CWDS team offered explanations of a general nature within the context of the Indian rural economy and the prevailing social attitudes. Women's subsistence level economic activities within a relatively less mechanized rural sector and a patriarchal family structure are the strong constraints on the Indian woman's capability to organize and assert herself. As shown in the Chipko Movement, men are eager to enlist women's participation in a crisis, and women do respond by breaking through traditional role patterns. In peaceful situations, however, women are mostly "invisible." If women dare initiate action on their own, village *Panchayats* and the males of the family turn against them because the male ego is savagely bruised.

During the peak of the Chipko Movement in 1977, women activists had insisted that women be consulted in the future whenever any forestation, deforestation, or any development activity was envisaged. This issue has not been taken up since then by any government agency or any voluntary association. *Panchayats* continue to exclude women, even though U.P. state's *Panchayat* Act requires that a village *Panchayat* must nominate two women members if no woman candidate is elected.

The Chipko Movement highlighted the partiarchal nature of the Indian society, as most of the women participants were older women or widows. In rural areas, young married women experience family responsibilities and social pressures that prevent them from stepping out. If a young bride does dare oppose, she can face total rejection by the family and the village.

Since various regions of India show a great deal of diversity, CWDS decided to conduct research in rural Panjab.[2]

The village of Tajpur in the Ludhiana district in the state of Panjab beam the site of scrutiny. Compilation of statistics showed that participation of women in Panjab is among the lowest in the country, having the lowest proportion of female workers to total workers. Out of the total female workers, 21.6 percent are agricultural laborers. That lopsided growth of industry in Panjab has affected the occupational structure of women needs no Savant's deduction.

The Tajpur study showed that women of landowning families undertake the supervision of pre-harvest and post-harvest operations, and look after the cattle in addition to the upbringing of children and general management of the family. During the afternoons and post-dinner hours, they spin cotton to be woven into bedspreads and trousseau for their daughters. They have little leisure to enjoy.

Women from landless families work as agricultural labor in various agricultural operations. In cash crops like potatoes, rice and cotton, female labor is found to be high. They also raise cattle to bring in extra income and to provide better nutrition for the family. Besides cattle care, they collect fodder from wastelands or roadsides, facing abuses of landlords by so doing. They help their men in "home-based" work along with full home care responsibilities like cooking and raising of children. Even though these women are working outside the family, it does not bring about any change in the role expectations of their families and males.

Because socially and culturally women are not considered breadwinners, they do not seek any gainful employment outside the house and fields. They participate infrequently in the organized sector. This situation allows the landlords to exploit these women, even though the women are sincere and honest at work. They are employed the most during peak season and are laid off when not needed. They are, therefore, the most insecure part of the population in the village. They also receive lower wages than do men, according to the Potato Research Institute of Panjab.

As the social education of women, which begins as early as her childhood, teaches her to be an ideal wife, mother, and an ideal homemaker, she is discouraged from seeking any education or economic independence. As the perfect wife, she is supposed to turn over all her earnings to her husband, who will squander the money on alcohol and tobacco and deliver her beatings in frenziness. Because women have no control over their earnings, they cannot raise any voice against such social evils.

We can summarize the status of the two classes of women in Tajpur village as follows. The first class of women in Tajpur is the landowning Jat women who are very hardworking, but social propriety requires them to work at home. Even the widows of the first group would not work outside the home or seek any other external employment. They may weave and spin at home form 7:00 A.M. to 9:00 P.M., but their work is not recognized as real work.

The absence of economic independence and the illiteracy tend to perpetuate the traditional status of women particularly among lower-caste women. Actually the general status of these poor women is deteriorating because married women cannot leave homes and children to learn new skills needed for modern and competitive economy. Reference here is to the agricultural sector where new technologies like threshing machines, tractors, and other gadgets have been introduced. Unmarried women cannot go out to learn a skill because of social constraints, as it means traveling to a distant place. Among the few well-off families, where girls may be allowed to learn in a residential facility, their families pressure them to stick to traditional areas which prepare women only for homework and do not give them any new economic skills for financial independence.

The economic dependence of women also leaves them incapable of participating in statutory bodies, such as the village *Panchayats.* Even through the Panchayat Raj Act requires the presence of at least two women either by election or co-option in *Panchayats*, either the law is ignored, or those two women of upper castes are co-opted whose husbands are member of the village *Panchayat*.

How to break this syndrome is a big task. The CWDS study team suggested the following strategy:

Organize women at the grass-root level with the assistance of an intervening agency, such as CWDS or AIWC, which could have a free discussion with them about their needs and aspirations. Experience has shown that, where Mahila Mandals or grass-root women's organizations have been formed by the central and state development agencies, they have become dysfunctional, because official agencies do not try to understand rural women's contributions to economy and society. This is the result of lack of understanding on the part of national developmental agencies, which have taken a narrow view of women's participation in the national economy.

At times, government funds remain unutilized; Mahila Mandals are not aware of them because the functionaries at village level, block level, and district level either are ignorant or show apathy toward these programs. These functionaries do not try to interact with the local women in a constructive way.

Occasionally, State Planning Departments are also sow in allocating funds to village agencies. For example, money for TRYSEM for Tajpur—money sanctioned by the central government—met a year's delay by the state government.

A few of the grants sanctioned by the government require grass-root organizations to provide matching funds to qualify. Most of the rural women have no control over their earnings, and they can not contribute. Women of better families may be able to get money from their husbands. As such women are the office-bearers in Mahila Mandals, they favor programs suited to themselves.

Since upper-class women control Mahila Mandals and relate well with village functionaries, the government programs like poultry raising and dairying are used to help women of richer families who have land and fodder to make use of these government grants. Even programs like kitchen hardening and storage of food-grains through the Farmers' Institute help women of landed families. Landless families are left untouched.

The grass-root organizations become so frustrated with the red tape of bureaucracy in obtaining grant money that they lose all motivation to apply. Besides, officials at the block, district, and state levels are so impervious that they do not attempt to research and identify a local product relevant to competitive markets. In some cases, therefore, Mahila Mandals or other women's organizations may get stuck with an unsold product due to lack of a market.

The study concluded, therefore, that an intervening agency like CWDS or AIWC must act as a channel of communication between the government's developmental machinery and poor rural women's grass-root organizations. These intervening agencies should provide necessary information to Mahila Mandals.

After a preliminary study of the village of Tajpur, the CWDS started an income-generating pilot project for women of economically depressed castes through the formation of a Mahila Mandal. The Panjab Development Authority had abandoned this village as a "problem" village for lack of community actions and prolonged hostility between the upper castes and scheduled castes. It had remained cut off from all development, although the village was well connected to nearby city of Jullundhur by several means of transportations.

The majority of the population of Tajpur consisted of economically weak scheduled castes who worked at home for leather and sports good industries on a piece rate basis through middlemen. Women were also engaged in other occupations like weaving, Ban to make sleeping cots. According to the observations made by the CWDS study team, this occupation exploited women. Tajpur women were facing a tough life, as they could not acquire new skills or upgrade existing skills in the leather and sports industries to meet the needs of a changing economy. So far as poor women of the upper castes are concerned, they are weaving and spinning cloth at home and falling prey to diseases like tuberculosis and asthma.

Even the Mahila Mandal has failed in Tajpur because of the shortcomings described earlier. In choosing Tajpur as a site for the pilot project, the CWDS team faced a gigantic challenge. The income-generating projects were started with the cooperation of the Ministry of Community Development. The Mahila Mandal was revived and activated. The intervening agency, the CWDS team, has stayed in constant touch with the financial and marketing institutions of the state government at all stages of the project. The team has also been in contact with private industries in Jullundhar to determine items of demand and suitable markets for them.

All of these efforts by the CWDS team and the Mahila Mandal sensitized the officials at the state, district, and block levels because the support of the state machinery is very important for the financial success of the pilot project.

CWDS has also familiarized the Mahila Mandal with how to deal with bureaucracy, how to manage accounts, and how to take care of banking procedures. Since village women have been exposed to the outside world, it has bred in them a sense of assertiveness, which is of great help in dealing with the business community and village *Panchayat.*

The pilot project has also served as a great catalyst in bringing about other changes in women's' lives, the most important being literacy. Women in Tajpur realized that basic functional literacy was required to keep accounts and to apply for loans from the nationalized banks, the Mahila Mandals started non-formal education programs to meet the need.

Today, the CWDS team makes periodic visits to the pilot project to collect data which help the Department of Women's and Child Development in the Ministry of Human

Resource Development in reorienting general policy and programs for women.

Four of the important findings are listed below:

1. Creation of employment among the poor and illiterate women in rural India is very necessary for a social and political change for women. This requires the organization of women in Mahila Mandals.
2. The intervening agency, in this case the CWDS, has to stay in a village for a long time to make a project self-sustaining. The intervening agency has to provide Mahila Mandal with researchers and activists who deal with problems as they surface.
   The other reason for a long stay of the intervening agency with a project is the mechanization of skills. The agency must continue to seek the upgrading of skill and search for new markets for the product.
3. Tajpur experience also showed that, as women engaged in the pilot project also have household responsibilities, their working hours in the project could not be the same as in a city factory. Flexibility has to be permitted.
4. Because poor women of upper castes and women of lower castes worked together in the project, it tended to loosen up the ago-old social barriers loosened.]

One other project of CWDS has been in Bankura. The CWDS chose West Bengal as an area of field study because, under the British, Bengal pioneered the social movements in the nineteenth century seeking emancipation of women from timeworn disabilities. Bengal also led the way in higher education for women and their recruitment into medical and teaching professions. Despite so much progressive background, the condition of women, particularly in rural areas and urban slums, has not much improved.[3]

The research study chose the district of Bankura out of sixteen districts in West Bengal because of its demographic and economic features. It is a drought and flood-prone district with high concentration of scheduled castes and scheduled tribes population, the majority of whom are marginal farmers or landless agricultural laborers. The district has uneven development; the eastern part is canal-fed and advanced in agriculture, while the hilly area in the west and the middle zone are comparatively poor and have a high percentage of scheduled castes and tribal population. The research team selected two villages from each zone—the hilly zone, the irrigated zone, and the intermediary zone. Then, twenty-five households were selected at random from each of the six villages for in-depth interviews. Officials at the district and block levels were also consulted.

The study revealed that rural women should not be viewed as a homogeneous group. Vocational training programs, therefore, should take into account socio-economic stratification in a village to meet the needs of rural women. The study also stressed that a system of monitoring and evaluating plans for training and employment of rural women must precede corrective measures.

The research team confirmed the finding of the report of the Working Group on Employment of Women, Planning Commission, Government of India, 1977-78 that a large number of occupations in which rural women are employed are low productivity, low skill, and low status occupations, the returns from which are highly inadequate in terms of labor spent.[4] To deal with this problem, rural women should be involved in those agro-based activities which are traditionally accepted but are profitable, such as animal husbandry, poultry raising, and livestock rearing for commercial reasons. The Working Group on Employment of Women further pointed out that increasing employment for women has to go hand-in-hand with the broader social policy of strengthening women's participatory roles in Mahila Mandals and rural elected bodies and their ability to exercise their rights with autonomy and dignity. These rights include access and control over the income generated by their own labor and supportive services like childcare centers, educational and health services, and lighter housework. The reader can easily discern that this policy statement by the Working Group is significantly different from the conventional approach which looks at women's economic contribution, whether within or outside the family, as marginal or supplemental for the family's subsistence.

The field investigators in the Bankura district came out with the following observations:

> Even though the Sixth and Seventh Five-Year Plans intend women to be one of the major beneficiaries in all plans of rural development like the Integrated Rural Development Program (IRDP), the Drought Prone Area Development Program, Small Farmers' Development Agency, and Integrated Tribal Development Program, none of the agencies at the district level, responsible for the implementation, have made any special efforts to bring women within their network. These programs are basically designed for asset creation and have no training component, and women are not viewed as specific beneficiaries of these programs. Nor have women been viewed as members of specific target groups like small or marginal farmers or tribal farmers even when women are occupationally members of such groups. Since the programs for poverty alleviation or employment generation depend basically on the transfer of assets like land, capital, credit, and inputs, a household is eligible to receive them, which means that the assets come to be controlled by men, although, indirectly women may also be the beneficiaries. Except in educational programs, women have never been viewed as individuals but only as members of a household.

Because rural women look upon families as basically their main responsibilities, the latter have first to be reduced by providing women with créche and Balwadis or pre-school facilities, so that they can avail themselves of developmental projects designed for women. The research team thus alleged that the official planners wrongly accuse rural women of apathy toward new projects because the underlying cause is entirely different. These women truly have no time to engage in developmental activities, as their full day is spent in the house.

Women often cannot enter training programs as entry qualifications are too high for them. The research team strongly recommended that they be lowered for women. So many times, women are not even aware of these training opportunities.

The CWDS research team also recommended that an appropriate organizational structure should be provided to supervise women's programs. At the state level, a Committee of the State Cabinet for Women's Development has already been formed since 1978. But the next step should be the inclusion of an officer within the departments of *Panchayats* and Rural Development who would supervise women's programs. They all must have special teams at the block level. The number of *Gram-Sevikas* should be expanded, and they should receive special training to identify needs of rural women with special reference to production and marketing.

It was further recommended that, at the state level, Women Corporations should be created. These Corporations should be multi-purpose agencies to carry on surveys and coordinate with other developmental bodies and credit institutions in states to implement various women's projects sanctioned in the Five-Year Plans. In addition to the Corporations, special cells must be created in all credit institutions, which would finance only women's projects.

Like the organizational structure at the state level, a similar structure should be created at the district level to guarantee that state projects for women are being implemented.

A high percentage of training seats in Community Health Volunteers Scheme (CHVS) and Short-Term Medical

Training Scheme (LMF) should be set aside exclusively for women. Efforts should be made to involve rural women in these training programs by raising the age limit so that mature or elderly women could become eligible.

The Indian Government gave the findings of the research team in the Bankura district due consideration and created State Level Corporations for women in all the states when the Ministry of Social and Family Welfare was reorganized in 1985 to become the Ministry of Human Resource Development. In the Seventh Five-Year Plan (1985-90) a specific high percentage of money has also been earmarked for women's programs.

The Bankura Project has been a great success in another way, too. Women organized themselves into a Mahila Samiti (women's organization) with the help of CWDS. Forty acres of wasteland was acquired to plant seedlings for Tassar cultivation. The women's cell in the Ministry of Labor agreed to provide financial assistance for the purpose. The CWDS also helped form Mahila Vikas Sangh, or Women's Development Association, the apex body of four Mahila Samitis. The Mahila Vikas Sangh has been registered as an official organization under Indian law. Its main function is to coordinate the activities of member Samitis and help to form more Samitis in the region so that women can participate in the development activities of the region.

The CWDS also organized a training workshop for leadership development as a part of the Bankura Project. In this six-day workshop, eight women *Panchayat* members, twenty-five Samiti members, and twenty *Anganwadi* workers of the Integrated Child Development Scheme of the Ministry of Health and Family Welfare took part. Participants discussed women of each category under their direct supervision with special reference to their rights and responsibilities and developmental activities intended for women. The purpose was to find areas of cooperation among the participants in order to maximize available benefits for women. Apart from these participants and

CWDS workers, officials of the district and the block developmental levels also joined to guide discussion and point out the developmental programs available to women. Women who participated in these workshops later on discussed their experience with their counterpart in their areas.

We may now turn to SEWA, or Self-Employed Women's Association, which has a powerful rural wing along with a wing for women workers in urban slums.[5] Started in 1978 with a tiny créche and a tailoring class in the poor village of Dholka Taluka of the Ahmedabad district in the state of Gujarat in Western India, SEWA's rural wing, in 1983, was working with three thousand rural women in various districts of Gujarat state.

The experience of SEWA has shown that rural women must be treated not as "beneficiaries" as in a welfare scheme, but as equal partners in decision-making. To help women exert their role, they had to be organized—the primary goal of the Rural Wing of SEWA. It seeks to train rural leadership organizers. These organizers are selected to participate in a course called Grass-root Organizers' Training. SEWA workers, however, reported that older males did create problems in the beginning. But younger village councilmen helped SEWA workers in organizing the Grass-root Organizers' Training Camp.

During their contact with rural women, SEWA workers also discovered that the women were ready to learn new skills and ideas. They were eager to escape from low-income and hazardous *bidi*-making (cigar rolling) activity. Income-generation projects through Khadi (handloom) weaving, Women's Milk Cooperatives, animal husbandry, and other craft revivals have come to occupy as major part in SEWA's interaction with Mahila Mandals.

Support services like créches, banking, legal aid, marketing, and linkage with government agencies act as supplementary to the main income-generation activities of SEWA.

The popular slogan "*Aage Chalo*" (march forward) has a very winning ring to it and this had been adopted by SEWA. Among some of the SEWA projects initiated under this slogan are the setting up of créches where children are well taken care of while mothers are away to work. That healthy children would serve as a deterrent to reckless childbirth was expected. The criteria for selecting a village for "*Aage Chalo*", créche include underdevelopment, distance from the main road connection, poverty concentration, and predominance of agriculture or female construction labor. The two districts of Gujarat-Ahmedabad and Junagadh—were identified for running "*Aage Chalo*" créche, or day-care centers. SEWA workers reported that untouchablity did come up as an issue in the beginning among upper caste women did not want their children to share food and other facilities with Harijan (untouchables since 1949). Gradually, the upper caste women accepted periodic picnics and health camps and cultural programs. Furthermore, joint mothers' meetings have contributed to the breaking down of caste barriers. The youngsters who have been raised in the créches mix together easily. This factor also contributes to national integration.

Besides créches, mothers' meetings or Mahila Mandals have served as vehicles to convey the basic needs to the rural women. For example, in scarce areas, availability of drinking water is more important than introducing wet toilets.

Literacy classes are also an essential part of the "*Aage Chalo*" program. Women are also being trained in crafts like carpentry, forestation, and handloom weaving, very significant in Gujarat, the center of the Indian cotton textile industry. The combined production of handloom and powerlooms has increased to 431 crore meters from 101 crores and the Indian Government has targeted the production of 410 crore meters of handloom cloth by 1985. The rural wing of SEWA decided to open up training centers for women to teach them weaving in new designs to meet the demands of a modern market. The project opened in the Dholka block, which had a large number of traditional female weavers who, had been displaced with the rise of machine-made textiles. Under this project, SEWA has been trying to revive the handloom industry in the area by enabling women to get loans from the SEWA bank. Male opposition menaced the start of this plan, as weaving at the loom had been considered a male prerogative traditionally, even though women had helped in washing and dyeing wool. Mother-in-laws also objected to the training program, as it took the daughter-in-laws away from home and essential housework. To resolve the latter issue, a more convenient time in the afternoon was fixed so that trainees could come after their domestic chores

SEWA workers invited the director of the weaving laboratory of the National Institute of design to assist in current design demand so that the finished product could compete in the open market. It was realized that women had to be assured of continuity of work because earning ability is an essential prerequisite in improving the status of women.

Finally the SEWA article warns that the urban women, the organizers in rural areas, must de-educate, de-urbanize, and de-glamorize themselves in order to establish a rapport with rural women. Only then will rural women discover their potential to learn new skills. Rural women of the Third World countries are not "beneficiaries" of a welfare scheme; rather, they are intelligent, equal, and decent human beings who have a vast reservoir of potential to learn and consequently to take the country forward.

The Indian Council of Social Science Research (ICSSR) helps to fund projects for rural women. Such plans hold vast significance for India's future:

- *Empowering Rural Poor:* Developing countries in the Third World have recognized the importance of people's participation in planning and implementation of development programs. Mobilization and education of the rural poor through their own organizations has, therefore, become a major component of rural development schemes in the sixth and the Seventh Plans (1980-90). The most fundamental reason for organizing the poor is to raise consciousness and awareness among them of their environment. Indigenous leadership, however, may not be available within the poor. An external voluntary organization often must provide leadership. A case study of organizing of the rural poor in Kuppam block of Andhra Pradesh in the south is presented below to indicate a new approach to rural organization.

The Kuppam Experiment: Popularly known as the Indian Rural Reconstruction Movement or (IRM), the Kuppam Experiment grew from the inventive mind of Dr. Goturi Reddy, who modeled the IRM along the lines of Dr. Yen's four-fold Integrated Rural Reconstruction Mode. The basic principles of the movement are to help the poor to help themselves; not to offer relief but release; not to show-case one instance but to establish a pattern and to permit outsiders to help but to insist that insiders do the job. Dr. Yen considers illiteracy, inequality, ill health, and civic inertia as the four basic enemies of mankind. These enemies are attacked through a strategy which has three components—"people," "power," and "released." It works as follows.

Attack	*Through*	*Release*
1. Illiteracy	Non-formal	Brain power
2. Inequality	Conscientization	Productive power
3. Ill-health	Community Health	Physical power Programs
4. Civic inertia	Self-government	Governing power

Kuppam block in Chittor district of Andhra Pradesh is the most distant from the capital of Hyderabad. Over a period of ten years, the IRM is expected to be replicated in the whole of Chittor district. This program is based upon a three-tier system of personnel organization: Program Coordinator,

Cluster Coordinator, and Animators.

The Program Coordinator holds the position only for three years. Then, he is sent for training at the International Institute of rural construction. After his return from the training program, the person is required to replicate the program in one of the adjacent areas of the Kuppam block by forming a new action group independent of the mother groups. Because the Program coordinator is not with the original group, the Cluster Coordinator becomes the Program Coordinator of this group for the next three years. He will be doing what the first Program Coordinator had done after three years. i.e., to go to the Philippines for training.

The method is designed to prevent institutionalization in an organization, and the trained personnel are required to replicate and multiply the program in other areas. During the past five years, seven persons were encouraged to form new groups. These groups, in turn, trained more workers in rural reconstruction work.

These groups keep one fundamental factor in view,—to reach out to the masses through the most progressive element in the village who are the young people. The youth also collaborate well with the Block Development Officials and try to maintain good terms with the government machinery as a whole.

Voluntary organizations develop awareness among the people which includes diffusion of information about local administration, institutions exploiting the poor, relevant legislation, and their rights and responsibilities. This cooperation occurs mainly through personal discussion with the people. Chorus songs and street plays on social problems also form part of the strategy to instill awareness among the target groups. Conscientious, or awareness, in turn creates a motivation to change. The organization of target groups into village associations enables the poor to strike a balance with the area's dominant interests, the landlords and the government officials. The strength of organized power won a victory when the associations of poor people triumphed in election for village *Panchayats*, cooperative societies, and youth associations.

The Kuppam Experiment demonstrated that the organizing of rural poor is a triangular task. Political empowering results from participation in local government and leadership training. Social empowering come about through education or conscientious. Economic empowering flows from asset-building and income generation programs. When all three aspects develop in a balanced way, the prospect of rural development escapes mere illusion to become tangible reality. Women account for nearly half of the Indian population; urgency to organize them is all too obvious, as they are the main mentors of the young generation.[6]

Cooperative Dairying: One other way to organize the rural women has been through the formation of Milk Cooperatives. Although cooperative dairying basically seeks to introduce technological innovations in order to produce large profits, it also has been used to transform rural society. As untouchables, or Harijan, are also the members, it has given them a status of equality within the cooperative societies. This egalitarianism has instilled a new confidence among them, and they now want to raise their status in ways other than just economical.

An All Women's Cooperative was set up in a very traditional village in the early 1980s. The district officials supported it. Soon, the cooperative was able to stand on its own; this success gave credibility to women that they can efficiently manage non-domestic affairs. The major change came when Women Cooperative could send two of its members as representatives to the village *Panchayat* to work along with men of the village. The Milk Cooperative, thus, has been instrumental in changing male attitudes toward women and in increasing women's participation.

The Milk Cooperative proved beneficial in another way, too. Rural people learned that, if a group could benefit in one way by a joint effort, similar efforts in other spheres could be equally resourceful. In addition, cooperatives provide a forum to discuss common problems and to seek solutions.[7]

Cooperatives can also act as "pressure groups" upon local village *Panchayats* and official developmental agencies.

The preceding discussion of the major issues facing rural women would demonstrate that the task of rural reconstruction is an enormous responsibility facing the nation and the Indian Government. The final success of the Indian democracy rests greatly on the success of rural regeneration. Only the future will deliver the judgment if India will succeed or fail.

Women's participation in Panchayat Raj institutions, or elected councils at the village, block, and district level has had a more checkered history. *Participation of Women in Panchayat Raj Institutions: A Case Study of Three Panchayat Samitis in Andhra Pradesh* is a revealing investigation, as it analyzes the reasons for the low level of rural women.[8] Before considering the results, readers must remember that, along with the three-tier system of Panchayat Raj, there is also the official hierarchy of the Community Rural Development Program (IRDP) with development officers at the district, block, and village level.

Legislation had created the Panchayat Raj in 1956. to ensure the presence of women in the Gram Sabha, Panchayat Samiti, and Zila Parishad, a new law was enacted in the 1960s to set aside a few seats for scheduled castes, tribes, and women. If women did not volunteer for election, they had to be co-opted.

The study revealed that women voluntarily did not stand for elections; they had to be co-opted. Even then, they would not attend meetings, as politics and participation in political institutions was considered unworthy of good women. At the village level, registers would be sent to these women's homes to record their attendance by their signature or thumb impression. The survey also revealed that women's lack of education and the presence of their own male relatives (older brothers-in-law or fathers-in-law) act as strong deterrents. A woman may be hesitant to speak up at a meeting of the Gram Sabha or village *Panchayat*.

The study pointed out that women members of the Zila Parishad (District Council) showed a greater degree of independence or participation than the Panchayat Samiti (block level) members. Many of them took good part in all discussions relating to communications, health, sanitation, schools, women, and tribal welfare. That there is a strong relationship between education and participation proved the truth. In general, women having secondary qualifications (sixth through tenth grades) participated well in the meetings. The economic position is another factor determining the degree of involvement. So far as caste is concerned, it had great relevance in the selection of members than in participation. Those women who had previous experience in politics or were related to persons in politics generally played a significant role. The study also revealed that women active in other social associations, did not necessarily become active participants in local political institutions. Somehow, women like social work but shied away from political participation.

A few reasons why women shunned political participation are given below:

Political is considered a male prerogative: Women culturally are not trained to accept qualities of leadership, initiative, independence, or organizing ability. In her upbringing, an Indian woman in rural India is taught to consider those qualities as undesirable for her. Women are made to feel weaker. Those women who engage in politics are considered masculine, thus abnormal. This leads to alienation of these political women from society.

Absence of Economic Independence: Most of the women members of local institutions did not have an independent income. They were only partners in the enjoyment of family income, not contributors to it.

Traditional Constraints: Women of upper caste and richer background are made to feel that if they participate in politics, they will be looked down upon. Talented, educated women do not accept membership, while ignorant, lower class women are left to be co-opted as members. The study revealed that bias against upper caste women's participation is so strong that, in some Panchayat Samitis (block level councils), two prostitutes and two widows were co-opted in order to comply with the legal requirements.

Absence of Awareness of the Political System: Rural people are not sufficiently educated about the aims of the Constitution and the need for equal participation of men and women in all fields of activity.

Defect Selection: Many times, women are co-opted, not because of their experience, but because of their connections to *Sarpanch* (head of the Village Council) or because of their submissive attitude.

Personal Inhibitions: Compared to urban women, rural women have fewer opportunities for social gatherings. They mainly move around in families where they do not develop qualities of individual thinking and individual decision-making. They are, therefore, not prepared to take active part in politics.

Defects in the Functioning of Panchayat Raj Institutions: In reality, these bodies are dominated by Sarpanchs and block-level officials. The result is that the presence of other members, including women, becomes merely a formality. These men control Panchayat Raj bodies by a number of devious methods like not giving enough notice about the meetings and agenda. Many decisions are made in advance of the session, and the meetings are called only to endorse them.

Non-Recognition of Equal Status: Several male members of the local institutions do not accept women as equal participants. This discourages women either from attending or from speaking up at the meetings.

Principle of Co-option not Conducive to Equal Status: Co-option creates among members a feeling of subjection to other members who have been elected. Co-opted women, thus, tend to sit very passively at the meetings.

After detailing the reasons for women's indifference to political participation, the study goes on to suggest remedial measurers.

Education: Both men and women should be made aware that they have responsibilities to society along with family duties. This can be done through the existing program of adult education.

Allotment of a Considerable Number of Seats to Women in Local Bodies: The seats for women should be very much increased to encourage their participation in politics and local democratic institutions.

Provision for All-Women Panchayats: The Committee on the Status of Women had recommended in 1976 that one positive way to encourage women's entry into politics is the establishment of all-women *Panchayats* by means of legislation. The Committee stated that these women *Panchayats* would not be parallel organizations to Gram Sabhas or village *Panchayats.* They would be recommended as a transitional measure to break through traditional attitudes in rural society which inhibit women's political participation. The way the present situation is, women find it very difficult to face the tug-of-war with men and are able to get elected or co-opted only from reserved seats. As a transitory measure, all women Gram Sabhas should be organized.

Strengthening of Mahila Mandals or Women's Associations as Real Agents of Women's Development: Experts in social development and change have noticed that, where women's organizations are strong, changes are introduced quickly and maintained easily. The question is how to strengthen Mahila Mandals. One way is to conduct common prayer and worship as a means to bring women together. Another inducement can be to pride some training to women to earn income. The richer families in the village must take the initiative in getting women together under the guidance of *Mukhya-Sevikas* or *Gram-Sevikas.*

Establishment of Village Cooperatives for Women: The economic dependence of women is one major reason for submissiveness and reluctance of women to enter politics. Co-operatives must be formed in villages. Those women who would become economically self-reliant would often possess qualities of confidence, courage, and vigor. These qualities would enable them to function as successful participants in village *Panchayats.*

Steps to Activate Women Members of Political Institutions: These "passive" women who sit quietly in village councils or other bodies should be given training by community Development Officers like *Mukhya-Sevikas* so that they could form definite views on village issues and contribute to decision-making.

Another way to activate these "passive" women is to bring together at regular meetings women members of the Village Councils or Gram Sabhas, Panchayat Samitis and Zila Parishads. *Gram-Sevikas* and *Mukhya Sevikas* should take the lead in this respect.

Contact with the Outside World: Rural people should be brought into contact with the urban world by organizing educational tours. As women may not volunteer to join such tours if only educational in nature, one inducement could be to arrange visits to holy places suiting the religious-minded villagers. Contact with the outside world would make the rural women more knowledgeable, alert, and assertive.

Sometimes a graduate or a post-graduate student majoring in Sociology could be asked to address the village *Panchayats.*

Opportunities for Key Positions: Women should be given key positions in Panchayat Raj institutions. This would increase women's participation and contributions. If a male is the President, the Vice-President should be a female.

Setting Up of Advisory Committees: These Advisory Committees should include women from different professional areas, such as women welfare officers, social workers, political thinkers, and members of political institutions. These

Committees can be of great educational value by bringing political theorists and social practitioners together.

Enabling Women of Urban Areas to become Members of Rural Political Institutions: Social researchers came across a number of urban women, originally belonging to rural areas, who are now willing to extend their services to rural institutions. If should be borne in mind that external agencies can only initiate the process of change which, in the final analysis, has to be managed and governed by rural women themselves through their Mahila Mandals.

ICSSR funded another important research project called: Functions of B.D.O., Block Development Officer: Need to Organize.[9]

The main discussion in this article is the administrative set up at block level which has assumed more responsibilities with the introduction of additional rural programs like IRDP (Integrated Rural Development Program), NREP (national Rural Employment Development Program), NREP (National Rural Employment Program). TRYSEM (Training of Rural Youth for Self-Employment), and MNP (Minimum Nutrition Program).

As the Ministry of Agriculture is greatly involved in these programs, it has a strong presence at the block level in the form of Agriculture Extension Workers. In the beginning, these workers were under the control of the B.D.O., but, with the increased number of activities, they have been taken away from the supervision of B.D.O. Now the Ministry of Agriculture supervises its program of extension, supply of inputs, and credit facilities, independent of the B.D.O., or Block Development Officer.

In addition to agriculture, the State Industries Departments are involved in the program of rural industrialization, like TRYSEM, through their District Industries Centers. Every state also has a number of different programs at the grass-root level for the rural poor. These programs vary from state to state and are implemented by the block-level functionaries.

The B.D.O. and his staff are over-burned with a heavy variety of activities. The author of this article has made a number of recommendations for reorganizing responsibilities of the B.D.O. to render him more efficient. Even though, the data has been mainly collected from the State of Madhya Pradesh in Central India, recommendations can be applied all over.

The B.D.O. has following responsibilities to discharge—

1. Implementation of programs under NREP.
2. Implementation of programs under IRDP.
3. Implementation of programs under RLEGP.
4. Work as the Chief Executive officer of the block level Panchayat.
5. As officer of the Panchayat department, carrying on liaison work with village *Panchayats* and conducting elections for them

Other work of the B.D.O. may vary from state to state; for instance, in Madhya Pradesh, he has to look after primary school in tribal areas.

To assist the B.D.O. at the block level, there are several officers.

NREP and RLEGP require the B.D.O. and his staff to travel extensively covering from twenty-five to thirty village *Panchayats*, as the basic work is building and road construction under these programs. Under the IRDP and TRYSEM , the B.D.O. has to survey and prepare a sufficient number of cases each year, submit them to the banks, and make sure that the required number of applicants get their loans and sanctioned assistance. By the end of the Sixth Plan (1980-85), the target was six hundred cases under the IRDP. The Seventh Plan has raised the cases to eight hundred and six per year per block. One can thus easily envision the severe strain of work on a B.D.O. This article recommends a reduction in his assignments to render him more efficient in a fewer areas.

The NREP and The RLEGP cannot be disturbed, as these programs are implemented through village *Panchayats* and the B.D.O. is the main Executive Officer in the block level *Panchayat.* To delink the B.D.O. from the IRDP would free him from the burden of seeing to it that, each year, six hundred families be reached, and the coordination between such varied sectors as agriculture, animal husbandry, rural industry, and fishery be provided, besides the arrangement of credit from financial institutions. A new administrative set up can be created at the block level under the previews of the DRDA (District Rural Development Agency). The appointment of a new block-level officer, subordinate in status to the B.D.O., would ease the situation. This new officer would have his own junior staff of specialists in agriculture, animal husbandry, and industries, in addition to V.L.W. or Village Level Worker.

As the preceding discussion would illustrate, the B.D.O. plays a very important role in rural improvement, and the latter determines the level of enthusiasm and participation on the part of the village people. It becomes necessary that the official administrative machinery be streamlined to encourage rural people to take more interest in village *Panchayats* and other elected bodies like Mahila Mandals. One of the chief goals of the Community or Rural Development Program has been to involve people in the important task of national development in all areas of life.

A field study, *Impact of Modernization and Irrigation on the Economic and Social Conditions of Rural women Workers*, grew from the efforts of Dr. Vithal Raj and Miss K. Lalita in a few villages in Kodal block in the State of Andhra Pradesh in 1982. The purpose of the research was to study the advantages and disadvantages accruing from developmental strategies to poor women and the change in their socio-economic status.[10]

The result of the study involves the implications of the "Green Revolution" of the 1960s. Rural men of poorer sections lost jobs with the introduction of tractors as traditional plowing was given up. These displaced men competed with women for jobs in rice transplanting. Many women quickly lost their only means of earning a living. The study showed that women generally were paid less than men despite development and gift publicity of the International Women's Decade of 1975 to 1985.

The study's other observations included:

> Many of the marginal farmers, who owned only about two acres of land, still had to do dry farming, as they could not get water from the new irrigation canals. The political clout of richer farmers enabled them to divert most of the water to their fields.
>
> Poor farmers, artisans, and landless laborers' debts have tended to increase sharply as they are imitating the rich farmers in the village. They go to cinemas regularly, drink tea and coffee, and offer expensive dowries in marriages.

The Raj and Lalita study concludes that the new developmental strategies like the "Green Revolution" have benefited mainly the rich farmers, who are also able to attend a nearby college, while the poor have remained where they were. Wages superficially have increased, but inflation has undermined the real power of money. The assumption of the "Green Revolution" was that prosperity would trickle down to poorer sections as a spontaneous outcome. Unfortunately, it has not happened. Women are faced with increasing unemployment because men are taking over their jobs with the increased mechanization of agriculture, which has reduced the demand for rural labor. Women, thus, bear the brunt of a most vicious cycle.

Impact of Technological Development in Agriculture on Women in Rural Areas, a study done in 1980 by S.P. Sinha, supports the conclusions of the preceding.[11] The Sinha's investigation centered upon villages in the Muzaffarpur district of Bihar in eastern India, and it also analyzes the effects of the "Green

Revolution" of the 1960s. Technological development in agriculture has reduced employment opportunities for poor rural women as they have lost jobs in traditional activities like threshing, de-husking, and flour making. To provide alternative jobs to such women, the State Handicraft Center must reach down to the village level to supply inputs, improved equipment, tools training, and marketing of goods. A large-scale publicity campaign must be undertaken to familiarize women with the existing government schemes and program.

A study of twenty-eight villages in three states of Kerala and Tamilnadu in the south and West Bengal in the east called *Women In rice Cultivation* was completed in 1986.[12] These states are paddy growing regions of India, and paddy rice is a very important crop in developing countries. Around 49.5 percent of women and 24.26 percent of men are agricultural laborers all over India. Around 36.86 percent of women and 55.26 percent of men are cultivators. In paddy cultivation, women transplant and weed while men plow, make bunds, or spray chemical fertilizers. Even though women's work is essential to rice cultivation, the study revealed that is has been regarded as less valuable. Sixty women respondents were interviewed in one village—all agricultural laborers and who cooperated with the research team for one full year. In the census report of 1981, this village had been listed either as "nil" or as having one or two female agricultural laborers. This could not have been a simple omission, as there are a significant number of households in this village where single women (widows, divorced, or deserted women) are primarily responsible for the upkeep of the family. As these agricultural women are not reported by the official data-collecting network, they are not "seen" by the agencies of the government in their plans. Again, discrimination resists detection.

As for the role of women of landowning households in paddy cultivation, they undertake such work as selection and storing of seed, supervision of labor if the fields happen to be close to the house, and taking care of cattle. In spite of their solid contribution, the commonly held belief is that these women do not work because only manual work is considered as work.

The study also showed that landless female workers have to seek alternative employment in the slack season to support their families. But recent modern developments have reduced or eliminated the availability of these jobs by substituting tile and concrete for roofing in place of coconut leaf matting. Similarly, permanent compound walls instead of fences are also taking jobs away from women. Use of plastic in many items has also reduced the demand for traditional goods, like baskets and sitting mats. Steady loss of alternative employment has forced many landless workers to migrate to urban slums where they face the problems concomitant with cultural estrangement.

Even in small-and medium-size land holdings, urban migration has grown along with the reduced size of land-holdings, which result from property division among children after the father's death.

A Sociological Study of Women Migration in Andhra Pradesh is a 1984 field study of tobacco women graders in the delta belt of Andhra Pradesh.[13] The research work shows that India ranks third in the world in producing all types of tobacco products. While some tobacco operations are performed both by men and women, the latter exclusively perform the tobacco transplantation and grading. Between 1951 and 1981, the total work force of grading factories shrank to forty percent mainly owing to mechanization of operations such as stemming. With more female labor available, women are willing to accept less wages. The other disadvantage is that, because these women are not unionized, they cannot insist on such statutory rights as maternity leave, créche, and subsidized canteens. With unavailability of jobs, women migrate first, then husbands follow. These migrants get information from relatives and other villagers who have already left. The analysis showed that most of the migrant households are living a life of austerity so that they might send money home to buy land, cattle, or gold for dowries. The study also pointed out that the proportion of women workers to male workers has gone down from 11.4 percent to 9.1 percent between 1951 and 1971 either because they do not possess factory skills or because of reduced employment in agriculture or agro-based industries. The contribution of these women to household income is still so great that families cannot survive without their income. Migration has noticeably affected the country's development, but it has created problems for the migrants placed in a totally unfamiliar environment. In turn, problems accompanying a rapid rise in urban slums have amounted to a monumental task for the residents and the official agencies. At the same time, one cannot ignore the positive effect of migration; plentiful labor is now available for industries springing up like mushrooms. For commercialized crops like sugarcane and tobacco, mobile and abundant labor is welcome. In addition, exposure to urban life is helping to break through the crust of old ideas and myths in the villages, although the process is slow.

With its subject, the unorganized women workers in big cities, *The Survey of Women Workers in the Unorganized Sector of Calcutta* (West Bengal), conducted by Nirmala Banerjee, is a survey of 411 women picked up at random.[14] The conclusions of the study highlight the following points:

The unorganized sector of economy employs a very large number of work force even in the urban regions of India. In the case of women, this percentage is significantly higher than for men.

The women in the informal sector included a significant number of children and old people, and nearly seventy percent of women belonged to families below the poverty level.

A large number of women are migrants to the city. These single migrants included married women with young children and unmarried girls.

Women workers were no longer confined to domestic service but were found in a number of traditionally male occupation or new occupations.

Whenever exact comparison between similar jobs in formal and informal sectors was possible, wage rates and incomes were less than half in the informal sector. No system of annual increment existed in the unorganized sector. To increase income meant increasing working hours.

Nearly half of the women earned forty percent or more of their family incomes. This was true even for the child female workers. Their earnings cannot be dismissed as "supplementary," as, without them, families could not buy the basic needs. Even though they contributed so much to the family income, one-third of the women were not allowed to manage family funds.

Even with a full working day, forty percent of women did the family cooking.

Even after working for five years, most of the women knew little about the Trade Union Movement.

Over sixty-five percent of women knew nothing about divorce law or abortion law.

Even though they were aware that women have to work, few of them were training their daughters to learn a skill.

Within the family, female children got fewer opportunities for education and were the first to be sent out to work in case of need.

Because so many of these women workers have migrated from rural areas, a number of programs for women in the Sixth and Seventh Five-Year Plans (1980-90) have given substantial emphasis to the creation of employment opportunities in rural areas themselves through the formation of women Cooperatives in agro-based industries.

To say that government programs have achieved much in relatively few years in the face of monumental problems may be to damn with faint praise; for, the bitter struggle and genuine suffering of Indian women persist. No matter how deserving is the valor of the vanquished in any historical content, their loss remains. India has accomplished much with astonishing rapidity, but will she ultimately prevail? Will time wait for India?

REFERENCES

1. *Women in Struggle: Role and Participation of Women in the Chipko Movement in Uttar Khand Region of the State of U.P.*, New Delhi: CWDS library, 1987.
2. Jhurani, Kamlesh, *Women Participation and Development—A Case Study from Rural Panjab*, New Delhi: CWDS library, 1985.
   CWDS publishes a journal called *Samya Shakti* or the organized power of people. Its volumes are available in the library in New Delhi, which list many other pilot projects of the CWDS.
3. *Extension of Vocational Training Facilities for Rural Women, Report on West Bengal, District of Bankura*, New Delhi: CWDS library, January 1983.
4. "From the Committee on the Status of Women," as reported in 1985 in *Samya Shakti*, New Delhi: CWDS, vol. II, no. 1, 1987, 80-87.
5. Dholakia, Anila, R., *Aage Chalo* (Move Forward), New Delhi: CWDS library, 1983.
6. Reddy, G. Narayana, "Empowering Rural Poor," in *Kurukshetra*, vol. XXV, no. 11, August, 1987, 20-22. (Reddy was the Assistant Director of Faculty of Human Resource Development, NIRD (National Institute of Rural Development, Hyderabad).
7. Brahman, D. Naga, "Cooperative Dairying," in Kurukshetra, vol. XXV, no. 11, August, 1987, 4-6.
8. Manikyamba, P., *Participation of Women in Panchayat Raj Institutions: A Case study of Three Panchayat Samitis in Andhra Pradesh*, November, 1981, New Delhi: ICSSR Library.
9. *Functions of B.D.O., Block Development Officer: Need to Recognize*, New Delhi: ICSSR library.
10. Kalkar, Govind, "Women's Work and Agriculture Technology,": Occasional paper, no. 3, 1985, New Delhi: CWDS library, 3-5.
11. Sinha, S.P., *Impact of Technological Development in Agriculture on Women in Rural Areas*, 1980, New Delhi: ICSSR library.
12. Saradamon, K., *Women in Rice Cultivation: A Study of Twenty-Eight Villages in Three India States*, April, 1986, New Delhi: ICSSR library.
13. Hemakumari, T.A., *A Sociological Study of Women Migration in Andhra Pradesh*, 1984, New Delhi: ICSSR library.
14. Banerjee, Nirmala, *Survey of Women Workers in the Unorganized Sector of Calcutta*, 1982, New Delhi: ICSSR library.
   Following studies are also available in the CWDS library.
   The Current Scene in Law and Education: Some facts for you to Consider,

1986.
The First Six Years and Forward, 1987.
Women's Work and Employment: Struggle for a policy, Selections from Indian Documents, 1983.
Forward Looking Strategies: For the Advancement of Women to the Year 2000, 1986.
Kalkar, Govind, *Women and Structural Violence in India,* 1985; Women's Studies in the People's Republic of China, 1983; Women's Work and Agricultural Technology, 1985.
Mais, Lucille Mathurin, *International Women's Decade: A Balance Sheet,* 1985.
Mazumdar, Vina, *Emergence of Women's Question in India and Role of Women's Studies,* 1985.
The Non-Aligned Movement and the International Women's Decade: A Summary of Decisions, 1983.
Pandey, Balaji, *Post-Independence Development among Women in India,* 1987.
Rural Women's Claim to Priority: A Policy Debate, Selected Documents from International and Indian Archives, 1975-1985, Shanti Chakraborty, ed. 1986.
Sharma, Kumud, *Interaction between Policy Assumption and Rural Women's Work,* 1985; *Women and Development: Gender Concerns,* 1985.
Swaminathan, M.S., *The Role of Education and Research in Enhancing Rural Women's Income and Household Happiness,* 1985
Towards Equality, Report of the Committee on the Status of Women in India, Department of Social Welfare, Ministry of Education and Social Welfare, Government of India, 1974.
Women and Development: Promise and Realities, 1985.

Reader may also consult the following works in the ICSSR library.

1. *Income-Generation Activities for Women: Some Case Studies,* published by UNICEF, New Delhi: 1979.
2. *Modernization of Traditional Handloom Weaving Industry in Kashmir Valley,* prepared for UNDP/APCWD, 1979.
3. *Role of Rural Women and Community Life,* prepared for Expert Group Meeting, Population Social Affairs Division, ESCAP, Bangkok, 1978.
4. *Women's Quest for Power: Five Case Studies,* sponsored by ICSSR.

Directories and Bibliographies

1. *Bibliography on Women at Work in India* by Suchitra Anant, S.V. Ramani Rao and Kabita Kapoor, sponsored by the Ministry of Labor and Rehabilitation, 1986.
2. *Catalogue of Agencies Reaching Poorest Women in India,* sponsored by Swedish International Development Authority (SIDA), 1981.
3. *Women's Studies in India: A Directory* by Suchirtra Ananta, S.V. Ramani

Rao and Shikha Goel, 1986.

4. *The Working Child—A Guide to the Literature,* sponsored by UNICEF, 1981.

General

Jain, Devaki, *Decentralization and Women,* paper presented at the Seminar on Decentralization, organized by Rajaji Institute of Public Affairs and Institute of Social and Economic Change, Bangalore, 1984; *Who will bell the Poverty Cat?* For Planning Commission, 1984.

Ideology

1. Jain, Devaki, *Nairobi Fever and Fall out—A Commentary,* paper for the UN conference for the Decade for Women, Nairober, 1985; *Report on a Lecture tour of Scandinavian Countries, 1983; Gandhi on Women,* Lecture delivered at the Conference of National Alliance of Young Entrepreneurs, New Delhi, 1984.

Memoranda

1. For Ministry of Education:
   Adult Education for Women, background paper prepared for Advisory Committee on Education for the 7th Plan, 1983.
2. For Ministry of Labor:
   Note on Women Workers, prepared for the Advisory Committee on the Implementation of the Equal Remuneration Act, 1983.
3. Notes for Sub-Committee on Unorganized Labor on:
   a. *Designing a Scheme for Organizing Unorganized Female Workers.*
   b. Women in Construction Labor.
   c. Women in the Handloom Industry.

Statistic and Data Collection on Women

1. *Adult Education for Women: Developing a Research Base through 8 Case Studies,* sponsored by Directorate of Adult Education, Ministry of Education, 1984.
2. Bezboruah, Rekha and Chand, Malini, *Employment Opportunities for Women in Forestry,* paper presented at the seminar on Role of Women in Community Forestry, Dehradun, 1980.
3. Bezboruah, Rekha and Jaishankar, Shobha, Role *of Income Generation in Adult Education for Women,* paper prepared for the Workshop on Educational Programs for Adult Women, organized by Indian Adult Education Association, June 1984.
4. *Domestic Work: its Implication for Enumeration on Women's Work and Employment,* paper presented at the Symposium on Women's Work and Society, organized by Indian Statistical Institute, New Delhi, 1982.
5. *Employment of Women from Kerala in the Fish Processing Units of Gujarat,* sponsored by the Ministry of Labor, 1984.
6. *Field Investigation of Rural households, for Indian Council of Social Science Research (ICSSR),* paper presented at Technical Seminar on Women's

Work and Employment, organized by the Institute of Social Studies Trust, New Delhi, 1982.

7. *Integrating Women's Interests into a State Five Year Plan*, Karnataka, sponsored by the Ministry of Social Welfare, New Delhi, 1984.
8. Jain, Devaki, *Background Note for the Technical Seminar on Women's Work and Employment*, organized by the Institute of Social Studies Trust, New Delhi, 1982.
9. *Statistics on Women, Children, engaged in Agriculture*, prepared for Food and Agricultural Organization (FAO) Rome, 1983.
10. *Utilization and Wastage of Training—Regional and National Vocational Training Institute for Women*, sponsored by Ministry of Labor and Rehabilitation, Director-General of Employment and Training, 1984.
11. *Women in Agriculture in India*, Background paper presented for Expert Consultation on Women in Food Production, organized by FAO, Rome 1983.
12. *Women's Employment as related to Rural Areas—India*, paper presented at United Nations Mid Decade Conference on Women, Copenhagen, 1980.
13. *Women in the Labor Force*, papers presented at Seminar on Women in the Labor Force organized by Asian Regional Team for Employment Promotion (ARTEP) and International Labor Organization (ILO), Trivandrum, 1981.

Technology

1. Banerjee, Jayanti, *Impact of Technology on Family Life and Changing Role of Women*, paper presented at the Regional Conference of International Council of Social Welfare, Bombay, 1981.
2. Banerjee, Jayanti, *Implication of Technology for Rural Women*, paper presented at the Regional Conference on Women and Technology, Surat, 1983.
3. *Technology Planning for Women*, paper presented at the Seminar on Science and Technology for Women, Delhi, 1982.

8

College Education for City Girls and their Dilemma

ALTHOUGH CHANGES associated with industrialization and urbanization have dealt a severe blow to many of the time-honored ideas about women, marriage, and the sanctity of the joint-families, urban society has not uniformly adjusted to these changes. Certain families have shown radical progressiveness in allowing their women to seek education and employment both, while some have limited their girls to education only.

Before World War II, education for the sake of education was accepted as an ideal before marriage among most of the urban families. A few exceptions were women in the medical profession, in teaching and in political participation in the National Movement. Employment as a more general practice is a phenomenon after India's partition in 1947, which threw many families out of their homes and forced them to migrate to new places to start from scratch. Partition also brought high inflation. Girls began to seek jobs outside the teaching and medical professions to support their families. A "working" girl came to be accepted favorably. Since the Constitution of India has heralded equality, more women have obtained a variety of jobs to supplement their family incomes. Since industrialization and technology have opened up new areas of knowledge and work, society has come to accept the "professional" woman. Many girls maintain their careers even after marriage. This trend has been a new event in the Indian middle-class society, as women of the lower classes have always worked. The problems and issues of married working women consequently gain significance while such women deal with stresses in their various roles as wife, mother, and employee.[1]

An educated woman wants her aspirations for self-expression and self-actualization to be fulfilled. She takes a job, but her husband complains as it leads to neglect of domestic duties even though he enjoys the earnings of his wife. Some men do not even approve of free mixing of their wives with other men at a job, which, in turn, raises problems of marital adjustment. Although the general nature of the problem may seem identical to the problem faced by Western women, important distinctions exist. The traditional concept of marriage in India, dying slowly, was a religious sacrament, indissoluble and eternal which made the couples adjust grudgingly or ungrudgingly. Marriage was a social duty toward the family and the community and there was little room for individual aspirations in the relations between husband and wife. On account of the traditional concept of marriage as a duty toward the family and the community, everyone did one's duty without ever thinking of one's individual aspirations. This caused little marital friction, and social norms also prevented the airing out of any friction in public because it would reflect badly on the whole family. At best, a spouse could only expect respect and a proper discharge of duties from the marriage partner. One did not expect happiness from marriage, therefore, one did not divorce if one was unhappy. When men and women were conditioned to accept little happiness from marriage, there were, as such, no unhappy marriages. The question of marital adjustment did not arise.

The Hindu joint family system was another factor, which lessened the occurrence of "unhappiness" in married life, as there were enough members of the same age and sex to provide companionship to the two spouses. This factor was very much responsible for marriage adjustment as wife and husband were not dependent on each other for affection and companionship.

The traditional Hindu joint family also laid down the roles and duties of every member of the family. So no conflict arose over one's role and status within the family. Each member's concern was to fulfill his duties as laid down by caste and society. Since the pressure on all was to conform, they were left with nothing to demand as their right. Under these circumstances, each person received ego-satisfaction in fulfilling his or her expected role. This lack of competition between man and woman as to their roles facilitated the achievement of marital harmony.

According to traditional Hindu norms a husband is expected to be the authoritarian figure whose will should prevail in the domestic scene. The wife should regard him as her master and serve him faithfully. The husband is superior, the wife his subordinate. A wife's prescribed role was more definite, her duties more specific, than those of her husband. Her husband was to be her sole joy in her life. She was to be a *pativrata*—thinking only of serving her husband. Dr. S. Radhakrishnan, one of India's Presidents, describes the Indian woman in these words: centuries of traditions have made her the most unselfish, the most self-denying and the most patient woman in the world whose pride is always suffering. It is this pride which sustained the marital harmony or did not allow marital adjustment to become a problem.

Processes of industrialization, urbanization, and secularization, however, have brought about social-psychological changes in the attitudes of educated urban women toward marriage and their own status. Women are now adopting a personal conception of marriage, which is fast replacing the religious conception. More and more educated women consider self-respect and the development of personality as necessary goals of life. The two pillars of Hindu society, sacramental marriage and joint family, are weakening. Both husbands and wives seek compatibility of temperament and common objectives. A surprisingly large majority of women expect a high degree of happiness in their married life and demand a personal gratification of their emotional, physiological, social, and economic needs.

Several demands are made by husband and wife on each other and varied are the satisfactions desired and expected of each other. So much is required of marriage now that, when expectations are not fulfilled, different levels of frustrations emerge causing problems in marital adjustment.

India is still passing through the transitional period. With old norms being rejected, the new norms have been fully accepted or defined unambiguously. This problem has caused a great deal of confusion among husbands and wives as to the new roles of spouses in the marriage scene. If only husband and wife could be absolutely positive about what is socially right or wrong, positive attitudes could be developed and conflicts avoided. Since in a period of transition it is not clear what is socially right or wrong, marriage conflicts are increasing. In the absences of clearly defined duties and responsibilities, one is apt to be unmindful of one's duties and to be unduly conscious of one's rights and other's obligations. This tends to create friction in marital relationships.

A working wife is called upon to play the dual role of wife and mother at home and an employee outside with a boss to monitor her productivity. The problem of adjustment for a working wife and mother is compounded because of her inability or unwillingness of the husband to adjust to the new situation. As Promilla Kapur pointed out in her study, strain can occur if the husband is called upon to take a new role of which he is not prepared as a child, particularly if the prestige of this new assignment is not equal to that of the former role. As women's tasks in all societies have less prestige than those of men, women taking over professional roles are moving to a higher level of prestige.

A working wife's behavior pattern and attitudes have both

changed because of the addition of the new role, but husbands have not shown the corresponding change in their attitudes. This lag in the change in the attitudes of the two partners is what makes martial adjustment more difficult to achieve.

Pressures on a working woman are great because, to be a successful wife and mother, she has to develop a certain set of traits but, to be a successful careerist, she has to exhibit very different qualities. To be a mother and wife, she has to have "self-negation" and cooperation, while, to be a successful careerist, she has to be self-enhancing and competitive.

So far as maintaining the home is concerned, a husband might help out considerably with the housework, but basic planning and supervision falls upon the woman. The handling of dual responsibilities contributes greatly to her fatigue, which, in itself, becomes a problem in marital harmony because she cannot devote expected time to her housework and wifely duties.

Marital adjustment can also become problematical because both husband and wife can have different routines outside of the house. They both will be called upon to adjust to this situation, and how well they do it will determine the level of marital happiness.

We can conclude by saying that a working woman has to achieve three kinds of adjustments. Have the husband and wife been able to adjust to their new roles? Have they been able to adjust as marriage partners? Have the two together been able to adjust to the changed patterns of family as a whole?

What is the marital adjustment? Marital adjustment can be defined as a state of life where both the partners tend to avoid or resolve conflicts, have a feeling of satisfaction with marriage and each other, share common interests and activities, and fulfill the marital expectations of each other.

Kapur has conducted a random study of three hundred working women to find out the objective and subjective variables involved in the martial adjustment of the Indian working women. It must be pointed out that, since marriage counseling as an institution has only just begun in a few major cities, like Delhi, it was difficult for Kapur to obtain an official list of maladjusted marriages from a public agency. She chose one hundred teachers, out of whom twenty-five were primary school teachers, another twenty-five taught in higher secondary schools, and fifty were college teachers. In the sample surveyed, another one hundred were office workers and the last one hundred were medical doctors. The sample chose women from different social-economic backgrounds, and each interviewee had to be married at least two years and in the age group of twenty to fifty.

Kapur points out that, in a direct approach of interviews, it was at times difficult to get information about maladjusted marriages; women were hesitant to reveal it due to social inhibitions. She did gather enough data to show that following factors were conducive to marital harmony:

1. *Consistent pre-marital social-economic background of spouses*—In India this factor assumes even more important than in the West, as the process of transition in which old values are either being rejected or modified is still going on. Families have reacted differently to this pull of change.
2. *Compatible and congenial personality traits of spouses.*
3. *Favorable post-marital circumstances*—because retired old parents do tend to live with their married sons, this aspect of family structure creates the additional problem of adjustment for both the spouses; the mother-in-law may be more traditional bound than the younger generation.
4. *Compatible attitudes of the two spouses toward wife's employment complex.*
5. *Harmonious sexual relationships between spouses.*

Factors discovered to be instrumental in bringing about

maladjustment were found to be similar in both groups of women—those who were maladjusted prior to employment and those who became so only after employment (except that employment was an additional factor found among the latter groups of women).

An analysis of the interviews also revealed that a working woman feels strained because she has to divide her loyalty and time between two equally important jobs. Even those women who reported their married lives to be happy mentioned this strain. They suffer from a sense of guilt that they are not giving enough time to either job. This is particularly true of those mothers who had young children. These working women live under great emotional pressure. If the husband is not understanding, he can make the life of the wife even more miserable. If a husband makes excessive demands on the wife because of male egoism, marital disharmony shall prevail.

What causes maladjustment is not whether a wife is equal or subordinate to her husband in the family; the existence of incompatible attitudes of the two spouses toward the roles of each other causes disharmony and friction. For example, how much control a wife should exert over her earnings can become a bone of contention. The interviews bore out another interesting point that, despite a wife's independent income and individual status, she ends up making more efforts than the husband to establish harmony in a married life.

Kapur offers a number of suggestions to the married couple, which can help establish marital satisfaction. These suggestions center around two set of factors, one relating to changes in attitude and expectations of spouses and in other members of the family, such as a mother-in-law and a father-in-law. The new, educated girls must also be informed through publicity and mass media about the feminine virtues of tolerance, sacrifice, and humility essential to performing the role of a wife and a mother. These young girls should not allow themselves to be carried away by the conceit of college education and economic independence.

Kapur also recommends the establishment of competent centers and institutions for both pre-marital and post-marital training and education. As the clue to marital adjustments is to be found in proper attitudes and personality traits, fostering of such attitudes should begin from early childhood. The final note is that marital happiness creates strong families, which, in turn, create strong nations. That is why so much importance is attached to well-adjusted marriages.[2]

Following are the results of a study conducted by Cora Vreede-De-Stuers of the young college girls in the city of Jaipur in Rajasthan state. It could be taken as representative of similar groups in other medium-sized cities (with a few reservations). The attitudes of these girls were greatly influenced by an ideal picture of womanhood they held, often conflicting with the reality of how women live. This combination of ideal and real—of what ought to be and what is—determined their reactions to vital issues of life, such as family and marriage.

The author has given a number of tables in which variables, such as level of study, family ties, and social-economic status of the parents, are taken into account while interviewing these girls.

Families of the girls interviewed were classified according to the father's incomes. Investigation revealed that the number of nuclear families in the highest income group was more than double than the joint families. At the same time, this highest income group has adopted modern life ways. The fathers and other members of the family had received Western education, and most of them had attended a university.

In the interviews, undergraduate girls were chosen from two colleges and were either first-or-second-year undergraduates. The graduate girls were selected from the University of Rajasthan and the Medical College.

An analysis of the research revealed that a significant

discrepancy occurs between the life of a girl at home and her life at the university. A girl, thus, has to be under constant stress to meet the variant demands of two different situations. This stress bore a great influence upon the girl's attitudes and expectations from life and marriage.

One of the questions asked in the interviews related to the girls' attitudes toward the joint family system, showing signs of decline in the cities. Even though most of the interviewers hinted at the inconveniences of the system (the domination and interference of the elders particularly of male members), a large number preferred to live in joint families. One of the reasons given was that children would be well taken care of, if the girls were to decide to take up an occupation. A joint family also takes care of widows and orphans. Paradoxically underlying their reasons for preferring to live in a joint family is their growing individualism, a major factor in the moral weakening of the joint family.

Among other factors leading to the incremental decline of the joint family system, occupational transfers have played a major role. The economy of India is predominantly state controlled which does award security of jobs and pensions upon retirement but it may also mean transfers.

The girls' response to the joint family system reflected the ambivalence of the post-Independence generation. The outside world is competitive and calls for an effort and ambition on the part of an individual to advance in a profession; whereas, the joint family compunctions call for subjugation of individual aspirations to family interests. The mixed response of the Jaipur girls toward the joint family showed the same ambivalence and definitely had a great impact on their attitudes and behavior in life. Even though a majority of the girls spoke in favor of joint families, they also showed a general aversion to the observance of traditional rites and rituals. They would much rather spend time attending movies, enjoying good music, and participating in other kinds of social entertainment. The reason for their lack of enthusiasm is that these girls' educated and occupational fathers did not observe rituals either because of lack of time or because of a disbelief in the viability of these ceremonies. These girls tend to feel that they ought to do the same, as they have a college education with a prospect of employment after graduation.

Why do parents give a college education to girls when it is producing such great mental confusion and creating an adjustment problem for parents and the structure of the joint family? It seems that college education has become essential for the girls of middle-class families to open the gateway to a decent marital match. A number of parents do envisage a professional career for their girls either to increase their marketability in the marriage arena or to satisfy their strong belief that a woman ought to take up a job for her own self-enancement.[3]

Manisha Roy studied the life histories of upper-class and upper-middle-class Bengali women in detail. These were married women between twenty-five and fifty-five. All had completed high school; seventeen has two years of college, fourteen had B.A. degrees and four had M.A. degrees. They all lived in joint families with the number of members from six to twelve. All women had at least one child, some as many as five.

Bengal is an eastern state of India. In its history, it resisted the imposition of Brahmin orthodoxy in the ancient period of India with the result that a number of pre-Aryan or pre-Vedic cults survived. The mother goddess is a highly venerated cult, and she is worshipped in her various aspects of fertility, endurance, and fierce rage to destroy demons and ghosts who seek to harm her children.

With the advent of the Indian modern period, Westernized education spread first in Bengal, as the British conquered it in the mid-eighteenth century. The early nineteenth century saw the emergence of radical social movements like Brahmo Samaj, aimed at improving the down-graded status of the Indian women. Bengal also saw the growth of an urbanized middle-class, as the British opened up new occupations and professions. The life-style of these men changed, but their women remained the same to a great extent until the post-Independence period.

Roy summarizes the personality of a Bengali woman raised in a rich and upper-middle-class family in these words: Her birth is not considered a matter of sad affair as is in the poorer sections and lower middle-class families; she is expected to bring honor to the family when she departs as a bride; and she is showered with enormous love by all members of the joint family.

While growing up, she learns about sex from her peers, Roy states. She may think that sex is dirty, as no one is supposed to talk about it. Only adult married people can indulge in it in privacy. The growing daughter does not see the mother and father spend any time together during the day. Her mother spends her time cooking special meals for male members, as servants are available for daily routine cooking. The girl notices that her father does not make any comment on any dish, as for a husband to praise his wife in the presence of others is immodest. He must pretend not to notice her.

The growing girl hears epic stories from aunts and grandparents, which instill in her the duties of a wife and a mother. To suffer is a woman's fate. The more she suffers, the more virtue she gains. She must also accept the willfulness of men. These stories also repeat the tales of women who won admiration because they suppressed their desires to adjust to ascetic, cold husbands who spent most of their time outside the house taking care of their external problems and their livelihood.

All these exposures create a conflict in the mind of the girls, for movies and modern magazines tempt her to a very different scenario of life. American movies are popular with the teenagers who marvel at the radical difference in life-styles depicted.

The "Facts of Life" do not come down to her as a part of

conscious and scientific instruction at home or at school; rather they trickle down to her in the form of distorted and scattered information from her peers, magazines, and women's gossip around the house. She does feel excited when she comes to know of this aspect of life, but she knows that she must not feel so as there is a big taboo on it socially and at home. She has to conceal it, as it is considered bad to feel that way. A girl is supposed to experience her first romantic impulse only when she meets her husband. Any outburst of this emotion other than in marriage is regarded as sinful.

While attending college, she prepares herself for marriage. Her parents prevent her from attending coed institutions as far as possible. Her only male companions are her cousins. Her elders arrange her marriage. She may go to a restaurant or a movie with her prospective husband but only accompanied by a male member, perhaps a cousin of her own family.

The marriage ceremony is a lengthy religious sacrament. The bride experiences a number of expectations while the bridegroom sits next to her in the performance of marriage rituals before the holy fire.

When the bride leaves her father's home, she is reminded of her duties as described in the epics which extol the high merit of a suppressed wife, a suffering mother, and a sacrificing woman in all her relationships.

The wedding night is a special night for an Indian woman, for the dating system is a social taboo. For most of the men also, this is their first sexual experience. His experience differs from that of his wife. He feels happy that now he has a woman with whom he can have sex with social consent. He is also proud to have a woman around him who belongs to him in all ways because she has left her father's house for good. In his upbringing, a man has also been taught not to entertain romantic notions about his wife. She is an object to be respected; she will be the mother of his children. So far as need for love and care is concerned, he continues to receive those from his mother and other female relatives. He prefers to remain an object of worship and reverence to his wife.

A wife begins to feel frustrated. Her husband's distant and unromantic behavior contrasts with the romantic throbs she had experienced as a teenager. A male child has been taught in a traditional home to look upon the act of sex with his wife as a means to procreate. Sex as an act of pleasure is associated with mistresses and prostitutes. In course of time, the wife resigns herself to her fate and feels utterly dejected.

Such a marriage does not break up because of the tenacity of a social tradition, which still denounces divorce. Besides, other members of the family in a joint family engage her attention and provide a slight outlet to express her unfulfilled emotions.

For an understanding of the husband's attitude toward sex, one has to look into the ancient and medieval religious literature. The Vedic gods and the epic gods (like the Greek and Roman deities) were sexual. This period was followed by a period of Brahmanical Puritanism in which sexual pleasure was held down, and procreation was the only justification for sex. If a man wanted pleasure from a sexual act, he must practice polygamy or engage frequent mistresses and prostitutes. Until his adolescent years, a Bengali man knows woman mainly in one category—as a mother whom he respects. As an adolescent, he learns about sex through the distorted portrayals of pornographic magazines where men are shown having sex, not with wives, but with mistresses and prostitutes. When he enters marriage, sex has been embedded in his mind not with respect. When he approaches his wife, whom he must respect, he cannot enjoy sex with her as an act of pleasure.

Another reason for a male's conflicting attitude toward sex is provided by the epics where males shunned sex to preserve power for constructive work. A male is consequently conditioned to believe that wives or women tend to seduce men and to reduce their physical power. Men must resist to preserve their masculine strength.

The husband-wife relationship undergoes a deep change when the first child is born. Now the husband begins to relate to her more openly as the mother of their child. This relationship represents the ideal of conjugal love, the main content of which is affection on the one hand as the wife is the mother of his child, and respect as a wife on the other hand, rather than erotic love between two equals.

Although the husband's attitude has changed toward his wife after a child, it does not compensate for the lack of romance in a woman's life. The two now interact more with each other during the daytime, as they have to talk about children. Such dialogue does not overcome her frustration, which lingers. She learns to live with him after fifteen or twenty years of married life with unfulfilled romance and other expectations, which she had before marriage. Their roles are well adjusted as a "husband" and "wife," but not as two equal human beings. They have learned to accept each other's nature without meeting on a common ground. Because her husband had never been taught to communicate with his wife on such issues as common interests, he may never know his wife's frustrations. On her part, she, reaches a stage where she does not expect any qualitative change in the behavior of her husband. While living with him, she tries to find satisfaction for her personal needs elsewhere within the family.

In her forties, her sex life with her husband becomes irregular and may even cease when she is fifty. Since the son has also grown up, occupied with his profession and marriage responsibilities, the mother may seek outlets in religious activities outside the house or in neighborhood concerns. When grandchildren come along they become the focus of her life.

The case of Bengali women has been presented to acquaint the reader with one other category of educated women in cities who have been raised in the traditional joint family structure. A woman of an upper or upper-middle class is socialized into accepting a number of cultural ideals as her expected roles and how she copes with real life roles which contrast with her dream world woven by magazines, Western films, and her natural instincts.[4]

The preceding study was published in 1970. Since then, rapid changes have been taking place in the outlook of the new generation. Western ideas of individualism and personal welfare are influencing younger people more than traditionalism. Again, the change would vary from family to family depending upon a number of factors; however, the emphasis upon dowry, the segregation of sexes with consequent emphasis upon the virginity of a bride, the non-existence of a dating system, the prevalence of arranged marriages, and the lack of adequate jobs prevent restless girls from open revolt against parents' control and social guidelines. Parents' guidelines in the 1980s may not be as strict as those of the parents in the 1960s and 1970s, reason being, mothers of the 1980s with girls of marriageable age have received a college education and like their daughters, might have experienced the same fluttering to free themselves from social taboos and traditions.

The following study presents the Indian women from a different perspective. In this research, Indian families are categorized as follows:

1. Tribal; lower-strata rural and urban families.
2. Upper-strata rural; traditional upper strata urban families.
3. Progressive urban families.

It must be stressed that none of these categories is exclusive.

In all these categories, distinction between a male and female will center on their respective spheres of activity, responsibility and initiative, authority and decision-making, rest and recreation, and participation in communal and national life.

Lower-strata Rural and Urban Families

Spheres of activity: Separate spheres of activity for male and female are not clearly discernible. Both must work to provide food to the family.

Responsibility and initiative: Management of the house is female work. Stereotyped routines of family chores leaves no time for unusual type of initiative to a woman.

Authority and decision-making: The male dominates. It is also considered mandatory to consult elders in the kinship in such matters as negotiation of marriages, holding of large feasts, and disposal of substantial property.

Rest and recreation: Most of the time is spent working. The only recreation is gossiping or watching other people quarrel. Occasional visits to fairs, towns, and markets provide some diversion. Religious festivals, marriages, performance of folk drama, and narration of mythical tales occasionally help break the monotony of the day.

Participation in community and social life: Both men and women participate in family, kin, caste and village affairs. As women work outdoors and contribute economically to the family, there are not many restrictions on their equal participation in these spheres. They participate in state and national elections, but women have no comprehension of their meeting.

Upper-Strata Rural and Traditional Upper-Strata Urban Families

Spheres of activity: Separate spheres of activity for men and women are clearly distinguished. Men manage outside jobs, and women take care of the house. Women are partially secluded as they do not meet men outside the family.

Responsibility and initiative: Men have full responsibility in outside affairs. The economic sphere is controlled by men, but women enjoy considerable autonomy in intra-kin, intra-caste, and religious affairs of the family.

Authority and decision-making: Male authority is most pronounced at this level. In the women's sphere, kinship status determines the authority. For example, a mother-in-law will have considerable authority over daughters-in-laws.

Rest and recreation: Although most of their time is involved in housework, they do have some free time. They may read a magazine and go to a cinema-hall but always accompanied by a male member.

Participation in community and national life: Men are participating increasingly more and more in these activities, but women are still limited to house chores.

Progressive Urban Families

Spheres of activity: At this level, spheres of male and female activities are less demarcated; however, families inclined toward traditionalism emphasize the domestic role of women but, at the same time, allow them a considerable freedom to participate in community and national life. On the other hand, families more Western-oriented recognize the principle of equal participation of women. Distinction between spheres of men and women gets blurred as the families go up in scale of sophistication or Westernaztion.

Responsibility and initiative: The responsibility for working and earning is still mainly that of men, but women may also work for economic reasons. At the lower economic level, women's earnings contribute greatly to the lifestyle of the family. At the upper economic level, women may still work for personal satisfaction of prestige. If they do not, they will participate in social work.

Management of the house and children still remains the function of women, but they always have domestic help depending upon how much they can afford. Their spare time is occupied by house decoration, social obligations and social visits which tend to increase as economic status rises.

Where women have professional duties, they have to divide time carefully between domestic responsibilities and professional obligations.

Authority and decision-making: Both men and women share decision-making. Minor decisions can be taken by each individual, but major decisions are a result of united consultation by both male and female.

Rest and recreation: Periods of rest and recreation increase at this level. Newspapers, magazines, radio, and television are there for recreation. Social visits are more often with coffee and snacks. Trips to shopping centers with stops at restaurants for lunch are common. Women may accompany men to bridge parties if more Westernized.

Participation in community and national life: Families of this type have contributed the most to the social, cultural, and political life of the country. Women leaders have come from this group who provide the push to the state-level and national-level policies which in turn affect the status of the Indian women all over the country.

It is interesting to note one feature about all these categories of families. The first category looks up to the families of the second level as its role model. Families of second level try to emulate the families of the third category, who are constantly trying to fight the general Indian conservatism toward women and to seek an equality between the two sexes as enshrined in the Indian Constitution.[5]

The following study is about typically professional women in the cities who are definitely the catalysts for change as they are so much more "visible."

The objectives of this study were to find out the reasons why professionally trained women seek employment or decide to stay out of the job market. A total number of five-hundred respondents were identified from four categories of occupations.

1. 250 secondary school teachers
2. 50 professional social workers
3. 125 hospital staff nurses
4. 75 library assistants

The study revealed that voluntary non-use of education and skill was very little in this group. Even those who were staying out of the job market would have entered it had more job opportunities been available.

Among the economic reasons given, the desire to reduce the burden of husband or parents financially was cited as the foremost. This admission is significant as it reveals how women of city background and plentiful education also consider their incomes as being only supplemental. They do not look upon their works as that of the bread winner of the family.

When these women were asked to specify what special economic advantages accrued to the family with their earnings, better education for children and family savings were mentioned. Curiously enough, these women did not state increased expenditure upon themselves as one of the main benefits of their earnings. When ability to spend more was mentioned, it was a reference to increased expenditure on furniture and buying kitchen gadgets (very expensive in India). The second reason given by these women why they worked was not to "waste away" their education. Professionally trained women thus felt that they must work to do justice to all the expenditure and long years they spent on education. The third reason given was to associate with different people at work and to get a feeling of freedom. The study further showed that seventy-five percent of the respondents included both economic and non-economic reasons in their decision to work.

Among occupational preferences, teaching was most preferred. Next came medicine and professional social work. Among the least preferred jobs were sales-girl, air-hostess, and receptionist. Women respondents tended to favor jobs where dominance in the professional role was marked. They did not like the "submissive" roles of the least preferred occupations.

In competing demands of family responsibilities and professional work, the respondents gave high priority to their role as a mother and a wife. Their responses showed that they felt guilty about not spending much time with their children. As for other family relationships, they did not care very much.[6]

The Center for Women Development Studies (CWDS) organized an informal discussion among prominent women journalists in 1985 both from the press and from the television media. The basic theme was how the media project women's image to the viewers. This projection helps form popular attitudes. Neerja Chawdhury, one of the journalists, related her own experience. Twenty years ago, many of the leading newspapers were unwilling to hire women because they would get married after a few years and leave the job; all the investment in terms of training would be lost. Since then, the attitude has so vastly changed that the newspapers are looking for women workers because they are more sincere and hard-working. We must also say that a change in women's attitude is also partly responsible for the new press policy. Now in the 1980s, women are more serious about their professions. They no longer look upon jobs as waiting rooms for marriage. Rising inflation has also made it necessary that two incomes be sustained to buy modern conveniences and to provide decent education to children. Mrinal Pande, another journalist at the panel, shared her experience in Panjab with a newspaper called Panjab Kesari. This newspaper prints women's news on the front page in blue ink to draw attention. Because women comprise the majority of the readers after men go to work, the newspaper should cater to that taste of the clientele.

The other group on the panel dealt with television, widely introduced only in the 1970s among middle-class households. One of the female television producers, Harsaran Birkaur, pointed out that, owing to the fact that the production business is male-dominated, she has to work extra hard to survive in the competition. She also has to fade away her existence as a woman to stay on par with men. Here, she was referring to a woman's responsibility toward reproduction. Birkaur had to come right back to work following the birth of her child so as not to interrupt the regular taping of her show. She also pointed out another disadvantage for women in a competitive situation. A male subordinate can socialize with the boss by having a drink after work, but a woman worker, because of her modesty and social taboos, cannot do so. This inequality can help a male worker get promotions and attractive assignments.

Chawdhury spoke about the importance of building close rapport with women's organizations working in rural areas as rural people are the majority and the "have-nots" whose issues should be given the widest airing. A number of women's shows are now being aired every week to highlight persistent problems. They relate to issues like dowry, early marriages, and family planning. Income-generation projects are given a great publicity so that women in distress may know where to go for training and government assisted projects. The message is that, if destitute women are willing to help themselves, there are opportunities. Usually, a retired movie star plays the role of a coordinator in these shows. As Indian masses enjoy movies tremendously, movie stars are their inspiration.[7]

In the 1980s, the number of black and white television sets sold to poorer people at the government subsidized prices has increased eight-fold, as reported in the 13 November 1989 issue of Time magazine. The author can confirm this information, as she found the use of black and white television sets in large numbers in the shanty dwellings of slum dwellers.

The possession of a television is becoming a status symbol among these people, as the owning of a color television, a refrigerator, an air-cooler, and a motorbike or car are the manifestations of prosperity in the rising middle-class in India.

City-educated girls and professional women set the pace of change in India. Even though the middle-class constitutes approximately two hundred million in a population of a billion, the emulation of the social class above one's own is more pronounced in India than in the U.S., thus helping in the process of modernization. Change is essential to break down the hold of religious and social orthodoxy, which has put the Indian woman at such a serious disadvantage.

References

1. Ali Baig, Tara, *India's Women Power,* New Delhi: S. Chand, 1976, 83-252.
   Dube, S.C., "Men's and Women's Roles in India," in *Women in New Asia,* Barbara E. Ward, ed., UNESCO, 174-203.
   Goldstein, Rhode L., *Indian Women in Transition: A Bangalore Case Study,* Metuchen, N.J., Scarecrow, 1972, 47-148.
   Mazumdar, Sudha, *A Pattern of Life: the Memoirs of an Indian Woman,* New Delhi: Manohar, 1977.
   Nayer, Sushila, "Our Changing Life in India," in *Women in the New Asia,* Barbara Ward, ed., UNESCO, 215-64.
   Sarma, Jyotirmoyee, "Three Generations in my Calcutta Family," in *Women in New Asia,* Barbara E. Ward, ed., UNESCO, 216-39.
   Thapar, Romila, "The History of Female Emancipation in Southern Asia," in *Women in New Asia,* Barbara E. Ward, ed., UNESCO, 473-99.
   Vreede-De Stuers, Parda: *A Study of Muslim Women's Life in Northern India,* Assen: Van Gorcum, 1968, 3-104.
   Women in Contemporary India: Traditional Images and Changing Roles, Alfred de Souza, ed., New Delhi: Manohar, 1975, 1-96.
2. Kapur, Promilla, *Marriage and Working Women in India,* Delhi: Vikas, 1970.
3. Vreede-De Stuers, Cora, *Girl Students in Jaipur,* Assen: Van Gorcum, 19970, 27-125.
4. Roy, Manisha, *Bengali Women,* Chicago: University of Chicago Press, 1972.
5. Since India is in a status of flux, it is not possible to give one standard characterization of the families in the urban-rural areas. *Women in Asia,* Barbara E. Ward, ed., UNESCO, 1963, 174-203.
6. Dhingra, O.P., *Women in Employment,* New Delhi: ICSSR Library, 1977, 380-415.
7. "Media and Women's Issues," in *Samya Shakti,* April, 1985, 98-108 (Samya Shakti is a publication of the CWDS).

9

All-India Women Conference or AIWC and its Role as an Umbrella Organization

FOUNDED IN 1925, the All-India Women Conference (AIWC) brought together Indian women of enlightened ideas who wished to change the social status and the traditional code applicable to women. This organization continued to expand and, in post-Independence days, came to be the major voice of Indian women. At present, the AIWC has a number of branches in all the major cities and has engaged in voluntary social work, in addition to printing its own journal called *Roshini* and a publication called *Annual Reports and Conferences.*

Earlier issues of *Annual Reports and Conferences* would show the concern of AIWC with such issues like abolition of dowry, reform of marriage laws, education of women, improving labor conditions, and securing political representation for women.

In the post-Independence period, the U.N.O. gave the AIWC a consultative status to ascertain the Indian opinion on world-wide women's issues.

In the annual session of 1956 held at Indore, the AIWC categorically announced that it was neither a political nor a feminist organization. Its purpose is to educate women who are classified as one of the most backward classes in India. The local branches of the AIWC greatly involved themselves in such activities as running schools for poor children, staffing milk centers, and establishing work and craft centers for women.

The urgent need for a uniform civil code for all Indian women began to appear on the agenda of the AIWC annual conferences as early as 1950s. Reference is to the Muslim women who can never rise to an equal status with men under the Personal Islamic law. The AIWC pointed to the example of countries like Turkey which have radically changed the Muslim religious law while remaining predominantly Muslim.

Because family planning is one of the vital issues facing the nation, the AIWC started the Family Planning Association of India (FPAI), a member of the International Planned Parenthood Association (IPPA) founded in 1952.

Even though the Constitution promised equal status to women, many states had not passed the necessary legislation, such as mandatory maternity leave or equal opportunity for work. At its annual session in 1973, the AIWC urged the central government to take necessary steps against the defaulting states.

The 1970s saw a general awareness in the country that women, along with other backward segments of society, have to be organized to bargain effectively and to exploit various income-generation schemes. The central government requested the AIWC to prepare a draft on women for inclusion in the Sixth Five-Year Plan. This draft appeared as "Women and Development" in the from of a separate chapter in the Sixth Plan (1980-85).

With adult functional literacy one of the high concerns of the AIWC because the 1981 census placed female literacy only at 24.88 percent, it called upon its branches all over the country to run such adult centers. A female education and training in modern skills have received increased support from the Indian Government in the 1980s, the Prime Minister called for inputs from voluntary organizations to prepare a government paper on education. The AIWC therefore organized a high-power Round Table discussion on 18 October, 1985 which emphasized adult education and named illiteracy one of the major enemies of the country.

To coordinate the activities of various social organizations, the AIWC helped in the formation of an All-India Committee for Eradication of Illiteracy among women in which all social organizations can participate. This committee makes recommendations to the central government to be included in five-Year Plans. The government has agreed to pay fully for the administrative costs of these literacy centers for women. The AIWC makes a special effort to enroll women belonging to scheduled castes and tribes.

AIWC is the key women's organization in India; it sends delegations to world conferences. One such conference was held in Kenya in 1985. With 1975 to 1985 declared the Women's Decade, the Kenya Conference was convened to review the positive and negative trends of the decade. One of the positive achievements has been that the number of women voters has increased thus reducing the gap between male and female voters from 12 percent to 6.89 percent. The report of the conference also showed that where more education is made available, more women turn out to vote.

The AIWC has been very active in the 1980s in mobilizing public opinion against discriminating civil code for different religious minorities The AIWC pointed out to Banu's case in 1986. A Muslim woman divorced by her husband according to Koranic law, Banu appealed to the Indian courts for maintenance (alimony) under the National law and not according to Muslim law which gave maintenance allowance only for four months. Although she won in the Supreme Court, the Indian Parliament overturned the decision because it violated the Indian Constitution, which guarantees protection to personal religious laws. The AIWC has carried on a great propaganda campaign against this decision, which was politically motivated. Like the earlier government of Indira Gandhi, Rajiv Gandhi's government was heavily dependent on the Muslim vote. The government could not afford to alienate the Muslim population.

The AIWC alleged that the Muslim Law had been

amended in 1939 to give additional grounds for divorce. If the law could be amended one time, it could be amended again to allow a Muslim woman to choose between her personal religious law and the National law. As of today, the AIWC had not succeeded in bringing about a uniform civil code, which would give equal protection to Muslim women.

The dowry has been another concern of the AIWC. Even though the Dowry Prohibition Act passed in 1961 was strengthened in 1984 to make the Act more stringent, marriage expenditures have been rising as the in-laws now demand modern appliances along with the traditional dowry. The media have been reporting the deaths of brides who could no longer endure the torture of in-laws who condemned them for not bringing sufficient dowries. Because of the high publicity given on television and the relentless efforts of the AIWC and other such organizations, Dowry Prohibition Officers have been appointed in all states to enforce the Dowry Act. These officers must report to the states annually. Dowry remains a serious problem besetting both the rural and the urban societies. The AIWC has pointed out that dowry symbolizes a certain attitude towards women that they are inferior to men. They can make themselves worthwhile to men by offering themselves and dowries in marriage. The dowry encourages male chauvinism. A male further feels that, the higher the dowry, the higher his status in society. In a place like Bombay, where shortage of accommodation is the number one problem, marriage advertisements in the newspapers ask for brides who own their apartments. Because the brides sought are in the twenties, they cannot own their own accommodations. Only parents who can offer housing are invited in the ads.

The AIWC and other organizations realize that legislation cannot abolish the dowry system. Social education has to accomplish a change in attitude to allow equal status for women. The result has been more television shows and press coverage of the evils of the dowry. In 1984, the AIWC also succeeded in getting the Indian Parliament to pass the

Family Court Act, which recognizes the right of women organizations to initiate criminal cases against dowry demands, dowry torture, and rape.

The AIWC has made other interesting observations about the dowry system based upon field studies in the cosmopolitan city of Bombay where neighborhoods consist of different castes and people from different regions. One such conclusion reveals that the dowry system is very common to most middle and upper strata of societies in all castes. Now the system is spreading into upper sections of the working class where men are employed in mills or serve menial functions in offices. They want to imitate what the next higher classes are practicing.

In another study undertaken by the AIWC, it was found that, because most political parties are made of men, women have little political clout to bring about faster changes for the benefit of women. Women have not been able to convince the average Indian man that women's problems affect the welfare of the whole Indian society. Prime Minister Raijiv Gandhi echoed this sentiment in his address at the Non-Aligned and Developing Countries Conference held in Delhi in 1985 when he stated that women are the social conscience of a country. The Prime Minister asserted that developing countries have fought against imperialism, domination, and discrimination in the past; now they must fight against discrimination in sex. Men have become a vested group against whom society must battle to secure equal rights for women. The AIWC greatly applauded the support of the Prime Minister.[1]

Besides agitating for changes in the law, the AIWC has been actively involved in many practical projects to help the poor rural and urban women. One project called Science Awareness may be mentioned. Workshops and training programs are held all over the country to acquaint rural and urban women with the use of science and technology in farming, energy-saving devices in the kitchen (like a solar oven), recycling of waste, improving of sanitation, and providing clean water.

A national and old organization with branches throughout the country, the AIWC has served as a powerful pressure group both at the central and state levels.

In the end, we may reiterate that the Indian society is experiencing the throes of a major change. Modern science and technology have shifted the emphasis from sacred to secular interests in the cities, and the villages are also being drawn into this vortex of cultural transformation because of the irreversible migration from villages to cities. The population of India has more than doubled itself since Independence, and land can no longer support even a fair proportion of this population. Many of the traditional village arts and crafts are losing the battle against the industrial goods.

Landless and jobless are flooding the cities in search of work. This exodus has shaken the stability of the joint family in the villages. The youngsters who migrate to cities from rural environs maintain contact with their families, but their exposure to urbanization and their separation from their joint families over a long period tend to instill a sense of individualism.

These village migrants begin to look after their own economic interests, although they may continue to fulfill obligations to their families and kin in the villages. The children of these migrants tend to receive limited education in the cities and work there. They may not totally change, but change does occur. For example, they may seek a new kind of husband-wife relationship more symmetrical than the traditional, subordinate relationship of wife to husband in the villages. At the same time, one dare not underestimate the hold of tradition on village emigrants and a large part of the Indian society in general. While change is irresistible and irreversible, it is slow in a society, which has been tradition-bound for centuries. With this dilemma the government and voluntary organizations must contend. New horizons have opened for women, but they are marked at the level of the urban middle class. Other women less fortunate have yet to be drawn into the mainstream. The nature of national policies, such as the Five-Year Plans and the rural Development Programs, underscores the effort of the Indian Government in this direction. How this process of change can be given an additional momentum so that the rural women and urban poor can, one day, experience the fruits of women's liberation and the new status accorded to them in the Indian Constitution before it is too late is the gigantic challenge facing the politicians in India.

History has yet to print its future pages with the sentences extolling the success of democracy in India. For now, many an Indian woman may only hope.[2]

REFERENCES

1. *Annual Report and Conferences*, AIWC, 1949-51, 8-12; vol. VIII, 1956, 23-27; vol. X, 1960-66, 32nd Session at New Delhi; vol. XI, 1967=68, 37th Session, 1968, Chandigarh, 48; 41st Session, 1973, Delhi, 74-84; vol. XIII, 1975-80, 43rd Session, 1975, Goa, 20-25; 1983, 44-52; 1985-86; 1985-86, 33-36.
Gupta, Ashok, "Call to Descend to Villages," in *Roshini*, January-February, 1986, 4-6. (*Roshini* is a publication of AIWC).
Roshini, January-February 1985, 5-7; May-July 1985, 7-9.
"Science and Technology for Indian Women," in *Roshini*, January-February, 1986, 1-3.
Ahuja, S.P., "Practice and Problem of Dowry in India," in *Roshini*, March-April, 1985, 25-28.
"Hindu Law and Married Women,: in *Roshini*, March-April, 1985, 24-25.
Manekar, Purnima, "Profile of Women in India," in *Roshini*, March-April, 1989, 4-9.
"Participation of Women in Political Affairs," in Roshini, January-February, 1986, 6-9; "Women and Panchayat," ibid., 13-14; "Women and Power," ibid., 14-16.
Ramji, Kamla, "Hindu Law and the Married Woman," in *Roshini*, March-April, 1985, 24-25.
"SITA and Prostitution," in *Lawyer Collective*, September, 1986, 4-8.
Subbama, Malladi, *Atrocities on Women*, New Delhi: AIWC, 1987; *Human Rights: Women's Rights*, New Delhi: AIWC, 1987; *Personal Laws and Women*,

New Delhi: AIWC, 1987.
"Two Sides of Muslim Women's Bill," in *Roshini,* March-April, 1986, 4-6.
"Women and Law," in *Roshini,* March-April, 1984-85, 21-22.
"Women are Social Conscience of a Country," in *Roshini,* March-April, 1985, 1-2.
"World Plan of Action for Women," was included in the declaration of *Women's Decade from 1975 to 1985.* The whole declaration is available in the AIWC Library.

2. Banerjee, Sumanta, "The System Produces Naxalites," in *The Hindustan Times* (New Delhi), September 30, 1987, 13.
"Bank Pressured to Drop Project," in *India Abroad* (U.S.A.), November 10, 1989, 11.
Chawla, Hanet, "Woman Power is also Birthing Power," in *Saheli* (New Delhi), April, 1987, 7-10.
"Death for Sati Abettos," in The *Hindustan Times,* (New Delhi), October 2, 1987, 1.
Drive to Rehabilitate Devdasis," in *The Times of India* (Bombay), September 13, 1987, 8.
"Family Welfare Program," in *The Hindustan Times* (New Delhi), September 24, 1987, 19.
Gandhi, Rajiv, "Deorala National Shame," in *The Hindustan Times* (New Dehi), September 28, 1987, 1, 12.
"India's First All Women Crew," in *India Tribune* (U.S.A.), September 23, 1989, 1.
Kalhan, Promila, "How to End Sati: Forever," in *The Hindustan Times* (New Delhi), September 28, 1987, 12.
"Manipuri Women Fight Alcoholism," in *India Abroad* (U.S.A.), May 19, 1989, 21.
"Onward Women," in *Time* (U.S.A.), December 4, 1989, 80-89.
"Pioneer Efforts and the 20-Point," in *The Hindustan Times* (New Delhi), September 24, 1987, 19.
"Puppies and Consumer Boomers," in *Time* (U.S.A.), November 13, 1989, 53-54.
"Role of Small Scale and Village Industries in Uttar Pradesh," in *The Hindustan Times,* (New Delhi), September 24, 1987, 19.
"Sati Does not Have Religious Sanction," *The Hindustan Times,* (New Delhi), November 27, 1987, 1 and 5.
"Slum Women Organized," in *India Abroad* (U.S.A.), November 10, 1989, 11.
"Wife Battering," *Saheli* (New Delhi), April,1987, 11-14 (*Saheli* is the Newsletter of Women Resources Center).
"Witch Hunt of Women," in *The Hindustan Times,* (New Delhi), October 11, 1987, 1-2.
"Women Mark Decades of Struggle and Organize for Further

Challenges," in India Abroad (U.S.A.), March 10, 1989, 12-14.

"A Youth Club Grows Up," in *The Hindustan Times,* (New Delhi), November 8, 1987, 5.

Central Social Welfare Board of CSWB has issued following pamphlet as an illustration of its range of activities *Cooperative and Speed Ahead: Schemes of CSWB,* 1986.

Ministry of Human Resource Development, Department of Women and Child Development, Government of India, has issued the following pamphlets as an illustration of its activities.

Scheme of Assistance for the Construction of Hostel Building for Working Women with a Day Care Center, 1986.

Scheme of Assistance for Setting Up Women's Training Centers/Institutes for Rehabilitation of Women in Distress, 1986.

Scheme of Assistance to Voluntary Organization of Education Work for Prevention of Atrocities on Women, 1986.

Scheme of Short Stay Homes for Women and Girls, 1986.

10

All India Women Conference and Center for Women Development Studies, 1990-2000

LET US START WITH AIWC, *All India Women Conference,* which was discussed in the last chapter. AIWC, today, has over 100,000 members in 500 branches all over India. At the international level, as mentioned earlier, it has a consultative status with the United Nations (ECOSOC): It is a member of the UNICEF Executive Committee, a member of WREN (World Renewable Energy Network), and a member of GEF (Global Environment Facility) of the United Nation's environment program; and it is affiliated with the IAW (International Alliance of Women).

AIWC objectives include the following:

1. To work for a society based on principles of social justice, integrity, equal rights and opportunity.
2. To secure recognition for the inherent rights of every human being: to work and to achieve the essentials of life such as food, clothing, housing, education, social amenities and security, in the belief that these should not be determined by accident of birth or sex but by planned social distribution.
3. To support the claim of every citizen to the right to enjoy basic rights and liberties. The AIWC;

    a. conducts awareness campaigns among women so that they utilize to the fullest fundamental rights conferred on them by the Constitution of India.

b. Cooperates with world organizations for the implementation of these principles, which alone can assure permanent international peace.

Activities:

1. Among the activities of the AIWC sponsorship of literacy programs is one. Both non-formal education programs for school dropouts and skill development programs for income generation are provided. Condensed courses for adult women at the primary, middle and high school level also receive due attention. AIWC's literacy campaign was intensified in 1996, and its 33 centers all over the country are running the non-formal education for female school drop-outs and condensed courses in education for adult women and girls.
2. Socio-economic programs are the second important activity of the AIWC. These programs were started in 1995 with the objective of capacity building for women by giving them financial support for their entrepreneurial endeavors. The goal is to make women economically independent. The AIWC central office in Delhi has sanctioned 33 programs in its different branches.
3. The Computer Training Center was set-up in 1996. The Computer Center has been granted accreditation for 3 years by the Department of Electronics.
4. The Micro Credit Program was created for the promotion of women of families below the poverty line. The direct beneficiary is the woman herself. The goal is to eradicate poverty by encouraging women to become entrepreneurs, and many AIWC branches have already created a large number of self-help groups. (In March 1997, the Ministry of Human

Resource Development, Department of Women and Child Development also approved a grant to train 120 girls belonging to the weaker sections of the society. Hair and skin care training has been included.).

5. The Women in AIDS Project was initiated in 1993 to create national HIV-AIDS awareness and sexually transmitted diseases control among poor women.
6. The Panchayat Raj Training program was created by the AIWC to train elected women Panchayat (village council) members.
7. Awareness Camps: AIWC conducts Awareness Camps on legal issues, female feticide, infanticide, health, and education sanctioned by the CSWBC (Central Social Welfare Board of the Central Government).
8. Health and Population Management has been actively pursued by the AIWC through all of its branches. Issues such as antenatal and prenatal care, vaccination, family planning services, and nutrition programs are among the main activities of the AIWC. In 1995, the Delhi Administration gave an ambulance van to the central office of the AIWC to carry on family welfare work in the slum areas on the outskirts of Delhi. The van is staffed with two Gram Sevikas (female village level workers) and a doctor who carries on the vaccination work and advocates the norms of a small and healthy family.
9. Rural Energy: As mentioned in a previous chapter, AIWC has been heavily involved in the development of non-conventional energy sources for the purpose of cooking in the rural areas. AIWC was selected as a Nodal Agency by the central government, (ministry of non-conventional energy sources) in 1985 to implement the national project for the improved Chulha (cooking stove) and in 1993 to carry out the national project of Bio-gas Development.

Additional projects include solar cookers, solar water

heaters and solar lanterns. The AIWC implements all of these projects through its branches and the partner NGOs (non-government organizations) at the grass roots level, with direct funding from the central ministry.

The AIWC was awarded Global 500 Roll of Honour at the United Nations' UNEP Conference in Istanbul in 1996 and won the IREDA award for outstanding work in the above-mentioned areas in 1997.

The AIWC organized a number of exhibitions and demonstrations at the Fourth World Women's Conference in Beijing in 1995 and at WREN (World Renewable Energy Network) Conference in Florence, Italy in 1998.

More than 3000 women have been trained by AIWC under the NPIC program (National Project on Improved Chulahs) to build and demonstrate the product. Village women, who have greatly benefited from these smokeless chulahs are happy as it saves their health from smoke and reduces cooking time. The women who construct and demonstrate the chulahs look upon the activity as income generating and confidence building.

The AIWC has also set-up a few permanent institutions for on-going care. The following are a few such institutions.

1. Old Age Home and Infirmary for Women was set up in 1994 in Vrindaban (U.P. State). Some of the branches of the AIWC are also running such homes where senior female citizens are provided with physical, social, emotional and psychological support. In addition, the AIWC branches are also running 'pay and stay homes' which provide residential facilities to senior citizens on payment of nominal charges.
2. Short-stay Homes—the philosophy behind short-stay homes is to provide a place where victims may stay for a short period of time before getting finally adjusted to their families and society. Short-stay homes are meant for women in difficult situations in their own homes, families and immediate

community. In a large number of cases the women have been divested of their rights—conjugal rights, property rights, occupational rights, etc. The dowry cases are the worst examples of women's torture. In order to overcome their economic deprivation women need better and modern work skills and ultimately they need employment or income or independent entrepreneurs. Short-stay homes attempt to train women in skills for employment, and provide them education, basic health services and needed legal advice and action. It may seem that these homes are attempting to achieve too much; but these are the basic needs of women in distress. The author had the opportunity to visit such a home in Delhi called Bapnu Ghar and talk to some of the officials about their work. They pointed out that they face a number of difficulties such as the lack of a proper building because there is not much appreciation on the part of the local administration for such work. The pay and allowances for the social worker, psychologist, craft teacher and physician are awfully low. The fault lies not only with the local administration but also with the inmates, many of them are not much interested in training, as they know that their stay is short. Experience has also taught that traditional craft, tailoring, sewing, etc., are not of much help in the ultimate settlement of those women who want to be self-dependent.

3. The third important institution of the AIWC relates to family planning. The Family Planning Center was established in 1977 and now it is called the Family Planning Association of India.
4. Fourth, in 1943 the AIWC established the Children Committee, now designated The Indian Council for Child Welfare. The author visited this group in 1987, and the ICDS (Integrated Child Development Scheme) is one of its very important activities.

The AIWC is represented on various committees and commissions on social welfare set up by the central government such as: Status of Women's Committee, National Vocational Training of Women, Implementation of Legal Aid Schemes, and the National Integration Committee. Whenever the Indian Parliament considers legislation about women, it seeks the comments of the AIWC. The organization has also participated in some very important international conferences, such as the United Nations Human Rights Conference in Vienna, 1993; UNESCO Conference on Education for All in Delhi, 1993; International Conference on Population and Development, Cairo, 1994; Fourth world Conference on Women, Beijing, China, 1995; and 42nd session of the United Nations Commission on Status of Women. A task force was set-up by the NGOs (Non-government Organizations) Committee and the Secretary General of AIWC was part of the task force on Violence Against Women; Seminar on the Follow Up Action to the Fourth World Conference on Women, in Beijing; June 1998; Micro-credit Summit in New York, June 1998; World Renewable Energy Congress (WREN) in Florence, Italy, September 1998. (An exhibition displayed various NRSE devices such as an improved wood-stove, bio-gas solar lantern, and solar cooker); and 43rd session of the United Nations' Commissions on the status of women, New York, March 1999. [1] At this session, the Secretary General made a presentation on behalf of AIWC and six other national level organizations.

Priorities and Concerns

After listing the various highlights of the AIWC, let us consider some of its recent priorities and concerns. The best source for this information is its serial publication called *Roshini* (Light). In the 1990's women's rights in India are being described as human rights, meaning thereby that the rights women demand are the rights of a human being. As Ms. Lalita Balakrishnan noted in the January—June, 1999 issue of *Roshini* (P. 5), only the acceptance of women as equal partners in society will generate the process of empowerment of women and accomplish the goal of total gender equality and equity in the next century (P. 7). One of the important international human rights treaties is the convention on *Elimination of All Forms of Descrimination Against Women* (CEDAW). The convention established an international bill of rights for women, and declared an agenda for action by countries to guarantee the enjoyment of those rights. In this plan for action the following goals and new priorities are included:

1. *Literacy:* The Indian constitution guarantees free and compulsory education to all children until the age of fourteen years. The sad fact is that one-half of India's children and two-thirds of the girls are deprived of education even today (*Roshini,* P. 8).
2. *Micro Credit Programs:* AIWC has started creating self-help groups of women in all their branches. Micro-credit programs are a means to expand economic opportunities for women. Increased incomes will greatly impact the well being of children and the entire family.
3. *Health:* The reproductive health of women is receiving a great deal of attention in the policies of the NGOs (Non-Government Organizations).[2] Education in this area should be imparted to adolescent girls too so that when they attain womanhood, they are knowledgeable about various facets of reproductive health. The AIWC and other NGOs also have great concern about the missing girls. This phrase refers to gender-selective abortion or neglect of girls. Societal attitude has to undergo a drastic change for the problem of the missing girl to be alleviated. Girls should not be considered a burden on parents but as equal, productive children like boys.

4. Violence Against Women: According to the Home Minister's statement (*Roshini*) in Parliament on June 9, 1998, violence against women is on the increase. There were 14,000 rape cases in 1997, 27,513 women were molested, and 11,153 were sexually harassed. The AIWC recommended to the central government that more stringent laws be introduced for such crimes so that the cases of the criminals are not lost in the procedural delay of court. The courts should be instructed to publicize convictions, both in private media and government publications. The AIWC requested the central government to put the issue of violence high on the agenda.
5. The 72nd and 73rd amendments to the Indian Constitution have made it mandatory that 33% of the seats in the village Panchayats (elected councils) and in municipal corporations be reserved for women (*Roshini,* P. 8). The AIWC has organized training camps and awareness camps for women at the village level so that women can fully participate in the grass-root level elected bodies.
6. The AIWC has taken a firm stand against women being portrayed as sex objects on television and other media. Television controlled by the central government and the private satellite channels must improve their act.
7. There is a new interest in the 1990's to reach out to the girl child and not just the adult women as in the past (*Roshini,* PP 27-28). AIWC has very well noted in one of its articles in *Roshini* that when you educate a man, you only educate him. But when you educate a girl child (who will be a future mother), you educate the whole family. On the issue of gender equity a number of NGOs in India are actively promoting fair treatment of the girl-child.
8. It is interesting to note the adverse reaction of AIWC and the NGOs to the new liberalization or market

economy policy forced upon India by the World Bank and IMF (International Monetary Fund) in the 1990's. India was requested to reduce the national fiscal deficit which was running very high by liberalizing the national economy (i.e. allow more native private initiative in industry and trade along with foreign collaboration to increase the national revenue). India was also asked to reduce governmental expenditure by reducing funding for various social programs. The argument of AIWC and other NGOs was that withdrawal of subsidy on fertilizers; etc. has hurt the small farmer. The export-oriented policy of the Indian government of agricultural goods threatens food self-sufficiency at home and encourages diversion of land to commercial crops like cotton and groundnut. The overall effect has been a reduction in the food allocation per person among the lower classes through the official food distribution system. (The middle class is able to buy the additional food in the open market.) As the male child is preferred to the female, it is the latter whose nutrition suffers.[3] Among the other adversely affected programs is the National Program for Women entitled DWCRA (Development of Women and Children in Rural Areas) and Mahila Samridhi. The goal was to assist rural women with the central government giving rupees 75 to every rupees 300 saved by a woman's group in a year.[4] AIWC and other NGOs want the central government to increase funding for various poverty alleviation programs and the projects targeted at women.

Another women's organization discussed in the earlier edition of *Women in India* was the Center for Women Development Studies (CWDS). The author visited the main building and the library of CWDS to research to archival collection and interview the high office—bearers. These discussions were very productive. Emphasis on children is to be noted in the various studies of CWDS, as children are the future adults of the country.[5] CWDS organized representatives from various NGOs representing street children and working children and formed a delegation that met with the heads of the Manifesto Committees of various political parties and handed over a memorandum of demands to be incorporated in their election campaign manifestoes. One of the demands was flexible good elementary education with provisions for vocational training and free school lunches. They demanded the establishment of hospitals with free medicine just for children, as adults have their own hospitals. Their third demand was for the police to improve their behavior toward these children. The Indian police tend to treat poor children as proven criminals. Juvenile Jails should not punish the poor children but should provide a friendly environment and vocational training.

The memorandum presented to the politicians also observed that poverty is the root cause of the problems of street and working children. To resolve this problem, their parents must be guaranteed work and rightful conditions. Only then will their children have a decent and encouraging future.

Sexually abused children were the theme of a recent article in *Indian Economics* entitled *Too Young to Know—Sexually Abused Children Need all the Help They Can Get.*[6] A 14-year-old girl had killed a man who attempted to rape her. She was arrested and put in jail in violation of the Juvenile Justice Act, which specifies that under no circumstances shall minors be incarcerated in a jail or a lock-up. The case was brought before the Supreme Court. Its three-judge bench directed the National Law Commission to study the issue to recommend how any kind of a child abuse could be made an offence under the Indian Penal Code.

The importance of this event is to stress that children are future adults and they have to be treated with justice and fairness. A democratic system like that in India has to inculcate these basic traits in human mind so that real democracy can be created.

Child marriage of girls has been an important social issue for centuries.[7] Grinding poverty leads parents some times to marry off girls too much older men to escape the burden of dowry. Not only are such marriages psychologically harmful to the child girl, early marriages of any kind preventing child girls from gaining any meaningful education or professional skill.

The author had an extended experience with the issue of dowry among lower classes in her recent visit. It just seems that Indian society is unable to break loose from this ages old custom which is one of the manifestations of the low value given to a girl.[8] Unlike in the west, a lower class girl with employment cannot rent an apartment or opt for a single life. A girl has to be married off. The earlier it is done, the better it is for the parents, as they can then feel free of a heavy obligation.

Organizations like CWDS and AIWC are greatly perplexed as to how to end the heavyweight of the dowry system upon the girl's parents. Income-generating activities on an ongoing basis for women is one solution because mothers can, then, provide education and some vocational skill to their daughters. The ultimate hope is that through education, societal attitude toward women will change. Educated and skilled daughters, once they become earning adults, will support their families with cash income and hopefully, societal attitude toward women will improve. If women could be looked upon as valuable partners in life, the dowry system might give way to the voluntary gift system at a marriage like in the western society.

However, the leaders of organizations like CWDS and AIWC are also aware of the fact that income-generating activities require a number of other concomitant factors.[9] One is that child care services, such as créches for working mothers be provided funded by the government so that older sisters don't have to stay home to care for the younger children. The older sister would then be able to attend school through the 10th grade to graduate. This scenario does not seem to be very promising in 1990's because since 1991 the central government has cut spending on social services because of increasing privatization of the economy and the requirements of the World Bank and IMF (International Monetary Fund).

One of the greatest challenges facing India is the population explosion which is now around one billion, while the physical land of India is only about one third of the U.S.A. Along with the earlier approach of the 1970's and 1980's, a new dimension has been added to the issue of population growth.[10] Swapna Majumdar, who conducted her research in the U.P. State of India, about 35 million are being added in the U.P. at the present rate of growth. A new program has been introduced jointly by the Indian government, the state government of the U.P. and the USAID (United States Agency for International Development). The name of the program is SIFPSA. This program is based on the thesis that just teaching the importance of a small family to illiterate people, urban and rural, will not achieve the goal. Family planning education has to be a part of a much larger effort, which should have the promotion of gender equality as the core idea. Education in gender equality can lead to a decrease in the preference for a son. This male preference is one of the main reasons for large families.

Sadhana Jauhri, the head of the SIFPSA, however, points out that ventures like this are few and far between. Unfortunately, politicians are still not worried, and health is not under the control of the central government but falls within the jurisdiction of state governments. But no state politician of any political party has taken a stand on this issue. There is an appalling lack of political will, although there are NGOs and autonomous bodies like SIFPSA which are working. Ms. Jauhri feels that unless the pace of work is stepped up considerably through political interventions and soon, it may too late to prevent a population catastrophe.[11]

Rita Manchanda, in her study, points out that in the joint family's pattern of rural India, a husband and a wife don't decide about the number of children but the mother-in-law does. She suggests that in any population education program not only the husbands but also the mother-in-laws have to be involved to teach about reproductive health and the benefits of a small family.

The central government still baffled with the population problem, decided in April 1996 to discard the earlier target-oriented family planning approach in favor of a need-based family planning approach.[12] With this new approach, village level health workers would no longer be under pressure to fulfill family-planning targets and health plans would be formulated at the primary health center located in the block town and not at the central or state level.

This would please health workers at the village level because their performance would not be based upon targets but upon informed choice. But is it happening? Not much, because people have not changed in the last five decades since family planning programs have been in operation. There is still the age-old desire for a son. Manchanda reported on the village of Chhaynsa in Haryana State, close to Vallabhgarh town. Chhaynsa is close to Delhi, but this proximity has not made much difference. The 70,000 strong, agriculture based village has a number of facilities like village school, aanganwadi, a health centre and access to Vallabhgarh by road. Many homes have television sets and television programs stress that the small family is the ideal aim for a couple. A woman named Om Vati was allowed to die during her seventh pregnancy when the village and her family elders failed to bring her to Vallabhgarh Primary Health Centre. She was pregnant the seventh time as earlier she only had daughters. The study points out many other cases where the mother-in-law pressed for more children until a son was born. The article concludes that family planning will follow over-all development and gender equality education, not the other way around. Otherwise, it will be like putting the horse before the cart.[13]

Another interesting approach to family planning is revealed in a Private Member's Bill on Population Control introduced in the Indian Parliament by Sukhda Mishra in the 1997 Parliamentary session to mark India's Independence in 1947.[14] This bill had a number of disincentives for not adopting a small family norm. Penalties included denial of the food ration card under the Public Distribution System, any government discount to purchase a piece of land as a member of a cooperative society, denial of free medical services from any government hospital, concessional loan from the banks or government institutions.

Incentives for adopting a small family are few. A sum of rupees one thousand is given to a couple who undergoes sterilization after having two children. But if both are unemployed, a job will be given to one if they go for sterilization after two children. The children of such couples, who adopt a small-sized family, would also have free schooling through high school with free books, free lunch and free uniforms.

Another facet of the steps to advocate a small family involves a giant step taken by industrial credit and investment corporation of India (ICICI), a large private bank. This effort by the bank aims at popularizing oral contraceptives, which have been widely misunderstood. James Bevar of USAID (United States Aid in Indian Development) in India has applauded the effort and has partially funded the program along with ICICI in the availability of a broad range of contraceptives and child health products in India.

In conclusion, both the AIWC and CWDS have not only highlighted the key issues facing women in their respective on-going studies, they have also undertaken new projects and continued the old ones with a new vigor to improve the general well-being of the women in India. The government of India is greatly by impressed with their achievements and continues to support them financially.

References

1 All India Women's Conference; *A Profile*, New Delhi, 1999.

2 "Sharing Responsibility: Women, Society and Abortion Worldwide", the Alan Guttmacher Institute, New York 1997. "Adolescent Reproductive Health: Making a Difference", *Outlook*, UNFPA, Vol. 16, No. 3, Dec. 1998; "Conveying Concerns; Women Write on Reproductive Health", Population Reference Bureau, Washington D.C., U.S.A., 1994; "Challenging the Culture of Silence: Building Alliances to End Reproductive Tract Infections," *International Women's Health Coalition*, Women and Development Unit, University of the West Indies, 1994.

3. Secretary General Kofiannan's message on the occasion of International Women's Day, March 8th, 1999, *Roshini*, January-June, 1999, p. 37.

4. "Towards Beijing-A Perspective", AIWC library, New Delhi, India.

5. "Children Demand a Happy Childhood", Hindu, August 7, 1999.

6. "Too Young to Know", *Indian Economics*, august 12, 1999, p. 8.

7. *Pioneer*, August 20, 1999, p. 10, *Telegraph*, August 23, 1999, p. 8, Swaminathan, Mina, "Women and Children Last", *Hindu*, August 29, 1999, p. 5; Singh, Rajesh, "NGO Leads Meo Girls to Education", *Indian Express*, August 10, 1999, p.4.

8. Siddiqui, "Abolition of Child Labour", *Legal News and Views*, August, 1999, pp. 25-27.

9. "Women and Children Last", *Hindu*, August 24, 1999, CWDS Library, Delhi.

10. Majumdar, Swapna, "Two Plus Two Makes Ten", *Young Indian*, July 4, 1998.

11. "Family Planning Lessons to be Learnt from Iran, Egypt", *Hindu*, June 14, 1999.

12. "State Cannot Decide How Many Babies is Enough", *Pioneer*, June 23, 1998, p 10.

13. CWDS publishes *Indian Journal of Gender Studies*. Following article may be consulted: Mitrachanna, Subhadra, "Gender and Social Space in a Haryana Village", Vol. 5, No. 1-2, 1998, PP 31-34; Mathur, Kanchan and Rajan, Sobhita, "Gender Training: Potential Limitations", Vol. 5, No. 1-2, 1998, PP 67-76; Basu, Aparna, "Women's Franchise", Vol. 5, No. 1-2, 1998, PP 127-134; Parashar, Archana, "Gender Justice for

Indian Women", Vol. 4, No. 2, July-December 1997, PP 199-230; Shasma, Kumud, "Transformative Politics: Dimensions of Women's Participation in Panchayat Raj", Vol. 5, No. 1-2, 1998, PP 23-45

14. Sharma, Alok, "Private Bill to Stress Small Family Norm", *Pioneer*, December 21, 1998, p 5.

11

United Nations Programs for Women in the 1990's

THE ISSUE OF gender equality has received heightened emphasis in the 1990's, and agencies of the United Nations have actively promoted it in India. On my trip last fall I visited the agencies located in the United Nations complex in Delhi and explored the main concerns and programs relating to women.

India's association with the United Nations started in 1945. It made its first contribution and started receiving technical assistance in 1951. Assistance has increased from $150,000 to an allocation of over $175 million for UNDP's Fourth Country Program in India (April 1, 1990 – March 31, 1995) covering a range of UNDP-assisted projects all over the country. The fifth program of assistance is from 1997-2001 AD. The UNFPA (United Nations Population Fund Association) is assisting India with $100 million and the work is spread over 38 districts.[1]

A workshop organized by the Mewat[2] Development Agency (MDA) in collaboration with the Gender Training Institute (GTI), Center for Social Research, Delhi, on gender sensitization for the Saheli and Sevika[3] workers of the Mewat region identified problems women face. It was held at the Haryana Institute of Public Administration (HIPA) June 10-12, 1997. Women from various blocks of the Mewat district were recruited and 30 women participated. Each block was also represented by their respective NGO members. The methodology followed in the workshop was participatory with a lot of visual exercises.

Sessions revealed the ten most important problems facing these women.

1. It is women's entire responsibility to look after the children, aged people and the whole household work.
2. Health problems.
3. Negligible time to rest and no outlet for entertainment.
4. Limited opportunities for educating girls.
5. Inactive role of women in Panchayat meetings.
6. Entire responsibility of women to fill drinking water and collect wood for fuel.
7. Lack of proper sanitation facilities.
8. Inconsequential right to property.
9. Minimal role in decision making
10. Unemployment.

At the end of the workshop, some recommendations and conclusions were made. The participants enjoyed the participatory and visual approach.

Women learned certain skills of effective communication. The qualities to be a good leader were discussed

The prioritization of the problems helped women focus on some of the issues, which need to be tackled immediately.

All the participants in the workshop agreed that the women should have a source of income. An earning member will earn respect in her family as well as in her community.[4]

(MDA has followed the "Gender and Development" (Coordination approach) with the Women of Mewat region after the conclusion of the workshop.).

Another gender sensitization workshop was conducted in Rajgarh in the state of Himachal Pradesh, May 21-29, 1998.[5] The name of the workshop was Training of Gender Trainers. The state government, in order to implement women's empowerment and development projects in three districts selected one woman in each village who was at least five grades pass and had basic leadership qualities. This woman was called *Sanjeevani* and was in the age group of 25-40 years. Her responsibility was the formation of a *Jagriti Mandli* (an association) in her village. Through this *Mandli* she is to impart basic knowledge of health, education, and legal rights on the empowerment process. But she herself is not aware of all the issues and the meaning of gender equality. So there is a social mobilizer called *didi* (sister) to supervise 8-10 *sanjeevanis* to help them understand the idea of gender equality.[6]

A training program for women in remote, hilly areas was conducted January 2-11, 1990 in Jagjit Nagar, in the state of Himachal Pradesh. The training was carried on by *Sutra,* a voluntary organization in Jagjitnagar, working for women's development in remote and hilly areas. Himachal Pradesh is a hilly area with a cold and wet climate. Its villages are located in remote areas and scattered far apart. The population of 65% of the villages is less than 200. The productivity of the land is low. The means of communication are limited.

As mentioned in an earlier chapter, forests have been mercilessly cut down to generate revenue for the state and for other purposes. After the forests had been destroyed, the next step to generate revenue for the state was to tolerate alcohol consumption among men.[7] The sudden flood of development carried away the traditional social structure with it. This change had the maximum negative impact on women. On one hand, women's traditional relationship with the forests started getting destroyed (forests had been used as toilets and to provide fuel. Forest produce was also used to supplement the diet). On the other hand, alcohol consumption led to increased physical and economic violence against women. The increasing demand for modern consumer goods became a burden for girls to be married in the form of expensive dowry demand from their parents.

Due to the villages being small and scattered the women remained isolated. Despite working for 15 hours a day, their participation in the cash economy has remained negligible. All the existing social organizations are male-dominated. For men, women have no value other than that of a child bearing machine and unpaid laborer.

It was in this context that some women of Dharampur block (Solan district) began to question the kind of development flooding the state. They started expressing their reactions through collective action such as the Chipko Movement and the Prohibition movement mentioned in an earlier chapter. Although this had little impact upon those in power, their level of awareness and the strength of organized action started inspiring women of other areas to come forward. They now wanted support for getting organized. SUTRA's area of operation began to expand and it decided to take up the *Sahayogini* Program (those who give support to an activity) under the *Mahila Samakhya* (Women's organizations) program. The aims of this program are:

1. To prepare two or three women workers in each development block for providing support to Mahila Mandals (Women organizations). These trained women will further develop the thinking of those women who have already started looking at their own lives in relation to the social context, and encourage them to take organized action against unscrupulous, hasty development.
2. To help women understand the nature of various local problems within the framework of regional development and to assist them to take steps to solve these through organized action.
3. To start adult education centres to increase awareness among women.
4. To open non-formal education centres for girls who have not been able to go to school to increase their

awareness through such education.

5. To assist Mahila Mandals to understand the social institutions presently working against women.
6. To support Mahila Mandals in taking organized action against rape, and physical violence.

SUTRA also decided that as a rule, one trained woman worker would be responsible for 10 to 12 Mahila Mandals. But in areas where a woman cannot travel alone, two trained women are appointed to share the work. SUTRA appoints a woman supervisor to oversee the work of the trained woman worker. So far as the training of the women workers is concerned, initial training for *Sahayoginis* is for 10 days. However, a three-day renewed training and discussion session is held every three months. Monthly meetings are held in each work area of the trained women workers or *Sahayoginis.*

The training program for *Sahayoginis* began on January 2, 1990. It was quickly determined that the *Sahayoginis* had to bring about change within themselves before being able to do so in other women. The trainees or *Sahayoginis* were divided into various groups to present role plays to dramatize some of the problems they faced in their environment. They are given below:

1. Crimes against girls and women are increasing day by day. Physical violence, rape, dowry demands and women's triple work burden have become common.
2. Despite working for up to 18 hours a day, women do not get commensurate compensation for their labor.
3. It is common for married men to bring in second wives.
4. Due to child marriage or unsuitable matches, the women's individual life is destroyed.
5. Physical violence on women because of alcohol is still widely prevalent.
6. The custom of selling girls several times through accepting bride price is still a significant problem.

7. Divorce or just simple abandonment.
8. Unemployment and poverty in villages is very acute.
9. Problems faced by a girl after marriage because the in-laws are unhappy with the size of the dowry.

One role-play conveyed how a mother-in-law strangles the girl on her son's instigation. When the case is taken to the village Panchayat *Pradhan* (Head) and the police, it is hushed by the family with bribery. Even the doctor is bribed to give a false medical certificate. This is used to prove that the girl died of cholera.

In the second session held on January 3, 1990, the issue of rape and early marriage was taken up. Participants or *Sahoginis* were divided into two groups to present the problem through a role-play. The woman is raped while waiting for a bus at the bus stop by drunken men. She had just attended a meeting of the local Mahila Mandal, which had delayed her somewhat. When she reaches home, the husband scolds her for coming home so late. He threatens to force her to retire from her job with the Mahila Mandal or bring a second wife if she continues to come home late in the evening. The sahayogini relates the problem to the Mahila Mandal the next day. She is advised to report the name to the police. When the policeman comes for her inquiry, the Panchayat Pradhan (head) and the police make a deal and the matter is hushed up.

Discussion on the role-play of rape brought out the following points:

1. Both the cinema and the television depict women as an object of entertainment, as a toy, which can be bought or thrown away.
2. Cinema and the television give wrong signals to boys that those who drink, commit violence and accept bribery are great men. Such a message tends to increase the helplessness of women who would like to step out of the house for a purposeful activity, but

are restrained from doing so because of the fear of rape or obnoxious teasing by men.

3. The police and the Panchayat Pradhan (head) cannot be trusted to respect law in defense of women.
4. The government is not willing to accept responsibility for the growing crime and violence. It just sidetracks the issue because some of the politicians depend upon the support of these male criminals or mafia men during election and after election.

In the session held on January 4, 1990 the issue of the handicaps faced by poor, particularly women, were discussed. Once again, the method chosen was a role-play. The woman portrayed is a poor widow who seeks a loan under the IRDP program of the central government.[8] This program, as explained in an earlier chapter, aims at pulling up the rural poor who are below the poverty line by extending loans to create durable assets. Somehow, the person in power, the Panchayat Pradhan (head), the bank officer whose job it is to sanction the loan, and the gram sevak (V.L.W.) all want bribes for doing something which is a part of their job. The Pradhan (head) is also interested in grabbing the widow's land. The most important point revealed was that the widow was not aware of her rights and the bribe money collected by various males was spent on alcohol. Mention of alcohol triggered a heated discussion of its impact on family life. The health of the man is affected with drinking. At the same time, over-all well being of the wife and the children is adversely affected with the availability of less money for food and other essentials. The *Sahayoginis* also felt that alcohol often was the main reason for family quarrels, rape of girls, etc. The government was absolutely unconcerned with the problems of alcohol consumption. It was opening more and more shops to net greater revenue. The sahayoginis also concluded that since the power structure is controlled by men, women should not expect anything from these institutions on their own initiative. What women need to do is to voice their concern collectively through Mahila Mandals hoping for some kind of an action of change in the long run.

What about the widow who is almost going to lose her land to the *Pradhan* (head)? The discussion concluded that the widow should go to the local Mahila Mandal and seek related information about her rights to land and a loan from IRDP. It was also realized that the widow should not approach the *Pradhan* (head) all alone. She should be accompanied by Mahila Mandal members. The *Pradhan*, the VLW or Gram Sevak all succumbed to this collective pressure.

The importance of the Mahila Mandal was brought home to the participants as it provided necessary information to women about their rights and showed the effectiveness of the weapon of collective action.

In the session held on January 7, 1990, advocate *Satyanarayan* provided legal information on marriage, dissolution of marriage, divorce and maintenance, physical violence (crime and rape) and how to lodge a complaint (FIR) with the police. Once again the persuasive method of role-play by the participants was used to heighten the legal problems faced by women. One role-play depicted the pitiful position of a woman who does not have any maintenance after her husband deserted her. The woman, then, finds out about the Mahila Mandal and becomes a member. The support she receives from the Mahila Mandal is great and the members are willing to spend the travel money from the Mahila Mandals funds whenever they go to see the Pradhan (village council head) or visit the courts.

The other role-play also stresses the importance of the Mahila Mandal or collective action when a girl is portrayed to have been beaten by her mother-in-law for not bringing enough dowry. The girl is forced to go back to her parents' house where she contacts the local Mahila Mandal. A collective action by the Mahila Mandal that involves a number of visits to the *Pradhan* (head) and the police pays off. Finally, the girl's husband is arrested.

In the session held on January 10, 1990, the topic turns to firewood. The role-play showed how the government security guard bothers the village women who have gone to the forest with sickles to cut and collect wood for cooking. The village women approach the local *Sahayogini* who accompanies them to the security guard. When nothing is achieved, they all go to the District Forest Officer who listens to the women and reprimands the guard. The Forest Officer tells the Mahila Mandal about the government plan to provide manure and plants for trees if the Mahila Mandal could identify some village land. The *Pradhan* intervenes by approaching the Forest Officer to work as a go-between. However, when the plants arrive, they are of pine and eucalyptus, which cannot be used as fodder. Mahila Mandal again approaches the *Sahayogini* who would go to the Forest Officer to explain the importance of fodder trees to village women. The situation is happily resolved in favor of the village women and the Pradhan's plans are laid to rest.
What are the lessons to be learned from this role-play?

1. The *Sahayogini* provided helpful information to the Mahila Mandal women and supported them whenever needed.
2. The District Forest Officer provided important information to women. The *Sahayoginis* felt that only if all government officials were so helpful would the people start trusting the government departments.
3. The Pradhan and his wife acted for their own interest ignoring the well being of the village women.
4. The *Sahayoginis* felt that the use of role-plays and films have been very effective in understanding the problems facing women.
5. The sessions helped the *Sahayoginis* to receive mutual support from each other in owning the problems facing them at home and in society and in working our solutions to them. No longer did the *Sahayoginis*

feel embarrassed or shameful about their problems and experiences.

The *Sahayoginis* training program concluded with a narration by each woman of her hard life with her in-laws and how they stepped forward to be somebody. Now they feel a sense of purpose in their lives to help other women through a collective action by Mahila Mandals.[9]

The preceding discussion has highlighted the point made earlier that the Indian government and the NGOs have realized even more in the 1990's than they did in the 1980's that leadership has to emerge from the ranks of the village women themselves. These potential leaders, no matter whatever title, have to be trained not only through traditional methods but also by incorporating new techniques like role-plays by women themselves to illustrate their issues and an extensive use of videos. With that in view, let us deal with the training program for trainers on Panchayat Raj (village elected councils).

References

1. *Poptimes,* The Population and Development Newsletter of UNFPA India, may also be consulted for more information, June, 1995, PP 2-3; *Outlook* is another publication made possible by a UNFPA grant. It features articles on reproductive health of women, which is linked to the population control issue.
2. Name of a district and a district is like the U.S.A. county within a state.
3. Women's Organizations.
4. Organizations like SEWA, Lucknow, India, work for the empowerment of girls and women through employment training and education. The positive effects of this approach are clear. Shy, new arrivals to the organization contrast greatly with the more confident longer-term women.

   There has been added a new dimension to the job-training program in the 1990's. Instead of just focusing on adult-women, organizations like *Prerarna* (Haryana) work primarily with adolescent girls and offer a wide range of programs. The new realization is that these girls are the future wives and mothers, so train them ahead of time. Since exclusive focus on girls was arousing the hostility of the local community, *Prerana* developed a parallel program for boys. In Karnataka, *Namma Maglu* enhances the value of a baby girl by opening a bank account in her name, which she can access after reaching the age of eighteen.

The Indian government (Ministry of Human Resource Development, Ministry of Health and Family Welfare, Ministry of Social Welfare and Ministry of Rural Development) has also intensified efforts and programs to address the needs of the adolescent girls. The UNFPA has collaborated in some of these projects ("South and East India: Investing in Adolescent Girls in India" by Margaret E. Greene, *Population Council,* (United Nations), Regional Working Papers, No. 7, 1997, Delhi).

5. "Report on Training of Gender Trainers" supported by European Union and organized by *Gender Training Institute Centre for Social Research,* New Delhi.
6. One may also review *"Fifth Program of Assistance, 1997-2001", UNDPA (United Nations Population Fund)*; "*Workshop on Gender Equality*", October, 1997, *India International Centre,* Delhi.
7. One may also read "Violence Against Women", *UNFPA,* June, 1999; "A Life Free of Violence-It is Our Right", *United Nations Development Fund for Women,* Delhi, March 1999, PP 6-7, PP 18-19; "Global Video Conference Urges Tough Stance on Violence Against Women"; *POPULI,* The UNFPA Magazine, Vol. 26, No. 1, March, 1999, p 9; "Trade in Human Misery", UNIFEM, UNICEF, UNIASU India, 1999.
8. Integrated Rural Development Program.
9. "For a similar program-Looking at the World Through Women's Eyes." *Mahila Samakhya,* "Karnataka (South India) Annual Report," 1998-1999, *U.N. Building,* Delhi.z

12

Training Women in Politics and Economic Development

AFTER THE 73RD amendment passed by the Indian Parliament in December, 1992 that one-third of the members in a village Panchayat and in an urban ward be women and that one-third of the head of the village Panchayats be women, it has become urgent that women be adequately trained to undertake this role seriously and effectively. The critics of the 73rd amendment ask that where women are illiterate and live in a male-dominated society, are they really prepared for grassroots administration? It is apprehended that the system may be made use of by certain vested interests to get their women candidates elected and gain indirect control over the functioning of the institution. In order to safeguard against such situations, NGOs are taking up the issue of mass mobilization to get younger, literate women into Panchayats and training institutes are conducting programs aimed at the empowerment of women. (Gender Training Institute also contributes towards achieving this.) This training program was residential and fourteen adjoining districts of Rohtas and Kaimur Zillas (an administrative unit in a state) participated. The two Zillas have 1930 villages with about 243 Panchayats in all and 1715 villages with about 160 Panchayats. The name of the NGO is Jayprabha Gram Vikas Mandal, which has been working there for quite some time. The local community members must elect their representatives (trainers in this case) with a solid understanding of the 73rd amendment of the Indian Constitution.

This training program at conclusion had enabled the participants to understand the 73rd amendment and clarify the need for this amendment.[1]

It may seem that the induction of women in grass-root politics is only a mattle of little time. Unfortunately, this is not the reality. Nearly 7.95 lakh (a lakh is 100,000) will be represented in the Panchayats when the Act went into operation in different states. (The 73rd amendment required all the states to bring their legislation for Panchayat Raj at par with it by April 1994). The Forum for Women in Local Government was formed in Delhi at the end of a two-day national workshop on "Panchayat Raj Institution: Strategies for Empowerment."[2] The workshop was organized on February 16 and 17, 1993 by the Centre for Development Studies and Action and Friedrich Ebert Stiftung (FES), Delhi. The Forum is a national body and works through a core group mainly to monitor the progress of local governments formation in light of the 72nd and 73rd Constitutional Amendment Acts.[3] It would also make recommendations and plan activities. The Forum adopted a few strategies for action of which the most important is to mobilize the rural women through Mahila Mandals and NGOs to participate in the Panchayat Raj elections in great numbers both as candidates and as voters. Secondly, the Forum recommended the setting-up of an Institutional Task Force,[4] consisting of concerned officials, members of related departments, National Commission for Women[5] NGOs and Women's Studies Persons. The Task Force formulated strategies for enabling women to participate in greater numbers and effectively in the Panchayat Raj institutions and monitor progress.[6]

The Forum for Women also suggested that every state must set-up an Advisory Committee consisting of, among others, all the women members elected to Panchayat Raj

Institutions, Mahila Mandals, local NGOs, women's groups working with programs for women etc. to advise and monitor whether the Panchayats are working for women's participation and development.

Another suggestion made by the Forum was that all development plans concerning the villages should be coordinated with Panchayat Raj Institutions and its women members. Such an approach would not only help in the more effective implementation of development but would also facilitate decentralization in planning, implementation and monitoring.

The Forum also recommended that funds should be allocated in the plans of the Department of Rural Development and in the Department of Women and Child Development (a branch of the Ministry of Human Resource Development) for undertaking political awareness and training camps on the model of awareness generation and other training camps. The Panchayat Raj Institutions Act should be disseminated with additional funding for publicity.

Provision should be made to pay the members of the Panchayat Raj Institutions in general and women members, in particular, such as a certain allowance for attending the meetings as they stand to lose their earnings for the day. This would act as an incentive for all the women to attend meetings regularly.

Since dissemination of information about the Panchayat Raj Institutions is very critical, the Forum stated that some of the existing institutions and programs like DWCRA, Mahila Samakhya Program, ICDs be utilized.

NGOs can contribute enormously by setting up mobile training units. However, there is a need for production of training material/manuals in easy style. Greater use of media (audio-visual) should be made in the training for Panchayat Raj Institutions.[7]

Since the 73rd Amendment, under Article 243-G and 243-E, envisages a three-tier developmental planning (the central government, state governments and Panchayats), the responsible and priorities of each would differ. Besides, regional differences would have to be taken into account while planning agricultural development.[8] For example, some crops may be suitable in the plains, but may be unsuitable in hilly regions.

Let us turn now to a higher level of political participation for women. From the Panchayat and Municipal elections women can forge ahead into State Assemblies and Parliamentary elections. This is the stage when women will have to choose a political party. The choice, among other things, will be determined by the gender concerns that the parties address.

The Draft Platform for Action—a document presented at the 4th World Conference for Women in Beijing, China, 1999, referring to the Nairobi (Kenya) Forward Looking Strategies, identifies the issue of inequality between men and women in the sharing of power and decision making at all levels. The Jakarta (Indonesia) Ministerial meeting of June 4-7, 1994, stated that governments, citizens and political parties are encouraged to increase the percentage of women in legislative bodies and ministries (central and state cabinets).

The Indian government appointed a group called the National Consultation on Women in Political Participation. More than 50 NGOs involved in gender issues were in this group. This group held meetings at all levels with grassroots women and finally the national meeting on January 21-22, 1995. Recommendations were then forwarded to the Department of Women and Child Development, Ministry of Human Resource Development. The Report discusses, among other things, the impediments that restrict active participation of women. It also draws up a charter of demands to create a politically friendly climate to enable positive participation of women.

As a background, the Report pointed out that since women's political participation spans decision-making at all levels; the question of women's empowerment is not only a political issue but a socio-economic one as well. Ms. Rama Devi remarked that no political participation is possible without revolutionizing the attitudes of the people in power, which includes the present body of decision-makers.[9] The Veteran Parliamentarian asserted that politics and economics are two arms of power and therefore inseparable. She also explained that men like Gandhi became popular leaders because they sought economic empowerment as a precursor to political power. She proposed that 1/3 of seats be for women, 1/3 for men and the remaining 1/3 open to all in the state assemblies and the Central Parliament.

The Report also included the poor representation of women in the major political parties of India-Congress (I), BJP (Bhartiya Janata Party), JD (Janata Dal), Communist Party—both wings. The figures reveal the representation of women in the decision-making bodies from 5.1% in the Communist Party (M) to 12.5% in BJP. Other parties lie in between. The Report then discussed the manifestoes of the various political parties as the general parliamentary election was nearing. Some of the manifestoes were interesting. For example, the Samta Party stresses the need to create an environment for equal participation of women by establishing appropriate support facilities such as day care and making career patterns flexible. The manifesto of Janata Party promised to expedite the creation of commissions for women in the states. It also promised that the allotment to a hut or to low-cost housing would be jointly in the names of both the husband and wife to give to poor women proprietary ownership. The manifesto also promised to fix a definite quota for women in jobs for scheduled castes, scheduled tribes and backward classes.

The report summed up some reasons for the poor representation of women in politics.

1. In the sphere of electoral politics, it is money and muscle power, and criminalization, which act as powerful deterrent to women participation in

elections.

2. Economic disempowerment of women has been made worse by the liberalization, globalization and structural reforms of the economy mandated by the World Bank and the International Monetary Fund (IMF) in the 1990's.
3. Patriarchy—male dominated attitudes toward women at home and in the workplace can be corrected only by gender sensitization, education and training countrywide.

Ms. Padma Ramachandaran, a retired bureaucrat proposed that 50% should be women administrators in the bureaucracy and that positive steps be adopted to sensitize the male, women's issues are a large societal problem.[10] She also suggested that women administrators interact closely with each other to plan out a strategy to resolve their issues.

The final suggestion in the report was the formation of a strong women's lobby cutting across party lines to capitalize on their immense strength derived from their 50% of the voters. The report called for more interactions between parliamentarians and women's movement activists. This could be a useful exercise. Formation of a data bank on women could be an effective way to influence parliamentary debates on women and other issues.[11]

Another approach to the issue of women's political participation is exhibited in a Report of the Inter-Parliamentary Union given in 1998.[12] That women's political participation increases with social and economic development is presumably supported by data from the Nordic countries where there are higher proportions of women legislators than in less developed countries. But not all women in the developed countries have satisfactory levels of representation in their national legislatures. Of the 46 developed countries that reported electoral data in 1998, 14 had fewer than 10% women legislators in their lower houses. Women in the U.S.A., even today, are only marginally better represented with 11.7% in the House of Representatives.

Increased participation of women in economic activity is considered a favorable factor for increased women's political participation. However, in the Asia-Pacific region, there are 11 countries where more than 70% of women above 15 years of age are economically active. But among them, only 3 nations have more than 10% women legislators.

Another hypothesis is that the type of political system has a bearing on women's political participation. But evidence shows that this is true only in the case of the Nordic countries where 37.6% of the legislators are women. Most democratic countries in other regions have less than 20% women in their legislatures.

According to the conclusion of the Report, even though the Nordic countries have a women friendly culture and have better levels of social-economic development with a higher literacy, the single factor most responsible for the higher representation of women is institutional. Most Nordic countries follow some variant of proportional representation for women in political parties that results in their electing a higher proportion of women representatives to their national legislatures.

Another commonly held belief is that the level of women's political participation is inextricably linked to the culture of the country. This belief is supported by data from most of the Islamic countries.

In India, the latest legislative initiative to increase women's political participation proposes to set aside 33% of legislative seats for women.[13] Some critics point out that the quality of the membership of Parliament can suffer because not enough qualified women are available to the political parties. The latter may be compelled to return a lower profile woman candidate rather than a stronger man candidate with the result that the over-all membership may be lowered in caliber.

But these critics have to be countered with the argument that proportional representation seems to be the only viable option as the Nordic countries have proved.

Training of women political leaders is one of the purposes of Women Studies Centers on university campuses. As stated in an earlier chapter, the Indian government and the U.G.C. (Universities Grant Commission) had begun to fund a few universities, which established Women Studies Centers. The Women Studies and Development Centre at Delhi University was set-up in 1987.[14] The centre has done an enormous amount of work in research, University curriculum development, teaching and documentation. It also carries on Awareness Raising camps, lobbying, social action and networking. The Centre functions with the help of an Advisory Committee consisting of university professors, college principals and experts from outside appointed by the university vice-chancellor and chaired by the vice-chancellor himself. The Advisory Committee meets at least once a year to monitor the activities and advise the Centre.

Curriculum development and syllabi redesigning has helped various departments to introduce special courses in Women's Studies.

Research projects undertaken by the Centre were based on field studies and action research and were both policies oriented and theoretical. Following are some of the research projects completed by the Centre:

1. "Evaluation, Study on Short Stay Homes in India": sponsor: Department of Women and Child Development, Ministry of Human Resource Development, Government of India, New Delhi.
2. "Women in Politics: Regional Cross-Cultural Research Project": sponsor: UNESCO, Bangkok, Thailand.
3. "Girl Child and Family": sponsor: Department of Women and Child Development.
4. "Child Labour Among Girls": sponsor: Ministry of Labour, Government of India.
5. "Women and the Population Issues": sponsor: UNICEF.

6. "Tenth Lok Sabha Elections": Study of Two Constituencies—Hapur-Ghaziabad and South Calcutta": sponsor: National Commission for Women, 1996.
7. "Appraisal of Awareness Generation Projects for Rural and Poor Women of the Central Social Welfare Board": sponsor: National Institute of Public Cooperation and Child Development.

The Centre has also organized a number of seminars and workshops on several themes about women. Some are as follows:

1. "National Workshop on Common Dignity of Women and Men: A Parameter of Social Change and Appraisal," February 27-28, 1990.
2. "Child Labour in Beedi (cigarette) making: Legislation and Practices, September 17-19, 1994.
3. " Workshop on Voters' Awareness", February 17, 1995.
4. "Women and Religion Across Four Boundaries", January 22, 1993.
5. "Decentralization and Devolution of Powers in Panchayat Raj System in India", March 22-23, 1996.
6. "Regional consultation on Proposed National Policy on Women for the states of Jammu and Kashmir, Himachal Pradesh, Panjab and Haryana", November 27, 1995.
7. "Masculinity and Violence," October 4, 1993.

In addition to above mentioned activities, the Centre's services have also been utilized by various governmental and non-governmental organizations in organizing seminars, workshops and conferences and providing background material for the same. Apart from working closely with the Department of Women and Child Development, the National Commission for Women appointed by the Indian government, the Centre has actively participated in all National Conferences of the Indian Association of Women's

Studies. The Centre has also worked in close collaboration with sister organizations to promote women's studies. After the passage of the 73rd amendment on Panchayat Raj, the Centre has participated in several training programs.[15]

The Centre also fulfilled a long-standing demand by bringing out a newsletter since 1993. The main purpose of the newsletter—*Women's News*—is to network and share information with Women Development Centres in various Delhi colleges, different departments of Delhi University, other university-based Women's Studies Centres and NGOs. Of the above organizations and institutes, we may give special attention to the Women Development Centres in various colleges of Delhi University. The university-based Centre works very closely with them and one of the primary objectives is to prevent atrocities against women through education and community action. Delhi University-based Centre also lobbys extensively with the Department of Women and Child Development to funnel funds into some specific programs. It lobbys with Delhi Administration to highlight the need for better police protection on the campus to allow free female mobility.[16] The Centre also provides family counseling through its Family Counseling Centre in collaboration with AIWC. On the issue of sexual harassment on the campus and in public places, the Centre has been organizing protests and has also lodged complaints against obscene advertisements with the concerned authorities.[17]

The National Commission for Women was set-up in the 1970's to celebrate the United Nations' Declaration of 1975-1985 as Women's Decade. Since then the Commission has spear-headed many movements and activities on behalf of women at the national level thereby weaving together many isolated, regional attempts of various groups and organizations. It is not possible to describe all the projects. But we may just mention two as an illustration of the Commission's endeavors.[18]

One endeavor has been to work out strategies and plans to provide easy credit for both urban and rural poor women.

A hopeful factor is that women are more aware of the changing economic and social life around them and are eagerly awaiting an opportunity to meet the challenges ahead through their own efforts. However, this awareness is more in the urban areas forming only 20% of India's female population of close to 400 million. The remaining 80% languish in rural areas exploited, illiterate and downtrodden. It is the goal of the National Commission to make economic development more balanced by bringing more women into the main stream of economic development. This goal calls for innovations in the banking system to enable women to be self-employed and generate income through various trades. The banking system can match the grant of loans to the requirements of women by having different types of loans to suit different categories of rural and urban women, literate and illiterate, skilled, semi-skilled and unskilled women.

The NCW,[19] following the example of Bangladesh, sent a letter to the Finance Minister, P. Chidambaram, requesting establishment of Gramin (village) Banks to enable the rural poor, particularly women, to obtain short finances at reasonable rates and repayment in easy installments for non-farm activities. This should be particularly helpful since normally the traditional moneylenders in the rural areas lend money at exorbitant and stiff repayment terms.

The mode of functioning of a Gramin Bank would be a manager assisted by six bank workers. Any person belonging to a household owning half acre or less of cultivatable land or other assets equal to that, is eligible for a loan. The Gramin Bank takes banking services to the very doorsteps of the rural poor because experience has shown that the rural illiterate poor are nervous to come to a city or a town to obtain a loan. The bank workers move around the villages falling within the purview of their branch to contact prospective loanees and motivate them to organize into groups of five each. A number of groups at the same place are federated into a centre and the elected chief of the centre conducts weekly meeting and recommends loan proposals of the members of the groups. The bank workers help in providing bank procedures and information to adjust the loan recommendations. The loans are granted without collateral. The loans are given to the borrowers by the bank workers at the centre. The loan is to be used for any training program or for any productive activity. The repayment of the loan in installments is insisted upon by members in the weekly meetings. The pressure exerted by the group play an important role in prompt repayment. The repayment is collected by the bank worker in these meetings. Every member also has to contribute a dime or so to a group fund at every meeting. Besides, 50% of the amount borrowed is deducted for deposit in the fund. The loan can be made by a group to a member from this fund at any time of emergency.

The NCW concluded that the overwhelming majority of the poor women, urban or rural, wants to improve the level of their living and are prepared to work hard for this. The report of the NCW lists the success stories of a few women who have improved their lives through their loans.

One other endeavor of the NCW relates to the abuse of liquor among poorer sections of the male population. Anti-Liquor Campaigns were being waged by grass-root workers in different parts in rural and urban India. In the face of this pressure, the NCW responded by organizing a National Consultation in March 1996, on the eve of the General Elections to the Indian Parliament. The workshop or consultation invited groups from various states. The goal was to network these groups so that collectively they could carry on their struggle more vigorously. The network would inform the broader women's movement as well as political parties about the significance of removing liquor from local shops by a legal measure.

The workshop or consultation narrated a variety of strategies adopted by women including sit-in-strike and compensation to liquor vendors for loss of revenue. Very moving incidents were narrated involving insults and threats that these women had to face. Yet all the women were aware that the anti-liquor could succeed only by the persistence of women who should be self-confident and not be intimidated by threats. The summary of the workshop also recommended that support from district (county in the USA) administration is very critical. Therefore, sensitization of administrative official is a key area for future action. A close link exists between literacy and the success of the anti-liquor movement. Therefore, women committees at the district and state level should be able to communicate with one another and share any new information to combat liquor consumption. Media also has a critical role to play in spreading the agitation from a local to a national level. One cannot stress enough the support of local police as the policemen are recruited from the same lower classes where alcohol consumption is abused and women's status is held very low. What is required is not the bribery of policemen but their sensitization to the bad consequences of liquor abuse. At the national level, all candidates must be made to take a firm stand on prohibition. Among the bad consequences of liquor abuse, the workshop or consultation highlighted the drain on household economy, (a male would spend 70 to 80% of the income on liquor), ill-health, malnutrition and lack of care of children, family disharmony, ill repute for the village community and gangsterism.

One of the myths ridiculed at the workshop was that prohibition would severely reduce states' revenue and, thus, their ability to finance a number of social projects. The activists at the workshop countered the myth by pointing out that except in Panjab and Haryana liquor excise is less than 10% of the states' revenue. This loss can be made up by increased sales tax and other taxes if the state resources are well spent.[20]

Though we have mentioned only the NWC here, the reader may be reminded that some other government bodies are also carrying on a range of similar activities for women. In the earlier edition of the book, *Women in India,* a mention was made of Women's Development Corporations mandated for each state by the central government as a sequel to the Women's Decade of 1975-1985 of the United Nations. One may consult the following for updated information on Women's Development Corporations.

Women's Development Corporation: An assessment. Sponsored by Ministry of Human Resource Development, Department of Women and Child Development; submitted by Institutes of Social Studies Trust, Delhi.

References

1. One may also consult "Women Claim Their Rights in Local Politics in *Strategies To Increase Women's Participation in Local Government,*" Documentation of a regional workshop organized by Friedrich-Ebert-Stiftung, Bangkok, Thailand, October 26-27, 1994.
2. *Forum,* p. 126.
3. 72ns Act reserves seats for women of the scheduled castes and scheduled tribes, *Forum,* p. 27.
4. Appointed by the Department of Rural Development.
5. It was set-up in 1970's.
6. *Forum,* pp. 128 – 129.
7. "Teaching Politics: Panchayat Raj", vol. XVIII, no. 3 and 4, 1992, *Department of Political Science of University of Delhi.* More on the 73rd amendment may be found in *Kurukshetra,* July 1997, pp. 37-40. The article suggests that as the situation stands today, the majority of the village masses specially the scheduled castes, scheduled tribes and other backward classes are by and large dependent upon the landlords for their living. In the absence of economic independence, they are not in a position to exercise their political rights freely. So, the urgent need is to restructure the economic set-up of rural society with a view to enabling the poor to become economically self-dependent and well off. The government has to take some very concrete steps like providing land to the landless and to promote cottage and small-scale industries. The village Panchayat also has to undertake some important measures to ensure the success of such industries, e.g., banning fully and partially the sale of goods such as soap, candles; etc. except those produced by the village industries.

   The article also suggested the offering of economic incentives in the form of sanctioning link roads, water-supply, primary school and a health center to those Panchayats which make the Gram Sabha (village assembly of all adults) an effective mini parliament at the village level. Under this amendment, the state governments have been given the power to authorize the Panchayats to collect and appropriate suitable local taxes. It also provides for giving grants-in-aid to the Panchayats from the state concerned. Besides, a Finance Commission has been constituted once in every five years to review the financial position of the Panchayats and to make recommendations to the states for the distribution of funds to local rural bodies to enable them to carry out their functions. This is definitely a great improvement upon the previous practice.

Since the Institutions of the Panchayat Raj are supposed to provide a sound base to the democratic superstructure in the country, education for the rural masses becomes indispensable for shaping them as responsible citizens, voters and representatives. Short-term training programs and refresher courses, workshops and seminars are sure to help the rural people understand their new status with the passage of the 73rd amendment.

Besides, the role of mass media in educating and awakening the masses can hardly be exaggerated. In brief, the overall constitutional and legal changes envisaged in the 73rd amendment are undoubtedly a step in the right direction; but these alone would not bring about the desired results. Much would depend on the attitudinal and behavioral overtones of the various functionaries involved in the working of the Panchayat Raj system because it is not the system but the people who work it that really matters.

8. "Panchayat Raj and Perspective Planning", *Kurukshetra,* July 1999, pp. 31-39.
9. "Rights of Women", produced by the *International Women's Tribune Centre,* New York, 1998, pp. 8-10.
10. "Employment Opportunities for Women in Village Industries", Dossier no. 4, *Institute of Social Studies; Trust, Women's Studies Resource Centre,* Delhi; "The Woman Worker and Her child", Dossier no. 5, *Institute of Social Studies Trust, Women's Studies Resource Centre,* Delhi.
11. "National Consultation on Women in Political Participation", held at YMCA, Delhi on January 21-22, 1995.
12. Rathod, P.B., "Women and Political Representation", *Manushi* (a journal about women and society), May – June 1999, no. 112, pp. 33-35.
13. This bill is shelved in the Parliament at present.
14. "Report of Activities (1987-1997)", Women's Studies and Development Centre, University of Delhi, Delhi.
15. Kaushik, Susheela, "Women's Participation in Politics", edited by Professor Susheela Kaushik; *Panchayat Raj and Women*; *Panchayat Raj*

in Action, Challenges to Women's Role, Knocking at the Male Bastion, Women in Politics, sponsored by National Commission for Women, July, 1992; *Women Pances in Position; A Study of Panchayat Raj in Haryana,* 1997. Vyas, Jayshree, "Political Empowerment of Women: Reservation for Women in Political Bodies", sponsored by UNIFEM, New Delhi.

The Centre also has extensive documentation on themes like Panchayat Raj Institutions and 73rd amendment; women in politics, bureaucracy and other decision making level; uniform civil code, girl children; the new economic policy and its implications for women, *Report of Activities,* 1992-1998.

16. Thirteen colleges of Delhi University have been receiving a grant from the Department of Women and Child Development for a decade under its scheme of "Prevention of Atrocities Against Women Through Education".
17. These were four basic centres set-up at different universities in 1987 under the UGC (University Grants Commission) India. The founding of these centres was a part of the women's movement in India.
18. All the issues may be obtained at the Women Studies and Development Centre, University of Delhi.
19. National Commission for Women.
20. If the current Parliamentary bill to set aside 1/3 seats in the Parliament for women is enacted, the cause of prohibition would receive a great boost. "A Study of Women Candidates for the Eleventh Lok Sabha, 1996", sponsored by *National Commission for Women,* Women Studies and Development Centre, University of Delhi, Delhi.

13

SEWA 1990–2000

WE SHALL NOW DEAL WITH SEWA located in Ahmedabad, in Gujarat State. This state lies in the upper western part of India and the review of SEWA would add to the large range of the geographical area sought to be covered in the book. It was established in 1972 and since then, it has undergone a wide variety of experiences. All of SEWA's work is with the reality of the every day lives of poor self-employed women and all of the efforts have been in how to make their lives better economically and socially to make them strong and self-reliant. SEWA has learned a number of lessons and the most inspiring is the growth of the women members themselves. Given the opportunity, women take leadership roles, assume responsibilities for their own organization and learn skills necessary to run them.[1]

As stated earlier, SEWA is an organization of poor, self-employed women workers. These are women who earn a living through their own labor or small businesses. They do not receive welfare benefits like workers in the organized (formal) sector. They are the unprotected labor in our country, constituting 93% of the labor force.[2] Of the female labor, more than 94% are in the unorganized sector. However, their work is not counted and hence remains invisible. In fact, 64% of GDP is accounted for by self-employed workers.

SEWA has three types of self-employed workers:[3]

1. Hawkers, vendors and small-businesswomen like vegetable, fruit, fish, egg and other vendors of food items, household goods and clothes vendors.
2. Home-based workers like weavers, potters, bidi (cigarette) and agarbatti (incense) workers, papad (waffle) rollers, ready-made garment workers, women who process agricultural products and artisans.
3. Manual laborers and service providers like agricultural laborers, construction workers, contract laborers, hand-cart pullers, head loaders, domestic workers and laundry workers.

As one can easily understand, if you are familiar with the labor conditions in India and the Third World that all the above three categories lead a very insecure and undignified life. The basic respect for manual labor is just absent.

Among the values of SEWA, stress is still on the basic philosophy of Gandhiji—truth, non-violence, courage and absence of fear, *Sarvadharma* (respecting all religions), *Swadeshi* by encouraging local employment including khadi (hand woven and spun cloth) and village industries, removal of untouchability and unity of all communities and castes, commitment and identification with the cause of the poorest, particularly women and self-reliance, both economic and in other respects.

SEWA's members and "aagewans" (local union leaders) are increasingly confident of managing their own economic activities and work-related campaigns. In Ahmedabad city they are leading the campaigns for home-based workers' and vendors' rights, for example. In the villages they have formed spearhead teams for each activity. They develop business plans as well as implement, monitor and evaluate their own activities.

SEWA's main goals are to organize women workers for full employment and self-reliance. Full employment means employment whereby workers obtain job security, income security, food security and social security (least healthcare, childcare and shelter). By self-reliance, women would be autonomous and self-reliant, individually and collectively, both economically and in terms of their decision-making ability.

SEWA organizes workers to achieve their goals of full employment and self-reliance through the strategy of struggle and development. The struggle is against the many constraints and limitations imposed on them by society and the economy, while development activities strengthen women's bargaining power and offer them new alternatives. Practically, the strategy is carried out though the joint action of unions and cooperatives.

SEWA is both an organization and a movement. SEWA's position as a movement is enhanced by being a confluence point of three movements—the labor movement, the cooperative movement and the women's movement. Through their own movement, self-employed women become strong and visible. Their tremendous economic and social contribution becomes recognized. More than ever, SEWA members know that they must organize to build their own strength and meet the new challenges. Towards this end, SEWA has been supporting its members in capacity—building, leadership building and in developing their own economic organizations. These economic organizations and other association all have the following characteristics—

1. They exist for the benefit of the self-employed women members of SEWA.
2. They are owned by the self-employed women.
3. They are managed by them.
4. They are democratically run.
5. They aim toward self-reliance, financially and managerially.

Since SEWA emphasizes employment and income, most of the organizations are trade or occupation related. They are poor women's organizations and the members own them through shares or control of working capital and other resources. They directly benefit from their own organizations. Some of the organizations are registered under the Co-operatives Act, and some are DWCRA (Development of Women and Children in Rural Areas) groups or producer's groups and are registered with the Ministry of Rural Development. All these economic organizations are small primary groups, village level or urban neighborhood level. They are all independent bodies.

I. Following is the breakdown of the Co-operatives—

a. Dairy Cooperatives-53 with 5182 women.
b. Land-based Cooperative (including salt producers)-7 with 192 women.
c. Artisan Cooperatives-10 with 1200 women.
d. Trading and Vending Cooperatives-5 with 1000 women.
e. Service and Labour Cooperatives—9 with 4036 women.
f. Including SEWA Bank, stone quarrying Cooperative, paper-pickers Cooperative, Health and Childcare Cooperative.

II. DWCRA (Producers') Groups are as follows: (These are 181 groups with 2981 women). These are village-based collectives of women engaged in various economic activities.

a. Craft-142 with 2106 women.
b. Land-based-21 with 395 women.
c. Salt production and gum collection-11 with 220 women.
d. Nursery raising and seed collecting- 7 with 140 women.
e. Food security program-10 with 12 women.

This totals 181 groups with 2981 women. All these DWCRA groups are organized by SEWA. However, they are linked to district-level rural development authorities and the Ministry of Rural Development at the central level.

III. *Savings and Credit Organizations;*

Women require banking and credit services in both urban and rural areas. In the latter, they have formed their own savings groups and are learning to manage their own collective capital. These groups then have formed their own district-level associations and include women workers of various trade in many villages. Four such district level associations are:

a. *Ahmedabad* Savings and Credit Association with 6868 members.
b. *Kheda* Savings and Credit Association with 9230 members.
c. *Gandhinagar* Savings and Credit Association with 1182 members.
d. *Mehsana* Savings and Credit Association (will be registered soon).

SEWA's urban members have their own savings accounts in SEWA Bank.[4] The Bank promotes and trains these associations in order to decentralize its own operations and build local self-reliance. It works closely with the associations in getting savings and credit to rural women. There were 1009 savings groups in nine districts of the state of Gujerat with a total of 26,508 women. In 1998, a total of 87,623 women were depositing their savings in SEWA Bank.

IV. *Social Security Organizations:*

There are 6 organizations of social security providers, including health workers and childcare workers. The members are the actual caregivers, while the self-employed women obtain services. For social security providers, this work also gives them employment.

V. *Federations:*

The economic organizations described above are all primary organizations, serving the self-employed women directly. But organizing at the grass-root level is necessary but not enough. Access to the markets, to training, to technical inputs and to policy making, requires organizations which can deal at state, national and international levels. The main purpose of the federations, thus, is to link the self-employed women, through their primary organizations to the economic structures, and in so doing, to mainstream them into the main economy.

These federations are of different types with different purposes, depending on the need of the primary organization. However, the main aim of all is to bring the self-employed women in to the mainstream. Following is a description of some such federations:

a. *Gujarat State Mahila (women) SEWA Cooperatives' Federation*—the need for this federation was felt by the Co-operatives mainly in the areas of marketing, capacity building for management of primary co-operatives and policy interventions with the state government and the central government of India. This federation has a membership of 84 Co-operatives with a total of 29,617 self-employed poor women. It was registered in 1993. In 1996, the federation became a member of the National Cooperative Union of India. In 1998, the federation organized several training programs in management, documentation, marketing, bookkeeping and accounts and technical training on design improvement. The Federation has license to export products made by its member cooperatives. The federation helped the artisans export Rs 10 lakhs[5] worth of their products in 1998. Within the country, the federation organized exhibitions and other marketing arrangements. The federation organized a state-level workshop on policy and on issues emerging from co-operatives' daily experiences. The Registrar of Gujarat's Department of Cooperatives participated and answered many of the questions.

For their active service and efficient management, the Gujarat State Women's Cooperative Federation was awarded an "A" grade by the government auditors.

b. *Gujarat Mahila (women) SEWA Housing Trust*—the purpose of this federation or trust is to deal with housing for poor, self-employed women, as their homes are also a productive assets where they conduct, manufacture or trade.

c. *Banaskantha DWCRA Mahila SEWA Association*—this is the north western desert district of Gujarat. Based upon local resources and women's own traditional skills, women have taken the leadership to develop their own district, Banaskantha, through economic activities. Eighty percent of the families, who once migrated during a part of the year to look for seasonal work, no longer do so. In 1996, rural women managers took over the running of their own activities.[6] An individual village level DWCRA group is too isolated and vulnerable to reach markets, raw materials and credit on its own. SEWA has undertaken the task of promoting DWCRA groups,[50] helping them to build their capacities and of linking with the state and the central governments.

SEWA found that cooperative structure was not suitable to form DWCRA groups as a cooperative is a very formal organization—it requires registration, maintenance of records, formal elections which is very difficult for every village as women are illiterate. (Milk industry is the exception as the cooperative structure already existed when SEWA stepped in.). Moreover, a DWCRA group only focuses on poor women whereas all sorts of women, rich or poor, have to be included in a cooperative. For each craft, separate DWCRA groups were formed and registered with the District Rural Development Agency (DRDA). As organizing is based upon an occupational activity, two to three different DWCRA groups could exist in a village like embroidery patchwork and bead work. (DRDA is comprised of officials from Health, Education, Forest and Industries Departments of the state. Since DRDA is within the purview of IRDA (Integrated Rural Development Agency at the state level, the members of DRDA decide the resource allocation for different development programs.). (SEWA has experienced some problems while dealing with the DWCRA officials. Somehow, these officials don't fully understand the importance of the Poverty Alleviation programs, particularly when it came to finding market outlets outside their own districts. (They feel as if the district funds are going out of the district.) SEWA has also found out that in order to strengthen the DWCRA program, a lot more needs to be to be done in human resource development like awareness and leadership building, skill upgradation, managerial training and financial management. The increased involvement of NGOs is stressed in the observation of SEWA because they can establish a rapport with the rural women which the government officials failed to do. (Why the poor don't trust the city-bred officials has been explained earlier).

Group formation under a DWCRA Program is very democratic. The Gram (village) Panchayat and the women together prepare a list of women below the poverty line. A SEWA worker assists in this. This is known as the IRDP list. Then the necessary forms are obtained by SEWA from the Taluka (block) Panchayat office and filled in. The head of the village Panchayat is constantly informed and involved, as his support is very crucial for the success of the program. Meantime, SEWA holds meetings with women groups in the village, village Panchayat and Gram (village) Sabha (assembly made up of the whole adult village population). The objectives of the DWCRA program are explained in detail including the income-generation activity and a revolving fund of Rs. 15,200 which is provided to a DWCRA group of 10-15 women by the government by opening a bank account. One just has to imagine how much time-consuming it is when one is dealing with illiterate village women whose whole horizon so far has been their village. The amount of Rs 15,200 is not handed over to one person or distributed among the members of the group. It is deposited in a bank and is to be used to purchase raw material for that particular economic activity of the group and to pay wages.

Then the group selects a leader with SEWA's guidance who can manage the bank account, purchase and distribution of raw material, distribution of work, supervision and monitoring, delivery of finished goods and conducting monthly meeting. A SEWA worker is very much present to facilitate in the selection of the leader and to train her in her responsibilities.

Once the group leader and committee members are selected, the DWCRA group is registered with DRDA at the district level. Upon registration, the group's bank account is opened in the nearest bank. Then the Taluka (block) level Panchayat releases the check of Rs. 15,200 in the name of the group. The signatures to the bank account are of the group leader, one committee member of the group and the VLW or Gram Sewak.

Based on the type of craftwork, the group leader or one of the committee members is accompanied by one of SEWA organizers or workers for the purchase of different raw materials like cloth, thread, mirrors etc. They visit two or three towns and obtain wholesale quotations from different traders. The committee, then, places before the whole group the quotations and a decision is made.

Then the amount of work is distributed to the members. SEWA insists that any artisan who asks for work should be given work. Employment is a basic right. This principle is strictly followed by every DWCRA group. Since DWCRA groups are small in membership, all are involved in decision making.

The next work on the list is collection of finished work. SEWA insisted upon observing the deadlines. Two days before the delivery of finished goods, the group leader and SEWA worker go to the bank to withdraw money for wages because SEWA insists upon the prompt payment of wages.

Marketing of goods is a very essential component of the whole income generation DWCRA Program. SEWA helps a lot in this effort. It was successful in persuading the Gujarat Department of Rural Development in opening a Craft Centre in 1991 in one of the rich areas of Ahmedabad. In 1998, this Craft Centre procured goods from 52 different groups in the districts of Banaskantha, Mehsana, Ahmedabad and Junagarh. SEWA also helped the artisans of DWCRA groups to receive assistance from the state Department of Industries for sales promotion and publicity of the Craft Centre. The total sale of the DWCRA groups through the Craft Centre was Rs. 35 lakhs in 1998. Today, the Centre has a display window at the Ahmedabad Airport. SEWA has also been instrumental in linking the Centre with the Gujarat State Handicrafts Development Corporation, which buys goods worth Rs. 2 lakhs every month. SEWA has also organized exhibitions in big cities like Delhi. SEWA has made the DWCRA women aware of the market strategies.

The experience of SEWA has illustrated that not only economically but also socially the status of women in the DWCRA groups has gone up. The women are respected in society and men have become supportive. At times, men are willing to collect fodder and fuel wood and allow the women to stay back and complete the craftwork. This had never happened in the past.

At least 18 DWCRA groups out of 24 groups in crafts have become self-sufficient with strong marketing linkages. The groups are also linked with the Craft Development Centre of SEWA in the distinct capital (Radhanpur) supported by All. India Handicraft Board (a central government agency) which provides input in design and product development to suit the market demands.

The Craft Development Centre has collected 400 traditional designs of different crafts like embroidery, leatherwork, patchwork and beadwork. Wooden blocks of traditional design have been purchased which help improve the quality of production and raise the productivity.

The Craft Development Centre also supplies raw material at reasonable prices to all the DWCRA groups and also provided a store to keep the raw materials and finished goods. The finished goods are sorted out, packed and then sent to the ordering party.

The support given by the Craft Development Centre has greatly increased the morale and the strength of the DWCRA groups.

Conclusions: working with these DWCRA groups SEWA has concluded that every craft activity has potential for great development if the proper guidance as to design and marketing is provided by a voluntary organization. SEWA has also launched a national survey of the market trends in 12 major metropolitan cities to further expand the market and establish a national network of marketing for various crafts. Since the craft skill has provided a good steady income to rural women, increased income helps improve the nutrition and living standards of their families. Now that the woman of the house can provide a good income, the elder daughters can attend school instead of looking after the younger siblings.

Since the craft is traditional, rural women learn to manage it quickly, thus making DWCRA groups self-sufficient.

DWCRA organization has been applied to other kinds of economic activities like Minor Forest Produce Collection. In the dry desert areas of Gujarat, gum collection is a major source of income for the communities from 6 to 8 months in a year. There is one tree called 'Proscopis Juliflora' which grows abundantly in the desert region. This tree is resistant to salt and heat and, hence, survives in the desert conditions. The gum oozes out from October to December, which is a white resin gum and is considered to be of good quality.

From January to March, red gum is available. With the onset of heat and hot winds, the gum turns black and is regarded of a lesser quality. White gum is used for eating; red in screen-printing and glue making and black gum is used in fire crackers and color chemicals industry.

The women in the desert villages which are far-flung and remote from a direct road, start the gum collection activity around 4:00 a.m. and walk eight to ten kilometers. They return around 2:00 p.m. The gum is collected either in gunnysacks or in tins tied around the waist. Since the gum crystals stick on the interior branches, women get hurt by thorns in reaching for gum. After working hard for eight to ten hours, a woman may collect only 2 kgs. Earlier, the daily collection of gum was sold to the local private trader who offered a very low price of Rs. 4 or 5.

SEWA stepped in and organized about 800 women gum collectors from 8 villages in DWCRA groups and obtained official licenses from the Gujarat State Forest Development Corporation (GSFDC) which issues the license as forest products are nationalized. According to government rules, the women are now authorized to sell directly to the Forest Corporation which offers double the price of an exploitative private trader.

SEWA's move to organize the gum collectors was not an easy affair. As usual, rural women (as the area is the remote region of Gujarat) were suspicious of SEWA organizers in the start. They thought that SEWA people were government agents who had come to arrest village women who were collecting gum without a license or illegally. I took a number of visits over a few months before SEWA workers could gain the trust of gum collectors. The formation of the group followed the same procedure as described earlier, i.e. it is fully democratic in composition and functioning. The group selects a leader. Women bring their daily gum collection to a collection centre in the village. Every Saturday the group leader along with the members of the group and SEWA organizers weighs the total collection of gum, completes the details in a register and deposits the gum at the local depot of the State Forest Corporation and collects the check. The check is deposited in the DWCRA group's bank account and the money is withdrawn for next week's collection payment.

The group leader, Ran Bai,[7] describes the radical change in her personality. She had never seen the outskirts of her village before. Now she goes to the depot of the Forest Corporation with other group members to deposit gum and collect the cheque.

Suddenly the official price of the gum began to fall and SEWA was shocked to learn in 1992 that it was because the Forest Corporation has started importing from foreign countries, hence the market glut. On August 22, 1992, a convention of all the DWCRA groups in Radhanpur and Santalpur was convened by SEWA and 2000 women members participated. The Gujarat Minister of Rural Development was the chief guest and the women described their condition to him. Women sought permission to sell gum in the open market where the prices were better instead of to the Forest Corporation only as mandated officially. The government took up the issue seriously.

The DWCRA groups thus learned the power of collective action and were happy to be relieved of the exploitative private traders and the mandatory sale to the corporation only.

In short, women in rural, remote areas cannot organize on their own. The help of the NGOs is very essential. The mission of an NGO, however, is to remain wary of the fact that the economic activity should be such that the DWCRA group becomes self-sufficient in the future so that the NGOs organizers could move on to another village. DWCRA program has a great potential to succeed in empowering rural, poor women provided the Indian government and the state governments are sincere and the NGOs don't let their effort slide.

SEWA also has a series of videos. Martha Statuart held a

video production workshop at SEWA with the assistance of United Nations University and Video Village Network in March 1984. There were 20 women to be trained. Some were illiterate and some semi-illiterate. These women were ambitious and learned to use various tools, shooting, sounds, recording, audio dubbing, etc. Today SEWA is still carrying on video productions with the support of an organization called Communication For Change. The author visited the video centre building and had the video screening to get an idea about the contents of the videos. One video may be mentioned—*Toilets-The Basic Necessity*. It was shown to Ahmedabad Municipal Corporation. Since then the Corporation has provided loan assistance along with SEWA Bank to build home-based toilets.

Video SEWA has been borrowed by Private Serial producers and BBC for broadcasting. In 1995 Video SEWA won a reward at the United Nations Women's Conference in Beijing, China.

SEWA has given due attention to Social Security services for the poor women, both urban and rural. Some 4,000 women were insured under a social security package, which covers a compensation of Rs. 10,000 in case of accidental death; Rs 1,000 as mediclaim in case of illness; and Rs. 5,000 towards damage to house or goods due to floods. More than 6,000 members have life insurance.

In 1992, SEWA and SEWA Bank started Integrated Social Security Scheme in collaboration with Life Insurance Company (owned by the central government) and General Insurance. A woman pays Rs. 60 as premium per annum. She can also insure her husband by paying Rs. 15. Since illiterate women can forget to renew, lifetime insurance is available by depositing Rs. 500 in the SEWA Bank. Interest from the deposit would pay the premium. A husband can also be covered by keeping a fixed deposit of Rs. 700. Lifetime members get additional benefits like Rs. 300 per child at birth and compensation for cataract, dentistry and hearing machine.[8]

One very interesting thing about insurance was that claims were settled at the local level by a committee of SEWA members trained by SEWA. Village people cannot travel to Ahmedabad for the settlement of claims.

Some other areas where SEWA has pioneered are in Dairying and Fodder Security System as cattle breeding is the next major occupation of the district of Banaskantha. SEWA, in coordination with Banas Dairy, has revived 75 defunct milk cooperatives. Today the daily collection is around 8,000 liters at Radhanpur Milk Centre. SEWA is now concentrating on involving women to form Women's Cooperatives in villages in the area.

Fodder Security System (FSS) deals with dry stacks of *Jowar* and *Bajara* (cereals). It is bought in the harvesting season and distributed to members of the cooperatives during summer lean months. With the assistance of SEWA, a committee of representatives of local communities manages the purchase, storage, distribution and financial activities. Some 2,000 cattle heads from six villages are supported by the FSS. The migration rate from the six worst affected villages has come down by 60 percent.

Eco-Regeneration Program (Nursery and Plantation) has introduced the women of Banaskantha to anti-desertification activities. Around 300 landless women are engaged in raising 10 lakh (1,000,000) fruit and non-fruit saplings annually. Training and technical input is provided by the Gujarat Agriculture University. SEWA trains them in plant grafting which provides additional income. Some 70 acres of Panchayat wastelands have been afforested under an agro-forestry program.

Water conservation in a desert region assumes one of the top priorities. SEWA has mobilized local communities and local resources for water harvesting activities including pond lining to harvest rain water. Cleaning of existing wells and canals and construction of minor irrigation structures has been undertaken very seriously. (*Women lead Watershed*

Development, SEWA Reception Centre, Ahmedabad.) SEWA wants all nursery raising to be done by local women and local groups. A message of rural women who manage the Watershed Development in desert area has the following points:

1. Unless women watershed users groups manage their own watershed resources, the watershed sector will remain unbalanced in favor of men and vulnerable to exploitative use.
2. Equity, not only between men and women but also between poor women and not poor women is important.
3. Women are good managers if given proper training.
4. To protect bio-diversity, the key to women's effective involvement in forestry is through their access to the watershed.

In the Watershed Development Program, 1994, 62 villages and 30,000 women are involved in water campaigns in the region. As a result of the efforts of the Watershed committee, 2500 hectare of land now has irrigation facilities, whereas before agriculture was only rain-fed. The availability of drinking water has checked migration of families and cattle. People's participation is unique in SEWA's program. While forming the Watershed Committee, every villager from the Users group and the Self-help groups remain present in the Gram Sabha (village Assembly) and are involved in the formation of the Committee. Out of a total number of 11 members, at least 7 are women and the chairman of the Watershed committee is unanimously elected from the women members. Thus, the planning and execution of the program is led by women. Women are more conservant with natural resources. So the planning execution is more positive. This reflects that women's competency cannot be overlooked particularly in rural programs. Rural women are at the centre in agricultural activity. Through soil and moisture conservation salinity of the land is decreasing and agriculture is becoming more productive and women are getting more sustainable income. About 3662 Hectares of land are treated under Watershed Development program. Cash crops are grown. Organic farming is also done. By this, environment and health are both protected.

SEWA launched the campaign—clean water is our basic right. In 1998, roof rainwater harvesting in Banaskantha and Surendranagar districts was initiated. Five hundred roof rainwater-harvesting tanks were to be constructed with support form the government. State level meetings with the Minister of Water supply, Gujarat were held to discuss an action plan whereby village women would develop and manage water sources contributing their own labor, resources and skills. The Gujarat State appointed SEWA to a state-level committee for re-charging water sources.[9]

Childcare as a Basic Service—SEWA has recognized this service as an integral part of any program, urban or rural, and it has been initiated. Poor women workers need to have daycare centers or crèches so that they can earn a wage and the older girls can go to school. SEWA has been campaigning for childcare as entitlement for all women workers for some years. It started the Gujarat chapter of FORCES (Forum for Creches and Childcare Services). I has been involved in a dialogue with other organizations rendering créche services at the state level to press the demand that childcare be made a part of the central government's Minimum Needs Program and to appropriate money both at state and central government levels. A number of campaigns have been undertaken at the international level too, to generate support for the childcare program as a right of working women. Process is slow, but SEWA leaders feel that the campaigns have helped make the concerns of poor women visible and a future part of mainstream development.

SEWA has launched a Food Security Campaign. It recognizes that the goal of full employment for its member, both urban and rural, cannot be reached without food security. For poor women their bodies are all they have in order to work and earn wages. Without adequate nutrition, they and their families cannot be healthy nor can they work.[10] SEWA has launched its own "Shakti Packet Scheme", a decentralized food-grain distribution system devised and managed by women. Food packets reach women and their families especially in remote areas of Gujarat.[11]

The Minimum Wages Campaign of SEWA seeks a minimum wage of Rs. 125 per day for the active unorganized sector workers. The majority of India's work force (300 million) people are in the unorganized sector, contributing 94% of the total labor force. It accounts for 64% of the total national income.[12]

Campaign for Recognition of Unorganized Sector Workers by SEWA calls upon the government to provide identity cards to these workers. Cards give a special status to these workers by making them visible to the public and the government. Some categories have been given to these cards like salt worker, construction workers, vendors, garment workers, head loaders, midwives etc. SEWA along with some other organizations hounded NCL (National Centre for Labour) in 1995—the first ever national organization of unorganized workers.[13]

SEWA has organized all kinds of workers in the cities. The author was present in Ahmedabad in 1999 and spoke to the leaders of some of these associations and unions. The experience with the rag collectors was very touching.[14] The leader, Sakriben, herself was a rag collector. She received a little literacy from SEWA like the fourth grade. She narrated how her in-laws had objected to her joining and working for SEWA. She stayed firm. She stayed in SEWA's hostel. Finally, she won. The rag collectors' union has contacted various offices through SEWA workers which now save their waste paper in plastic bags. Sakriben mentioned very proudly that now she could travel alone, read the number on a public bus and talk to any officer. If an official tries to stop her collection truck to look for a bribe, she and others refuse to pay. They point out confidently that they are SEWA workers and threaten to report to higher authorities if harassed anymore. It seems that the police and other officials in Ahmedabad have become fully aware of the presence and strength of SEWA. Organized action with proper guidance has paid off. Some of these SEWA workers went on to describe other success stories. For example, they have taken a loan from SEWA Bank and built concrete homes. The author saw television sets in their homes! And a glowing sense of confidence in the colony of rag collectors.

The author had a long conversation with SEWA organizer, Smita Ben, of the vegetables' vendors in Ahmedabad. She herself was a vegetable seller along with her mother on the streets of Ahmedabad. Since it was not permitted by the city municipal law, the police would come and nab them. Their vegetables would be seized and the vegetable sellers received court orders to appear in court. Smita Ben told me how at times the women would offer bribes to the policemen to recover their seized goods. Now after becoming a member of SEWA and being appointed the organizer of the vegetable seller, she no longer fears the police. She, along with others, has gone to court with a SEWA worker to explain to the judge that the vegetable sellers are not being mischievous when they sell on the sidewalks. It is their livelihood to feed the family. Lately, Smita Ben and SEWA have been able to convince Ahmedabad City Council to set aside marked areas in the old markets and the new markets where the vegetable vendors can sell their produce. Smita Ben has taken a loan from SEWA Bank to build a concrete house. Her Husband works as a transportation worker. With their steady incomes, their children are going to school regularly.

To conclude the section on SEWA, let us review the ten questions SEWA asks to measure its own success—

1. Have more members obtained more employment?
2. Has their income increased?
3. Have they obtained food and nutrition?

4. Has their health been safeguarded?
5. Have they obtained childcare?
6. Have they obtained or improved their housing?
7. Have their assets increased?
8. Has the worker's organizational strength increased?
9. Has workers' leadership increased?
10. Have they become self-reliant both collectively and individually?

SEWA has spread its activities to some other cities like Indore in Madhya Pradesh. The extension of activities in itself testifies to the success of SEWA in mobilizing the support and enthusiasm of the unorganized poor women. Whenever the author talked to the women workers of SEWA or the poor women who have been organized by SEWA, their sparkling faces and positive answers left no doubt how big a success story SEWA has been in Ahmedabad. These women not only reported their economic gains, but also exulted a measure of confidence in them, which was a spectacle to behold.

References

1. Tomoo Hozumi, state representative, United Nations' Children Fund, writes "I was very impressed with level of efforts you have been putting into and the results you are getting out of DWCRA (Development of Women and Children in Rural Area) scheme. I met many of the women whose profiles are written in the report I received from you, and saw myself how they are empowered and managing things themselves. This experience convinced me that DWCRA does work, provided that there is right inputs and expertise." "WE CAN: WE WILL", SEWA Academy, Ahmedabad, working paper no. 3.
2. *SEWA Report*, 1998, Ahmedabad, Gujerat, India.
3. The structure of SEWA is as follows: Any self-employed woman worker in India can become a member of SEWA by paying a membership fee of Rs. 5 per year. Every three years SEWA's members elect their representatives to a new Trade Council made up of worker-leaders. This council then elects the Executive Committee of SEWA. (Executive

Committee (25 elected) and Trade Council (393 elected leaders)). Worker-leaders meet in their monthly members trade and area committees.

4. The author visited the Bank in 1999 and was impressed with the rows of simply dressed women waiting to do business with the Bank.
5. One lakh is 100,000.
6. Nanavaty, Reema, "We Can: We Will, Women's Empowerment & DWCRA Program", SEWA Academy, SEWA, Ahmedabad, India, working paper no. 3, 1998.
7. Poverty alleviation has been one of the goals of the Indian government, especially since the Fifth Five Years Plan (1980's). About ten percent of the central government's annual budget is allocated directly toward schemes for poverty alleviation. These schemes include:
    1. Food security through Public Distribution system.
    2. Work security through various schemes such as IRDP, RLEGP and ICDs.
    3. Credit schemes through HUDCO and National Housing Band.
    4. Insurance schemes through the National Insurance Companies.

   There are other sector-wise schemes. In the Agricultural sector there is the Small Farmers Development Agency in addition to some other schemes through the Department of Agriculture for small and marginal farmers. In the dairy sector, the Dairy Development Boards are very active.

   In the forestry sector there are Forest Corporations. In handloom and handicrafts sector the Handloom and Handicrafts Corporations are included. There are also some special schemes for special groups such as women, scheduled castes and tribes.

   In short there is a wide range of agencies and programs and a great deal of funds are available for the development of poor people including women. However, as was mentioned in an earlier chapter, there are leakages in funds, which lead to delays, high overheads, low performance and inefficiency. As a result of above factors, so many funds remain unutilized or under-utilized. Also in the absence of organized groups at the village levels, the developmental efforts by the government doesn't yield desired results.

   It was in this context that SEWA began to work with the rural development programs by assisting the women to form groups to benefit from these programs.
8. "We Can: We Will", SEWA Academy, p. 20.
9. The author interviewed Shilpa Ben at the SEWA Reception Centre. She is in charge of the Insurance Schemes.
10. "Women Lead Watershed Development in Desert Area", SEWA Reception Centre, Ahmedabada.
11. "SEWA", 1998. P. 16, SEWA Academy, Ahmedabad.

12. The central government a Public Food Distribution System at low prices. But it is limited.
13. "SEWA", 1998, p. 16, SEWA Academy, Ahmedabad.
14. Ibid, pp. 18 and 19.
15. The author took pictures of this neighborhood.

14

Seva Mandir

SEVA MANDIR[1] IS LOCATED IN Udaipur, Rajasthan, a state, which is dominated by a huge desert and a tribal population living far away in remote areas. However, Udaipur district has a range of hills and had deep forests which secluded it from the social and political change. Historically, Udaipur was the capital of the princely state of Mewar under the British colonial rule and the feudal rulers of Mewar, known for their conservatism, discouraged education and further contributed to the alienation of Mewar. However, tribal life was characterized by independence and self-sufficiency and an interdependent relationship with resources. When India became independent in 1947, feudal structure ended along with princely rule. The gravity of economic and social power shifted to the educated elite who could take advantage of economic developmental opportunities offered by the Indian government. As a result, forests have been cut down ruthlessly in the name of economic progress and the traditional linkage between forests and the tribal people has been destroyed.

The initiation of Seva Mandir in 1969 by Dr. Mohan Singh Mehta dreamed of a socially just society. Dr. Mehta's ideology was to empower the underprivileged so that they would be able to assert their rights and at the same time reconfirm their faith in traditional beliefs and institutions. Dr. Mehta also believed that education was the only appropriate empowering tool to bring about the necessary social change. Thus adult education was started among the tribal communities in the rural hinterland of Udaipur City. But soon it was realized by Seva Mandir that education alone was not the all-inclusive cure. It represented an effort in vacuum. The poor and marginalized people need assistance for survival. This became all the more compelling in the early decades of 1970's when the state of Rajasthan was struck by a severe drought, which threatened the very existence of project communities. Immediate concerns such as deepening of wells and digging new ones were taken up. This was followed by an extensive program of agricultural extension work. Seva Mandir participated in a project called "Lab-to-Land" launched by the Indian Council of Agricultural Research of the central government. About 1000 farmers were selected and given assistance and training in adopting modern agricultural techniques. The peasants benefited and SEWA Mandir was on the threshold of entering much greater (or more significant) development work. This agricultural success also inspired the younger generation of poor peasants to develop a closer relationship with SEWA Mandir's activities. SEWA Mandir recognized the leadership potential of the younger people in handling all kinds of community work and launched the "Peer Leadership Program" in the mid seventies through awareness training sessions. But soon Seva Mandir found that when these trained young people sought to be the agents of change, the elders and the status quo opposed. The youth contested the village council pr Panchayat elections in 1978, but found their efforts futile because of village status quo resistance. This experience was of great significance to Seva Mandir's strategy because it realized that the poor adult had to be conscientized in order to make them accept the youthful leadership and to make all developmental plans really meaningful to them. The poor must not just sit back waiting for the government to hand out programs. The poor must demand specific kinds of developmental projects to become self-reliant. This meant, in turn, that the elected representatives at all levels, particularly at the village level, be made receptive and accountable to the wishes of the people. The process can be described briefly as making the people participatory in their future economic and social betterment. The structure of Seva Mandir also was recast to meet the new challenge and the period 1980-1985 was one of laying the foundation for "people-based" development. In this new strategy, a group of people at the sub-village (hamlet or a cluster of homes) level was to identify issues and problems that confronted them and which they wanted to act upon. It was here that the concept of a "group fund" emerged which was to be used for developmental work such as forestry, water resource development, education and health etc. The period after 1985 has seen an immense effort by Seva Mandir to develop the necessary support systems to make the villagers' dream come true. Seva Mandir at present is working in six blocks of Udaipur district, Badgaon, Girwa, Jhadal, Kotra, Kherwara and Gogunda totally about 400 villages.[2] Each block is divided into zones and the zonal office is staffed with full-time field workers like at the block level. The zonal workers are assisted by bare-foot professionals and each village may have 3 to 5 of them. The field workers made up of the zonal workers and para professional are the source of Seva Mandir's strength.

The objectives of Seva Mandir have emerged from its deep-rooted conviction, which emphasizes that people must involve themselves in their own development to experience the true democratic freedom. Some of the objectives are as follows:

1. To help create awareness, appropriate skills and processes so that villagers can assert their rights and also demand accountability from their representatives and system at large.
2. To promote the idea that people prepare their own developmental plans village-wise or group-wise.

People must be trained and assisted by organizations like Seva Mandir to develop their capabilities to implement these plans and thus move toward self-reliance.

3. To promote cooperation among the poor so that they recognize the benefits of an organized effort.
4. To promote an understanding of the external environment, particularly how to deal with the official agencies and how to play a more active role in the new Panchayat system.
5. To make a determined effort to bring women into the mainstream of developmental activities.

To achieve these long-term objectives, Seva Mandir has laid out a few short-term objectives:

a. Education, including adult and non-formal education.
b. Water and Watershed Development.
c. Agriculture
d. Forestry Development
e. Health and Sanitation
f. Women's Development

Literacy and Education—Dr. Mehta said that literacy is both a basic right, which everybody should enjoy, and a necessity for a society, which wishes to be sincerely democratic.

At first a few volunteers cycled out to neighboring villages to hold literacy classes in the evenings; but in 1969 a formal literacy program was undertaken in Badgaon Block which was expanded in 1971 with the assistance of World Literacy of Canada, into a full-fledged Literacy Project. Some five thousand men and women were enrolled from 1971-1974. The sole criterion for opening a centre was that there should be a primary school teacher available who was prepared to conduct the literacy class. Later on this restriction was dropped as long as a teacher from the young, literate could be found.

In the mid-seventies, non-formal literacy education was made functional (agriculture-oriented) literacy with instruction in improved farming techniques with the support given by the central government. A crash program was launched in 1978 to train over 250 instructors in functional literacy. This program suffered a temporary setback because of political changes in the Indian Parliament, as the expected government grants did not come through. It was not until the early 1980's that Seva Mandir was able to regain its momentum as the Rajasthan State Government asked it to implement the National Adult Education Program in tow of its blocks—Jhadal and Kotra. Three hundred centres were opened by 1992. Seva Mandir has changed its policy to "Total Literacy Campaign" which used around 2000 volunteers. The instructors continue to be villagers who only have eight years worth of formal schooling. They are highly motivated, as they are a part of the village community. Around 9,000 students are enrolled as of today. Seva Mandir's experience has shown that rural adults are still not very anxious to gain literacy skills and that a way still has to be founds to break this deadlock. One of the reasons is that only about fifteen percent are literate in a village and of those, only two to five percent may make even a limited use of literacy. Tribal people still rely on oral information. Literacy is sought only as a threshold to finding a job. Seva Mandir has learned that there has to be a direct linkage between literacy and the practical problems faced daily by a villager. A lot of research has been done to create the new teaching materials to establish this linkage. Books relate to subjects like agriculture, animal husbandry, forests etc. Since conditions vary from a village to village, literacy material has to be readjusted. Seva Mandir has, therefore, written songbooks in local dialects and has compiled collections of local folk stories, etc.

Seva Mandir also recognizes the need to generate

enthusiasm for literacy. It had organized a Mela (Fair) in 1990 when its staff and villagers headed by a cultural group, reached some 18,000 people in over 40 villages in Jhadal Block. The experience has been repeated since then.

Post-literacy centres called Jan Shikshan Milyams have been set-ups in Jharot and Kotra for those who want to pursue literacy further and for those who want to be trained as instructors. A Nilyam has a reading room, mobile library, meetings and camps on difference issues like agriculture, animal husbandry, Panchayat Raj etc. A Nilyam is thus a forum for information dissemination.

In addition to the adult education centres, Seva Mandir has also taken part in a non-formal education program for young people in the 6-14 age group. Some 3,000 children attend these centres, girls exceeding the boys in number. The policy of Seva Mandir is to have the village group recommend a list of instructors and the one selected is given appropriate training by Seva Mandir.

In the non-formal education program, the policy of Seva Mandir is to record local traditions and pass them back to the tribal people in the form of literacy. This approach achieves a very basic goal—strengthen the pride of the tribal s in their culture while furthering general development.

References

1 The name of the NGO. It means Temple of Service to others.

2 "Anubhav", Experiences in Health and Community Development", Seva Mandir, Udaipur, 1992.

15

Water and Watershed Development

DURING THE EARLY PART of the 80's, creating village groups became the main focus of Seva Mandir's work. It was felt that the organized village groups would then demand their rightful entitlements from the government. The key idea was that instead of waiting for the government to dole out developmental projects to the villagers, they themselves must initiate and implement their own developmental projects, with the help of Seva Mandir. Various programs were started and village committees were set-ups to manage and monitor these programs. Additionally, Seva Mandir trained a number of village based people (call paraworkers) in the fields of health, education, forestry, childcare and community organization etc. They were also given a small stipend by Seva Mandir. These paraworkers have proved to be a great asset to the village as some of them, bold enough, have been elected to the Panchayat.

Seva Mandir was disappointed in the beginning with these village groups as the demand for watershed development; wasteland reclamation and afforestation did not emerge in a significant way. Similarly, people's involvement with health, literacy and women's programs was very little. Seva Mandir's leader did some soul searching and found out the reasons. Village people were still dependent on patrons (feudal legacy) which made it difficult for them to demand development as a citizen's right. This realization led Seva Mandir to help village people reduce their dependency on patrons by having the villagers work together on private and common property resources and reap the economic benefits. Seva Mandir gave special attention to those village communities, which took up such activities as pastureland development, pooled private land development and watershed development etc. Finance is very important to every economic activity. So Seva Mandir started the following:

a. *Gram Vikas Kosh Program (GVK)*[1] —the concept of such a fund is that people save money to build a corpus of funds to be managed by a village committee trained by Seva Mandir. The GVK savings come largely from contributions that villagers make from development programs initiated in their village by Seva Mandir. The GVK village committees are democratically made-up so that authority does not come to rest in the hands of a few. Committee members are elected by the villagers. The members then are trained by Seva Mandir to manage funds and provide leadership. As of March 31, 1998, there was a capital base of Rs. 2,069,723.75 in all 219 GVKs put together.
b. *Water Resource Development:*
1. *Anicuts*—under the direction of a small group of civil engineers, Seva Mandir built 15 anicuts between 1989-90 and has been adding since then. They are based upon the concept of participatory approach to development where the beneficiaries themselves take the initiative and decide for themselves what development they should have and then in the creation of community assets with a major help coming from Seva Mandir. Antiquates is a simple earth damfaced with stone and cement to contain the run-off from a watershed which is enclosed by a stone wall. Side gullies were plugged with small walls to check erosion. Grasses and legumes were sown

along the hillsides to prevent run-off. Regular community meetings were held to share fodder and fuel wood available from the enclosed land.

The central government issued guidelines in 1994, which gave NGOs parity with government departments in supporting local associations to implement watershed works on a micro-watershed basis. The guidelines require that 80% of the funds for watershed treatment be routed through local village associations of the watershed inhabitants. Seva Mandir, soon after the guidelines were introduced, geared itself to help local associations avail of this scheme. Guidelines further require that implementation work is to be done through local authority structures and through people's participation. The strategy of Seva Mandir is to build poor people's institutions so that the well to do in the village do not siphon off all the benefits of the new projects to themselves. This is at the heart of the Third Comprehensive Plan, 1999-2002 AD, of Seva Mandir.[2]

2. In relation to agriculture, *Lift Irrigation Project* deserves our attention.[3] Six irrigation schemes are currently being carried out in different blocks. The work involves masonry stone to make the well pucca (concrete). The existing wells are deepened and a pump house is constructed. Trenches for laying the pipe are dug.[4]

c. *Bio-gas Plants*—the first bio-gas plant was installed in 1982. The advantages of the technology are a clean source of fuel while limiting the use of firewood, which involved cutting down of trees, and enhancement of the soil with animal manure.

d. One of Seva Mandir's efforts has been to encourage tribal people to grow vegetables as a part of their diet. The staple food of the tribals has been maize or coarse grain bread eaten with slices of onions or occasionally lentils. Seva Mandir also encourages the planting of fruit trees.

Seva Mandir's experience has shown that when the villagers are consulted about their development priorities and the type of support they need from the outside, their main insistence is very often to become more 'food secure'. Therefore, the aim of Seva Mandir is to offer a package with the people themselves leveling their land, improving their irrigation systems, preparing composite pits and so on, while Seva Mandir gives better quality seeds and other inputs. Seva Mandir also encourages the introduction of new crops and animal husbandry.

e. *Mini Chak Scheme*[5]—The individual plantation scheme was first started in the year 1985-86. This area has benefited 11,968 families and has afforested an area of 4335.68 ha to 1997. This scheme was found useful in enabling small and marginal farmers to develop their private wastelands. The farmers are expected to plant 150 to 500 seedlings of various silvi-cultural crops.

The grant by Seva Mandir is made at the rate of Rs. 5 per plant and the payment is made in three years. The condition of fencing is a must before any plantation activity can be started.[6] (The work in the wasteland development schemes is done through Gram Samuh (village group), which identifies the kind of work that can be done. It also monitors the work closely. It works in consultation with the paraworkers). An estimated are of 50 ha per year is to be afforested through "Individual Plantations" during the Third Comprehensive Plan from 1999-2002 AD.

The 'mini chak' scheme was first started in 1993. This scheme was evolved by the field workers of Seva Mandir in 1993 after considering the limitation of the Private Wasteland Development Scheme. A total of 1, 259 families have benefited from this program up to 1997-1998. This program has led to the development of 889.76 ha of wasteland and a total of 399,783 seedlings have been planted.

This scheme targets the small and marginal farmers of the area. Mini chak model is adopted for a pooled wasteland of 2 to 5 households. Each family must contribute at least I bigha (1/5 of a hectare) of land to the proposed pastureland. Seva Mandir finances 50% of the fencing.

The beneficiaries participate in various activities related to the program. Their contribution in form of labor and material is about 50% of the total program expenditure. Besides, the beneficiaries also contribute to the GVK (Gram Vikas Kosh or Village development Fund) a token amount of Rs. 100.

One main fall-out of the mini chak program has been the increased cooperation among farmers. Besides the beneficiary families are given training on the various aspects of the program which leads to skill development and exposure to new ideas.

The target of the 'mini chak' plantation is put at 250 ha per year in the Third Comprehensive Plan. So a large tract of land would be afforested

f. *Assisted Natural Regeneration Silvi-Pastoral Model*—this scheme was developed in 1997. The proposed site should be devoid of agricultural land. The land should have at least 300-400 trees as growing stock, and should have substantial presence of rootstock. The land should have potential to regenerate naturally after cattle-proof fencing provides protection to it. Seva Mandir provides 50% of the fence expenditure incurred. The area should remain closed for grazing at least for five years.

This scheme enhances the natural growing stock of the area, which already has a good amount of tree cover. It will also help in the soil and water conservation. This scheme is relatively new.

g. *Panchayat Pastureland Development*—this scheme was first implemented in the year 1989-1990 and it has covered 35 community pasturelands up to 1997-1998. Seva Mandir gives a 100% grant for the development of these pasturelands. However, villages are required to contribute to the GVK (Gram Vikash Kosh) to the extent of 10% the grant given by the Seva Mandir. An annual fodder collection fee is charged which is also deposited with GVK.

   The village community derives several benefits from this scheme. The major beneficiaries are the poor and marginal farmers who depend a lot on community pastureland.

   This scheme would develop around 70 ha of degraded pastureland every year.

h. *Joint Forest Management or JFM*—the Indian government issued new guidelines in June 1990 for the management and use of forests.[7] Under JFM, local people protect forestlands and help in their regeneration and management in collaboration with the local Forest Department (FD) of the state. The villagers in return are entitled to fodder, fuel wood and a share in the timber proceeds at the time of harvest.

As must be very clear from the previous discussions about the village people, and intervening agency like Seva Mandir has to be there to organize them in the first place and, then, to protect them from the arrogance and arbitrariness of any kind of bureaucracy—here the officials of the F.D. Seva Mandir started on this project by forming Forest Protection Committees (FDCs) in the villages and having them registered with FD. The degraded forestlands of these villages were afforested with financial aid from Seva Mandir. Till 1997-1998, Seva

Mandir has developed 137 ha of forestland under JFM.

The people of villages where afforestation has taken place under the JFM program have already started receiving benefits.[8]

Seva Mandir has promoted the networking of the various FPCs by bringing them under an umbrella FPC federation. It has also taken up forest, soil and water conservation work through the FPCs. As is one of the goals of Seva Mandir, capacity building of the FPCs is continually carried on.

i. *Raising of Seedlings*—this is another activity of Seva Mandir to give employment to farmers. They raise three kinds of nurseries.[9]

Horticultural program of Seva Mandir aims to build upon the soil and water conservation work done by Seva Mandir and other agencies. As the horticultural crops are more profitable, introduction of improved varieties of fruit bearing crops can generate additional income for the farmers.

In the end it should be stressed again that all the preceding efforts at improving the livelihoods of the villagers are carried on through village level institutions under the guidance of the Natural Resource Management Unit of Seva Mandir. The primary village institution is the 'Gram Samuh" (village group) selected from the 'Gram Sabah' (village assembly made up of all adults). Gram Samuh coordinates all the developmental activities taken up in a village or in a hamlet with the support of Seva Mandir. For specific activities like forest protection and community pastureland management, separate working committees are formed which function under the umbrella of Gram Samuh. Seva Mandir carries out a number of programs like workshops and training camps, to build further the capabilities of these institutions so that one day they may become self-reliant.[10]

Women and Child Development as a Part of the Capability Building at the Local Level.

As was mentioned earlier, Seva Mandir mainly works among the tribal people. They live on hills scattered with small land holdings with poor quality soil as the pattern. Agriculture is mostly rain-fed. Thus poverty is the common feature. Men migrate to nearby towns to obtain seasonal employment while women are left behind to take care of land and the family. Girls either take care of the siblings while the mother is working on the farm or the small girl grazes a few sheep or cows the family may own. Schools lay vacant. For Example, in Jhadol block, out of 456 posts of teachers, 126 are vacant.[11] The literacy rate for the tribals in Udaipur district is 12.7% while for men and women separately it is 22.2% and 2.9% respectively.

Let us review the literacy program of Seva Mandir. It had started its Adult Education program in 1969 in rural areas close to the city of Udaipur. Government had also started its own Adult Education programs like Farmers Literacy program, Farmers Functional Literacy program and National Adult Educational program in the 1970's. All these interventions were useful; but there was limited demand for education on the part of adult learners. Seva Mandir, based on its experience, realized the need to integrate education with larger developmental activities. The Indian government launched its Total Literacy Campaign and Seva Mandir received partial funding. The new approach of Seva Mandir was the setting up of village education committees to take responsibility for supervision of the program.

However, despite this people based approach, Seva Mandir could only give literacy to 9000 adults out of a total target of 15,000 persons. Seva Mandir consulted with instructors, learners etc. and a 'New Education Policy'[12] was adopted in 1996 which has the following aims:

1. To create a demand for education among the poor.
2. To make education more holistic to cater to the educational need of different age and gender groups.
3. To create capabilities at the local level to service and manage their own educational needs.

What the 'New Education Policy' aims to achieve is to hand the management to the village group. The power of selecting and paying the instructors will now be with the 'Gram Samuh' (village group). Money will be deposited with village GVK (Gram Vikash Kosh). The teachers will be appointed for a year. Renewal will depend upon performance. The 'New Education Policy' will build the self-reliance of village communities and also spare the daily supervision by Seva Mandir. As explained earlier, these village communities live in scattered villages or hamlets in very distant and remote areas.

Moreover, the Village Education Committee also undertakes all responsibility for developmental work. Thus education and developmental work is integrated to create a demand for literacy on the part of the villagers. Seva Mandir also seeks to integrate its non-formal centres with formal education.

Lok Jumbish Parishad is a state program of Rajasthan. The primary goal of the program is to hand over the management of primary education from the State Department of Education to the people's committees. NGOs are expected to play a big role in motivating families to send their children to school and local education committees will monitor and supervise the performance of teachers. Lok Jumbish program also receives support form the central government and till very recently, from the Swedish International Development Agency (SIDA). It has become responsible for primary education in almost one-third districts of Rajasthan State. The non-formal education centres of Lok Jumbish target the non-school going kids in the age group of 5 to 14 and teach them till class five. Lok Jumbish has also evolved mechanisms like Seva Mandir's 'Gram Samuh' concept to involve communities in development projects. Proposals have to come from village education committees. They also select a group of people from the villages to train them to motivate others to educate their children.

Yuva Shiksha Kendra (Youth Education Centre)—this is a new activity undertaken by Seva Mandir under its 'New Education Policy'. The target group is the illiterate young, both girls and boys, in the age group of 13 to 25. Emphasis is on providing functional literacy and information on subjects like agriculture, health, etc.[13]

Adult Literacy (women)—in 1995, Rajasthan state recorded the largest gap in the state for the population, male and female, over 15 years old. Only slightly over 18% of females and 56% of males are literate in Rajasthan, while at the national level the figures are 37.6% for females and 64.2% for males.[14]

Poor health of women in Rajasthan has been attributed to factors like low status, child marriage, frequent childbirth, malnutrition, over work and lack of access to medical facilities. Figures for 1995 show that in Rajasthan infant mortality is higher for females at 91% than males at 83%, while the figure for India is 76% and 73%, respectively.

Another component of the background to study women in Rajasthan is to understand that due to traditional division of labor, it is men who migrate to cities with the growth of market economy and, again, it is men who had participated in the government development projects. Seva Mandir, therefore, started its Women's Development Unit in 1980. The unit has worked on building women's capacities and confidence levels, and giving direction to their collective strength. Women's groups have been created in the villages so that both men and women would participate in the decision-making outside of the home. Since this effort pre-supposes a male society willing to accept women as equal partners in life, gender sensitization of village men and the male workers of Seva Mandir was a must

After nearly 15 years of involvement in the areas of women's development, the Third Comprehensive Plan of Seva Mandir has targeted the following key areas in order to empower women.

1. Leadership development, capacity building, awareness raising for women through grassroots level workers and field workers of Seva Mandir.
2. Addressing Reproductive Health needs.
3. Economic Development Schemes.
4. Setting up childcare services such as pre-school centers (Balwadis) and daycare centres (créches) to help the mother and reach out to the girl-child.

1. *Leadership development, capacity building and awareness raising for empowerment* is a manifold strategy. The objective is to make women more confident and aware of gender issues. Grass-roots level workers called paraworkers, who are a part of the village community, are trained by Seva Mandir and they in turn form women's groups and associations in the village. The author attended one of the camps to build leadership. Women were dressed traditionally. But they were asking questions. They had traveled on their own to attend the camp that lasted ten days. The author chatted with a few of these workers who were very assertive and willing to take off, given the opportunity. The number of these paraworkers is scheduled to be increased to 70 by the end of the Third Plan period (2001). These paraworkers don't just vanish from the imagination of Seva Mandir after they are trained as leaders. They have to report each month to the block office of Seva Mandir to inform about progress at work. Paraworkers or leaders will be provided a continuous training about every three months. Subjects such as literacy, knowledge of numerals, information on health, environment and other subjects will be disseminated. It is expected that women's groups in the villages will thus be

gradually empowered receiving information on different issues from paraworkers. Since women's issues are male issues too, the reports of the monthly meetings of the paraworkers at the block level are passed on to male groups in the village.

Seva Mandir also proposes to hole more of the three-day awareness camps in each zone in the Third Plan. A total of 20 camps will be held in a financial year. About 35-40 young and elderly women will participate in each of these camps drawn from various villages.

Seva Mandir organizes educational tours to other states or other districts of Rajasthan. About 50 women from a particular area participate to visit other NGOs and learn from their experiences.

International Women's Day is celebrated with great gusto. In different blocks, the celebration is held and about 500 to 1000 women participate. Besides a free meal and some recreational activities, women are divided into different groups to discuss issues very important to the welfare and empowerment of women. International Day celebrations make women feel as important human beings in their own right and not just the addendum to men.

The Women's unit of Seva Mandir publishes a quarterly journal "*Cheto Behana*" containing information on different subjects and giving space to paraworkers or women leaders for self-expression. (The author read some of these articles of the paraworkers, which were very stimulating.).

2. *Reproductive Health*—the health status of women and girls in Rajasthan is very poor because of poverty, illiteracy and a low status of women in the family and society.[15]

Seva Mandir carries out awareness camps in selected villages. The purpose is to sensitize men and women, as well as adolescents, to reproductive health issues.

The zonal and block level workers of Seva Mandir will be given intensive training lasting from 3 to10 days in reproductive health issues. The grassroots level workers or paraworkers will receive similar training. These workers will be provided with medical kits to cure some of the medical problems of the women at the basic level (village). Medicines will be provided at cost price to women and the money collected will go to the GVK or village fund.

Seva Mandir has set-up Referral Health Centres at the second level attended by regular doctors. At the top level, Seva Mandir facilitates medical help provided by its doctors in Udaipur city.

Since population growth is one of the major problems facing India, making women aware of reproductive and gynecological issues can go a long way to help women have control over the number of births.

3. *Economic Program*—Seva Mandir has a few economic programs to provide women with skills and income. Literacy and awareness is made an integral part of these economic programs. Seva Mandir provides the initial capital and skill training, like patchwork, to help women with their economic activities.

Women are also encouraged to form Savings and Credit groups. Each woman puts away a small amount in this fund on a monthly basis to make women's groups self-supporting. These self-help financial groups tend to strengthen the position of women in the household and give them control over their savings.

Besides the patchwork, Seva Mandir started a new income-generating program in 1993 with a grant from UNICEF. A women's group receives a revolving fund of Rs. 10,000 to take up an economic activity. A few women's groups bought small lift irrigation pumps, goats and flourmills. Seva Mandir plans to carry on with this project and extend it to more women's groups even though the UNICEF aid has run out its time limit.

The author attended the meetings of some of these women's groups to search for new economic activity that generates income. In the case of tribals, one has to remember that they don't live in compact villages. They live in small clusters or hamlets and these hamlets may be far away from each other. These clusters are so remote that the tribals cannot access a town easily to sell their products. So new economic activities should increase the nutrition level or in some other way add to their well being locally.

4. *Childcare Services*—they include Balwadis for 3 to 5 year olds and daycare centres for 0–3 year olds.[16]

The Balwadi program has resulted in the higher enrollment in primary schools and a decrease in the dropout rate in primary schools. At the household level, balwadis help the mother by taking care of the children for sometime during the day.

Balwadis are run by local women (paraworkers) trained by Seva Mandir. Zonal and block level workers of Seva Mandir pay periodic visits to check attendance and curriculum material. A snack is a part of these balwadis to help the nutrition level of children. Snacks help to encourage mothers to send their children to balwadis.

Seva Mandir has its own balwadi unit in Udaipur to supervise balwadis and daycare centres in Udaipur slum areas.

5. *Gender Sensitization*—Seva Mandir is planning to integrate gender issues awareness in all its programs like GVK, JFM, and Watershed Development.

Seva Mandir holds mixed meetings at the community level so that men can learn to work along with women as equal partners.

But Seva Mandir has experienced that gender equality is a long way off. Tribal men are used to having two wives for no good reason. For them, to accept women as equals will require a lot of cultural change on their part. But a start has to be made and Seva Mandir has made that start.

As it has been mentioned that there are three broad categories—Education, Women and Child Development, and Health—in the Component of Capabilities. Two have been discussed and now we turn to the health. The Health program is being carried out in 250 villages of Udaipur district and 235 paraworkers are involved in carrying out this work.[17] Paraworkers are members of the community and receive training and information from Seva Mandir. The aim of the Health program is to improve the vaccination coverage of children, improve the nutritional status of children, minimize complications of pregnancy, childbirth and post natal period, increase the number of contraceptive users, lower the mortality rate and create a demand for these services.

The last area of emphasis by Seva Mandir is Institution building. GVK or Gram Vikash Kosh is the centerpiece in this component.[18] So far 219 GVKs exist in Seva Mandir's areas of activity. Contributions are normally from individuals who participate in various developmental programs supported by Seva Mandir. Membership to GVK fund is open to every family or adult person. The members elect a management committee of 7-9 members to supervise and manage the funds. It is mandatory that 33% of the members be women. Unlike the central government's developmental plans, decisions regarding benefits from the GVK are taken by the stakeholders themselves. Experience has shown that the GVKs serve the long-term purpose of village solidarity by teaching people to reconcile differences through shared goals and development.

In concluding the work of Seva Mandir the author commends and congratulates the organization and its leaders. Its basic idea is that local people be empowered by a NGO to determine their own developmental needs, not only reduces deprivation and dependency, but also contributes to the development of a more just and decentralized democratic society.[19]

Conclusion

Since the author is from India and has been visiting the country off and on, what are her conclusions? NGOs like SEWA and Seva Mandir are the beacon lights in the right direction. The number has increased, but it is still very small in relation to the population. The Indian government made the right decision in the 1980's to involve the NGOs increasingly in developmental work as they rapport better with locals than the government's own bureaucrats who are still very arrogant and authoritarian. The NGOs made the right decision to involve the local groups in their own economic and social betterment projects rather than imposing decisions on them made by the NGOs. The training of local leaders, who are a part of the community, makes the local groups more effective in their assigned work of development and other projects. Women as leaders in a village are a new scenario. Their emergence as leaders not only raises the status of women locally, but also truly creates a democratic, egalitarian society we strive for.

But the disheartening point is the rise in population. Will India be able to stem it? With the rapid rise in human numbers, it seems that after a while those who benefit from the NGOs is very small in relation to those left on the sidetrack. How to resolve this issue? Politicians have to forget their squabbles and corruption and like Mahatma Gandhi, rise to the occasion.[20]

References

1. Village Development Fund.
2. Seva Mandir prepares its own plans to get funds. *Third Comprehensive Plan (1999-2002)*, Seva Mandir, Udaipur, India.
3. *Annual Report, 1997-1998*, Seva Mandir, Udaipur, India, p. 22.
4. "Anubhov", Experiences in Health and Community Development, pp. 12-14, Seva Mandir, Udaipur, India.
   It was not until 1979 that Seva Mandir embarked on agricultural development in any substantial way after the drought of 1973. The Indian Council for Agricultural Research had launched "Lab to Land" programs and Seva Mandir was invited to select 150 farmers drawn from six villages. The farmers were to be taught new skills and diversification into new types of farming skills. The second year, enough seed banks and group funds were created so that the farmers could continue with the increased farming practices after the present subsidies had ended.
   With the coming of the prolonged drought of the mid-eighties, Seva Mandir began to give attention to programs of water development and reafforestation. A Land Development Program was accordingly started with Oxfam support which aimed at checking land-erosion, improve existing fields, create new cultivatable land—all by means of leveling, terracing, contour building and construction of small check dams.

There was a lot of opposition from landlords and other vested groups in the villages, but Seva Mandir continued its effort and a substantial progress were made.

5. *Third Comprehensive Plan,* 1999-2002", Seva Mandir, Udaipur, India, pp. 39-40.
6. *Third Comprehensive Plan,* pp. 37-40.
7. All the forests are the government's property.
8. *Comprehensive Plan,* pp. 42-44.
9. *Third Comprehensive Plan,* pp. 44-48.
10. The author was present at one such camp where capability building training was being given in 1999.
11. *Third Comprehensive Plan,* pp. 62-63.
12. *Third Comprehensive Plan,* pp. 64-65.
13. *Third Comprehensive Plan,* pp. 68-69.
14. T*hird Comprehensive Plan,* p. 78.
15. *Third Comprehensive Plan,* pp. 83-86.
16. *Third Comprehensive Plan,* pp. 87-88.
17. *Third Comprehensive Plan,* pp. 90-94.
18. *Third Comprehensive Plan,* pp. 100-102.
19. "Project application submitted to the European Commission", Seva Mandir, Udaipur.
20. Readers may also consult the following:
    1. Dreze, Jean, "A Surprising Exception", *Manushi,* p. 12, no. 112, May-June, 1999.
    2. Rathod, P.B., "Women and Political Representation", *Manushi,* p. 33, no. 112, May-June, 1999.
    3. Rastogi, Florence, "Ram Dei", *Manushi,* p. 36, no. 112, May-June, 1999.
    4. "Reader's Forum", *Manushi,* p. 43, no. 112, May-June, 1999.
    5. "A Journal About Women and Society", *Manushi,* no. 111, March-April 1999.
    6. Bhattacharyya, S.N., "Integrated Rural Development Programmme: Need for Revamping", *Kurukshetra; India's Journal of Rural Development,* July 1997.
    7. Veerabhadraiah, Dr. V and Thejaswini, C.N., "Knowledge Assessment of Rural Women on DWCRA and Their Problems", *Kurukshetra,* July 1997.
    8. Dwarakanath, Dr. H.D., "Policies and Programs for Rural Development", *Kurukshetra,* July 1997.
    9. Rao, Dr. (Mrs.) Meera, "Development of Women and Children in Rural Areas—An Appriaisal", *Kurukshetra,* July 1997.

16

Child Labor in India—Why

CHILD LABOR IN India is a grave and extensive problem. Children under the age of 14 are forced to work in glass-blowing, fireworks, and most commonly, in carpet making industries. The exploitation of children has become an accepted practice, and is viewed by the local population as necessary to overcome the extreme poverty in the region.

Child labor is one of the main components of the carpet industry. Factories pay children extremely low wages, for which adults refuse to work, while forcing the youngsters to slave under perilous and unhygienic labor conditions. Many of these children are migrant workers, who are sent away by their families to earn an income sent directly home. Thus, children are forced to endure the desperate conditions of the carpet factories, as families depend on their wages.

The situation of the children at the factories is desperate. Most work around 12 hours a day, with only small breaks for meals. Ill-nourished, the children are fed only minimal staples. The majority of migrant child workers who cannot return home at night sleep alongside of their loom, further inviting sickness and poor health.

Taking aggressive action to eliminate this problem is difficult in a nation where 75% of the population lives in rural areas, most often stricken by poverty. Children are viewed as a form of economic security in this desolate setting, necessary to help supplement their families' income. Parents often sacrifice their children's education in order to help families with their petty earnings

The India Government has taken some steps to alleviate this monumental problem. In 1989, India invoked the law that made the employment of children under 14 illegal, except in family-owned factories. However, this law is rarely followed, and does not apply to the employment of family members. Also in rural areas, there are few enforcement mechanisms, and punishment for factories violating the mandate is minimal.

Legal action taken against the proliferation of child labor often produces few results. Laws against such abuses have little effect in a nation where this abhorred practice is accepted as being necessary for poor families to earn an income.

Thus, an extensive reform process is necessary to eliminate the proliferation of child labor abuses which strives to end the poverty in the nation. Changing the structure of the workforce and hiring the high number of currently unemployed adults in greatly improved work conditions is only the first step in the legal process Establishing schools and eliminating the rampant illiteracy that plagues the country would work to preserve the structural changes.

The Child Labor Deterrence Act of 1993 prohibits importing to the U.S. any product made, whole or in part, by children under 15 who are employed in industry. Such pressures should be applied to India by other members of the international community to move toward the elimination of abusive child labor in India and in other South Asian countries.1 (Congressional Record: July 25, 1995 (Extensions), page E1507, Hon. Dan Burton of Indiana in the House of Representatives.)

Mr. Prabhakaran did a study of child labor in the match making industry in a small town in South India. Children, mostly around 10 years of age, sat in rows to insert matchsticks in the frame which the child held in his lap. This was "D" unit of the Standard Match Industries at the Madathupatti village crossing, not very far from Sivakasi, a small municipal town in Tamil Nadu's Ramanathapuram district, only one of the hundreds in the region. Sivakasi is also famous for the fireworks it produces. Most of the workers are children, some above the age of 14, but a lot below 14 years of age. The foreman at the Tayyalpatti village unit says that child labor is preferred as children work faster, work longer hours and are more dependable.

Out of a total population of 100,000 workers in the match and fireworks industries, the child worker population is around 45,000. The children, most of them from neighboring villages, work either in small cottage units in their own villages or are brought into Sivakasi town by organized transport. Children are rudely awakened around 3 or so in the morning by their parents, handed a small lunch packet, and bundled into vans or buses belonging to the factory owners. Each of these villages has an agent who "enrolls" children, and who ensures that the children are awake when the transport arrives in the predawn darkness. Each agent gets a monthly salary and parents are offered a "salary advance" for each child they pledge to the factories. Late in the evening between 6 and 9 p.m., the children are dropped back to their villages after they have put in a 12-hour day, with no relaxation periods.

An estimated 44 percent of the child workers are below the age of 15. Legally, every child has to possess a doctor's certificate clearing him or her for employment. Girls outnumber boys in every factory, for they are considered dexterous at filling match frames, making matchboxes, counting sticks, or pasting labels; while in the fireworks factories, they newsprint with the distinctive red of the crackers, roll gunpowder, and package the final products.

Most of these children have never been to school. Their childhood is spent dangerously with chemicals and noxious fumes, dust from chemical powder and the heat of the boiler rooms.

The security arrangements in every small-scale and cottage

factory are elaborate. Visitors are stopped at the gate, and by the time entrance is gained by a visitor into the factories, the children have been whisked away to nearby fields or hidden in large storage sheds.

The children usually ignore simple illnesses, but when questioned, they tell of headaches and skin ashes. Doctors report a higher than usual incidence of tuberculosis and respiratory ailments in these children.

Often children are the sole support of their families, and thus, school is out of question. Of those who do attend classes, 80% drop out by the end of the fourth grade by which time-such is the poor quality of public education-they have learned little and soon forget even that. They grow up stunted in mind and body and become the mothers of generation like themselves.

Prabharakaran himself was a Dalit(an untouchable) though all caste systems are declared abolished by the Indian Constitution. His father was a forest guard which enabled Prabhakaran to complete his High school in 1973. He was hurt and appalled how people of his caste were humiliated by other so-called upper-castes, even though untouchability was declared illegal by the Indian Constitution in 1948.Prabhakaran wrote that girls of Dalit community are raped. He decided to do something about it and other vices against Dalits. Finally, a British agency, Action Aid, wanted to get beyond welfare and offered to pay him and his friend if the two could develop something different to help.

Prabharakaran tells how the two of them had to go from one village to another as people thought they were terrorists or some other kind trouble-makers. Finally, one small village called Minakshipuram, let them in and set up a small non-formal education centre for children. It was a village of 43 houses. The two started schools in the morning and at night in the street and played with the children. But the children were so tired in the evening that they fell asleep in the classroom. Besides, their parents were not motivated and had no thirst for knowledge. Prabhakaran and his friend concluded that they would have to try something different.

Prabhakaran went to his own village as his friend Balakrishnen took up a job somewhere else. He formed the Malarchi Trust as an agency to get government grants to start health and income-generating programs. Soon drought hit the region stretching for four years. There was no water or fodder for the cattle. Thousands of people migrated to the rock quaries of Kerala. School attendance dropped and the children in the match factories had to work harder. People believed that it was God's anger for their sins.

Prabhakaran mentions that they had to provide work so people could buy food. Government had some projects but they were not enough. Action Aid and Oxfam gave money. The Malarchi Trust staff and the village people deepened wells, cleared streams, and built new village ponds to store water when the drought ended, The Malarchi Trust generated 18,000 man-days work.

The success of the Malarchi Trust helped it to spread to 23 more villages.

The lesson learnt was that adults have to have an income flowing to them so that the children could attend school.

Prabhakaran asked the village people and others, why do the match factories hire so many children? Village people replied that there exists a nexus between the factory owners and politicians who receive campaign funding during elections from these factories. So the politicians ignore the issue of child labor in the match making factories. Greed to make money has overtaken them- so explained the village people.

Prabhakaran asked a 17 year old girl who had worked in a match making factory since the age of 5 and she had the same rate of production; he asked a girl who was 15 years of age and she worked in the match-making factory since she was 7; he asked a girl who was 13 years of age and had started working since the age of 7 in a match-making factory- he found out that in some cases, these girls were the sole supporters of their families. The girls also told Prabhakaran that it was the custom with match factories to hire children from certain villages as these children had specialized only in one work of match-making since their childhood. Girls did not mind it as they could also socialize with each other while working because they all came from the same village. These girls learnt little in after-work classrooms as they were so tired in the evening.

Prabhakaran asked these girls, would they like to something else in life? Girls replied that they went to work in these match-making factories when they were small. Now this was their life. These girls had some pocket money which gave them a false sense of confidence.

Prabhakaran pondered to himself that something new had to be tried. Public schools run by the government had poor teachers. Teaching was monotonous and children did not learn much. His new experiment would be costly as he realized that the children cannot attend school unless they receive a stipend and have a mid-day meal. Prabhakaran applied to an agency in Belgium for funding to start a small pilot project involving 150 children. Children would learn literacy and vocational subjects. But there would be games and plays to make the school experience interesting. Children themselves would write plays and act them with their traditional music. This approach would also help revive their own culture.

Population of India is a big hindrance to the success of such programs. Resources either from within or from foreign agencies are limited. The rate at which the population is growing leaves the unsolved problem at the zero starting point. Population control is a must. India cannot adopt China's forced policy of one kid. Being a democracy, population control has to be achieved through the persuasive work of NGOs. Only the future would unfold the success or failure of the democratic India. (THE LITTLE MATCH GIRLS-Through Indian Eyes by Donald J. Johnson, Jean E. Johnson and Leon E. Clark, pp.290-297.)

We now come to the new theme of Structural Adjustment

Changes being imposed by The World Bank and The International Monetary Fund since 1990's on the developing world to bail them out of economic crisis. The result has been what we call the globalization of economy. How globalization of economy has affected the poor sections of the Indian population with reference to women labor and child labor will now be discussed.

Structural Adjustment Policies have hurt the poorer families with the women bearing most of the brunt. Social services provided by the government have been drastically cut or eliminated. Inflation in India has been rampant. Under these circumstances, women in the poorer sections of society have to rely more on the income from child labor. If women themselves are forced to undertake outside work beyond home, mostly in the informal sector of the economy, the education of girls has suffered as girls must take care of the siblings while mother goes out to work. In situations of extreme distress, children are sold off into bondage to pay off family debts or just to stave off starvation. Thus, one of the consequences of the adoption of Structural Adjustment Policies has been an increase in child labor and an increase in the drop-outs from school. Multinational Corporations which have subsidiaries in India sub-contract part of their production to small firms which rely heavily on child labor and woman labor. These are usually labor-intensive and low-skill jobs.

In the urban areas child laborers are concentrated in informal sector and in the small-scale cottage industries where they work for paltry wages and horrible working conditions.

In a recent study of workers in the informal economy in Gujarat titled Foot-loose—Labour- Jan Bremanhas analysed the saga of the workers in the informal sector, their journey from being small and marginal peasants and agricultural laborers through seasonal or permanent migration to their status as casual workers in the rising informal sector at the bottom rungs of the urban economy. Needless to say that these workers are those who have been at the bottom rungs of the Indian caste-based social hierarchy, i.e the Scheduled Castes and Tribes, the other backward castes and minority groups.

This is a far cry from the World Bank's perception where the self-employed peasants on leaving the countryside first become waged laborers in the urban informal sector, earn some money and learn skills during their stay at the bottom of the urban economy, save and finally set up an independent business. (Globalisation and Child Labour by Vasantahi Raman as Occassional Paper No. 31, 1998, published by Centre for Women's Development Studies, New Delhi, India)

A Study on the "Social Cost of Economic Reforms" conducted by Gupta and Pal for the Indian Council for Research on International Economic Relations, New Delhi reveals that

The poverty ratio shot up from 35.5% in 1990-91 to 39% in 1993-94, and that the number of poor increased by 48 million in the three year period.

The artisan groups are also facing an uncertain and bleak future. The handloom sector is a major employer next to agriculture. Official policy leading to an increase in cotton yarn prices led to a severe crisis, leading to suicides and starvation deaths among the weavers. The plight of other artisan groups is no better. Under the Structural Adjustment Policies mandated by the World Bank and International Monetary Fund, subsidies to the yarn growers had to cease leading to a rise in prices.

Thus the artisans once the backbone of the Indian economy are facing a tremendous survival crisis. There was a net decline in the number of workers in the artisanal sector in all the groups. Very hard hit were also the jewellery work, leather work and textile work. These artisans both female and male are swelling the ranks of agricultural laborers. (Social Security for Indian Workers: Performance and Issues by Mahendra Dev in *Indian Journal of Labour Economics, Vol.*

40, No. 4, 1996).

Thus, the agricultural laborers and artisans constitute the bulk of the rural poor. These are the very people who migrate in droves to the cities with every periodic drought or famine or due to "development projects", and they are the urban poor who provide bulk of labor to the rising informal sector. The recurrent disasters seriously hamper the capacity of these families to physically survive. These workers are, thus, forced to sell their labor far below the subsistence level thus making child labor in return, a necessity to survive.

Malnutrition leads to a high rate of maternal and infant mortality, vulnerability to disease, and appalling level of illetracy. Thus the phenomenon of child labor becomes an integral part of general human welfare.

In industry, children work as full-time workers in the carpet industry located in the Mirzapur-Bhadohi belt in the state of Uttar Pradesh and in Jammu and Kashmir state; the match and fireworks industry in the state of Tamil Nadu; the diamond-cutting units of Surat in the state of Gujarat; the glass factory in Ferozabad; the brassware industry in Moradabad in the state of Uttar Pradesh; silk weaving in Varanasi in the state of Uttar Pradesh; the pottery units in Khurja and in the tea plantations of the states of Assam and Bengal.

If one were to look at the spatial concentration of child labor, the states of Uttar Pradesh, Bihar, Madhya Pradesh, Orissa, Karnataka, and Tamil Nadu account for most of child labor.

We may now look at the impact of agricultural changes in India since 1960's. The agrarian structure is still marked by large inequities with a small handful of landowners. owning and controlling most of the land and the vast majority of the small and marginal peasantry operating small and uneconomic landholdings which forces them to turn to agricultural labor for a period ranging from 3 to 7months. Those who are landless have of course to rely on agricultural labor and other work to earn a livelihood. The inequities of the traditional social order have further been aggravated due to the development model followed by the Indian Government from 1960's to 1991. The number of small and marginal peasantry slipping into the ranks of agricultural laborers has steadily increased. The same can be seen with the issue of child labor. Between 1961 and 1991, the proportion of child workers who were cultivators earlier has gone down sharply while those who were agricultural laborers' has gone up. (A Policy Perspective on Child Labour in India Ö by D.P. Chaudhri published in *Indian Journal of Labour Economics,* Vol. 40, No. 4, 1997,p.796). This means that a vast section of the Indian population dependent on land and agriculture for their livelihood are getting pauperized and getting alienated from land. The tribal people who are about 8% of the population are losing land either because of the manipulation of vested interests or through development projects. The adoption of Structural Adjustment Policies has further aggravated the above trend.

The unemployed and underemployed are too poor to remain unemployed for any significant length of time. They have no choice but to take up any work irrespective of the wage return. The hordes of these workers suffer from frequent unemployment and mostly remain in abject poverty.

Strategies for the Elimination of Child Labor

UNICEF has come out with the position that child labor is inhumane and should be abolished as a final goal. Ironically, this current of abolitionism is mounting precisely at a time when the developing countries are being forced to undertake Structural Adjustment Policies which are increasing the incidence of child labor as explained earlier.

One of the major elements of the strategy for the total abolition of child labor is the emphasis on education. The UNICEF sees education as the cutting edge of the strategies to prevent and eliminate child labor. Having said that, the

UNICEF is also constrained to state that strategies complementary to education need to be concurrently implemented.

These include income-generation, payment of minimum wages, empowerment of women, law enforcement and convergence of social services on identified families of child laborers.

Many NGOs in India have been articulating a view point which undercuts the approach that shocking poverty , arising out of unequal access to productive assets and resources, structurally in-built inequities and a pattern of development which further intensifies these factors, is the root cause of the prevalence of child labor amongst the poor. The formulation which has emerged from this school of thinking is : poverty is not the cause of child labor, child labor is the cause of poverty – compulsory education, according to these NGOs is the only weapon to tackle the problem of child labor.

The strategy of compulsory education as the core of policy *initiatives* to end child labor glosses over the complex social structure within which child labor operates. This matrix or structure is marked by stagnation in agriculture and handicrafts, fast eroding control over means of livelihood of the mass of peasantry, artisans, fisherfolk etc. and a commercialization of the entire economy which wipes out the basic producers.

The most important drawback of compulsory education position is that it ignores the present day international context. The example of Sri Lanka is quoted as a success story. But the high literacy rates achieved by Sri Lanka was due to heavy state expenditure in health and education. One wonders whether such examples are relevant when the state is withdrawing altogether from its commitment to social welfare.

What is distressing is that the Government of India's position while acknowledging the deep structural roots of the problem and advocating a phased abolition of exploitative child labor , has been characterized by a deplorable lack of political will. Of late even the Government's stand point is undergoing a metamorphosis in the forces of globalization.

An example of the radical-sounding but ill-conceived initiative of the Government of India is to be seen in the recent Eighty-third Amendment Bill which attempts to make the right to education a fundamental right. One of the major drawback in the Bill is the fact that a whole of children in the age group 0-6 are left out . The underlying assumption seems to be that the education of children and child-care in this age-group belongs to the domain of the family. This is a retreat from the commitments made in Article 45 of the Indian Constitution which talks of education of children up to the age of 14.

Apart from the obvious fact that early childhood care and education is so vital for the full and healthy development of human beings which the Bill has ignored, the more disturbing aspect of the Bill is that in the prevailing socio-economic context the overwhelming majority of the families cannot provide early childhood care and education without the support of the state. There are almost 200 million children in the 0-6 age group of whom a vast majority are below the poverty line.

There is also a provision in the Bill which allows for penalizing the parents who do not send their children to school. The presumption behind such an initiative is that this will be a major step towards eliminating child labor. This approach completely ignores why these poor families have to send their children to work.

Among the children working , a distinction has to be made between two kinds of groups. The first group are the children working in the family/household. The second group are the children working for wages in industry or agriculture. Even in the second group we need to identify the children working in the most exploitative and hazardous industries. They are bonded children, street children and child prostitutes. Needless to say, policy initiatives will have to focus on the families of these child laborers.

These families need to be identified and a multi-pronged approach, the core of which would be to address the poverty of these families, along with a package of health and education for the children is called for.

Even while dealing with hazardous industries, a specific analysis of each of these industries has to be undertaken. The fact that most of child labor in these industries is really in the informal (unorganized) sector, specifically small units which come under the category of "cottage industry" is a fact that has to be taken into account.

One question that we need to ask is ourselves is: in the attempt to get rid of child labor in these industries, are we going to contribute to process whereby the entire small-scale, informal sector is going to be wiped out? Or can we not devise strategies and policies which while addressing the supply dimension of child labor can also alter the structure of industries in such a manner whereby the small-scale/informal units can be made viable without having to take recourse to super-exploitation of women and children? Let us take the example of carpet industry which employs a large number of children. In this industry there exists a large number of intermediaries between the manufacturer and the weaver/master craftsmen. Probably one solution is the formation of co-operatives of the small loom owners/weavers who would have direct access to the market. Here the example of NGOs like SEWA in Ahmedabad is relevant which has encouraged the formation of co-operatives of small producers/workers which could have access to the national market in India and even in the international market.

In the end, we must stress that a piece-meal approach to the problem of child labor will not work. Getting rid of or even drastically reducing child labor in one particular industry will not deal with the unrelenting supply of child laborers. A holistic approach is necessary wherein the structural roots of the problem are addressed.

In the end, we have to recognize the interconnection

between globalization of economy and social unrest in the third world. The restructuring of the world economy denies individual developing countries the possibility of building a national economy, *transforming the third world into reserves of cheap labor and thus, globalizing poverty*. (Economic Reforms and Social Unrest in Developing Countries by M. Chossudovsky in *Economic and Political Weekly, July 19, 1997)*

Above information has been taken from *Globalization and Child Labour in the* publication of Centre for Women Development Studies as Ocassional Paper No. 31, 1998, a research institute funded by the Government of India. It is located in New Delhi, India.

One may also consult the following articles or books on the status of child labor in India:

1. Chambers, Robert, *Bad Times for Rural Children . . .*, Ford Foundation, 1983.
2. Grant, James P, *The State of the World' Children,* Oxford, New York, 1989, 116p.
3. Bhangoo, K.S, *Child Labour in India. Social Change, Centre for Women's Development Studies, 1990.*
4. Burra, Neera, *Exploitation of Children in Jaipur gem industry, Economic and Political Weekly,* 16-23 January, 1988.
5. Chandra, Sharmilla, *Is There Anybody Out There? Pioneer* (The work focuses on the plight of the working children and states that while there are laws protecting children in the organized or formal sector economy, none cover those in the informal sector, who account for 90 percent of the child work-force.), 18 October, 1992.
6. Jayal, B. N., *Child labour and exploitation in the carpet industries. Mirzapur, Indian Social Institute,* **1987.**
6. Mahender Kumar, *Child labour in agriculture, Yojana, 1-15 November, 1983*
7. *Women and Child labour in unorganized sector:* non-government organization's *perspectives,* ed. By K. D.

Gangrade and J. A. Gathia, Concept, xii, 1983.
8. *Battle against child exploitation, India Abroad,* November 16, 2007, p.M2-M5.
9. *The Challenges of Development, India Abroad,* November 2, 2007, p. A27.
10. *Documentary addresses farmer's plight, India Abroad,* November 2, 2007, p. A22.

17

Crimes Against Women

WOMEN ARE ALMOST half of the world population. Their well-being and status in society is very important not because they are the equal citizens, but also they are mothers responsible for the nurturing of their children as decent citizens of society.

Let us start with the evils of the dowry system in India. As we know that the history of India is very old and goes back to 3,000 or 2,000 BC when an Indo-European tribe moved into India through Afghanistan, probably, from Central Asia. Their four Vedas deal with various themes; but the most important is *Rig Veda,* foundation of what later on came to be called Hinduism which is the religion of about 80% of the people in India today. Rig Veda talks about the divine force and birth and re-birth which are parts of the Hindu religion. Besides religion various other topics are discussed, very notably about women. In the Rig Veda Women had a high status; they could seek education like males; there was no veil and remarriage of widows was allowed. Marriage was regarded as a very sacred institution in which the bride participated on an equal basis sitting next to her bridegroom. Relatives gave voluntary gifts to the newly-wed as is the custom in western societies so that the newly-wed would have the necessary things to start their household. There is no mention of mandatory dowry custom.

However, in course of time, with the declaration of early

marriages as the divine act as enshrined in Manusmriti, a religious discourse written by a man called, Manu, around 400 or 300 BC, the status of women plummeted all the way down. Widow marriages were prohibited as a widow was held responsible for the death of her husband because committed some sinister sins in her past birth. Widow's life was a living hell living like a slave in the house of her in-laws. Since child marriage was declared a divine will before a girl starts menstruating, a father was very anxious to marry off his girls even though it required offering huge prices, later on called dowries , to the boy's family. Since the boy's parents were in a superior bargaining position, they could demand whatever they wished for. This dowry demand also created another heinous sin, female infanticide, so that the father would not have to worry about dowry and other humiliation from the daughter's in-laws as their demands would continue through the whole life of the daughter. Here I can bring in the testimony of my own mother and my aunt who described how sometime the number of girls would dwindle so much in a village as both my mother and my aunt came from a village. They had good information about the social practices and events in their village and in other surrounding villages.

In 1961, the Indian Government enacted the Dowry Prohibition Act, and in 1986 made dowry death a crime. However, this law id riddled with loopholes which allow the majority of the perpetrators, i.e., husband and in-laws to be acquitted, leaving them free to remarry and start the vicious cycle again. While the National Crimes Bureau of India reported 5,199 dowry deaths in 1994, unreported estimates run as high as ,11000 to 15,000 Indian brides killed annually. One of the reasons why so many dowry-related deaths go unreported is that they occur in villages where 75-80% of the Indian population still resides. The media may not be there to report these deaths. Moreover, some villages are in tribal areas, very remote, and access to them is not common. In towns, the in-laws will pour kerosene over the bride and then kick her over a gas stove sitting on the floor, setting her sari (woman's draped material around her is called a sari) to fire. These deaths are then reported as kitchen accidents, not murders.

Bride-burning is not a crime committed solely by men against women. In many cases, the mother-in-law, who may herself have suffered dowry abuse when she was young, is the perpretrator.

Hitendra B. Thakur, who founded the International Society Against Dowry and Bride-Burning in India, argued that bride-burning will cease if the young women of India refuse to marry as soon as the groom's family ask for dowry, or if the women leave the marital home at the first sign of abuse. But members of the audience noted that they lack alternatives such as jobs and shelter because the women's parents often refuse to take them back.

Conference participants listed practical steps aimed at eradicating dowry and bride-burning. They include constructing residential training centers and apartment complexes for young women., forming support groups for students and parents opposed to the dowry system, and creating loan funds for students to eliminate some of the financial pressures that underlie the practice. Hitendra B. Thakur also said in his book Don't Burn my Mother, a fictional account of dowry death, that novels, newspapers, and movies should be used to convince the bride that instead of the option to marry with dowry and die, it is far better to remain unmarried and alive.

(ELEVEN THOUSAND WOMEN MURDERED FOR THEIR DOWRIES EVERY YEAR- Patricia Schroeder of Colorado in the House of Representatives, January5, 1996, *Congressional Record: January 5, 1996-Extensions- p. E26-E27).*

CWDS or Centre for Women's Development Studies in New Delhi, India, reported in its annual report of 2002 that all kinds of crimes against women in India have been increasing over the years. 337 cases of CAW or crimes against women are reported every day. Daily, 42 women are raped of which are children. Cruelty by husband and his relatives consistently records the highest rate. Every hour, 5 women face cruelty at home. Rajasthan, Madhya Pradesh are the two states in India with CAW rates above 200. Among other prominent states where CAW rates are high and rising are: Gujarat, Kerala, Haryana, Andhra Pradesh and Mizoram.

The hydra-headed problem of violence confronts all women. It assumes hideous forms and faces at home, on the street, at work, in school, by night or day. Where does this violence come from? What are its roots? How do we fight it?

Over the past 30 years or so the Indian Women's Movement has addressed itself to these questions, since violence and crime are the most hideous expressions of female oppression. In fact, the Movement was sparked off in the late 1970's when women took to the streets of major cities in dramatic protest against crimes like dowry deaths and rape. Alarmed by the high incidence of violence, women actively documented and investigated incidents of violence. They studied legal judgements and critiqued the gender bias inherent in judiciary's approach to certain crimes. They agitated for changes in police procedures when dealing with women victims and they lobbied strongly for changes in laws that lacked the teeth to punish those guilty of crimes.

Despite the women's movement's painstaking documentation of the many dimensions of violence, including its personal, domestic, caste, and other forms, both government and society have been slow to respond.. When the protests reached a high point, public opinion was temporarily appeased by amendments to the laws on rape and dowry. For example, the government enacted Protection for Women from Domestic Violence in 2005.The Act provides for comprehensive remedial and rehabilitative framework to deal with domestic violence, defined to include both commissions and omissions involving physical, sexual, verbal, emotional and economic abuse. The complainant can only be a female who is or has been in a domestic relationship with the respondent, which, in turn, is defined as living , or having lived together at any point of time when the two are related by consanguinity, marriage, or through a relationship akin to marriage, adoption, or living as part of a joint family. The complaint is maintainable , irrespective of whether the complainant has any right, title, interest in the shared household, and irrespective of the nature of shared household., be it leased, freehold, jointly or individually owned.